SERVING TWO MASTERS

Moravian Brethren in
Germany and North Carolina,
1727–1801

Elisabeth W. Sommer

THE UNIVERSITY PRESS OF KENTUCKY

Publication of this volume was made possible in part by a grant from the National Endowment for the Humanities.

Editorial and Sales Offices: The University Press of Kentucky
663 South Limestone Street, Lexington, Kentucky 40508<n>4008

04 03 02 01 00 5 4 3 2 1

Library of Congress Cataloging-in-Publication Data

Sommer, Elisabeth Watkins, 1958-
    Serving two masters : Moravian Brethren in Germany and North Carolina,
    1727-1801 / Elisabeth Watkins Sommer.
        p.   cm.
    Includes bibliographical references and index.
    ISBN 0-8131-2139-6 (alk. paper)
    1. Moravians—North Carolina—Salem—History—18th century.
    2. Moravians—Germany—History—18th century. 3. Salem (N.C.)—Church
    history—18th century. I. Title.
    BX8568.S25S65   1999
    284'.67585—dc21   99-28731

In Memoriam

Elisabeth Müller Sommer
1893–1990
and
Rebecca Bullock Watkins
1910–1991

To the new generation

Caleb Sebastian Otto Petersen
March 3, 1995
Maximillian Donald Sommer Petersen
December 13, 1996
and
Annelise Thomas Hornack
January 7, 1999

Contents

Illustrations

Preface

SEARCHING FOR THE AMERICAN FREEDOM

The story told in these pages began as a search for the meaning of American freedom in the eyes of the German Pietist group known as the Moravian Brethren in America and as the Unity of the Brethren in Europe. It became a story of change and resistance to change on two continents. One historian has referred to the eighteenth century as a "crucible" for many "passages to modernity."[1] It was a transitional period for the attitude toward marriage and family relations, the triumph of reason over revelation, the spread of political consciousness, and the accompanying appearance of politically driven revolution. The latter developments and their impact are reflected in the quotation given above. The Brethren found themselves in the midst of their own inner transition, as their second generation grew to adulthood, and the transition of the world around them. The generational conflict became an integral part of a cultural conflict that pitted those who had chosen the life of piety against those who were born into it. The fact that the membership of the Brethren ranged in social status from artisans to nobles gives added dimension to their "culture wars." It also allows for a fascinating view of the social dynamics of eighteenth-century Germany and America during a period of political and social upheaval on both continents.

It became clear in the course of the search for "American freedom" that, like a Russian nesting doll, the issue of the definition of American freedom lay within other issues. The hunt itself originated with my earlier examination of the relationship between the Moravian settlement in Salem, North Carolina, and the central ruling body of the Brethren, the Unity Elders Conference, based in Germany. My focus in that study was on what happened when a group with a unified ideal for living as a godly community and a governmental system forged and based in Germany faced the challenge of the American Revolution, which resulted in a new nation. This study involved looking at the development of the Brethren's peculiar settlement towns (*Ortsgemeinen*), which, in turn, allowed for an intimate view of the impact of the Pietist movement on social organization. The nature of the Brethren made their story particularly intriguing: although they formed protective religious settlements, they did not withdraw from the world. In fact, many of their leaders were familiar with and at home in the royal courts of Europe. The fact that the German settlements were concentrated in eastern Germany, where the manorial system was generally strong, rather than in the southwest, where peasants had a greater measure of independence, added to the comparative interest.

What became known as the Unity of the Brethren originated with a group of Protestant exiles from Bohemia and Moravia who, in 1722, settled on the east Saxon estate of Count Nicholas Ludwig von Zinzendorf. Five years later, under the guidance of Count Zinzendorf, they drew up a set of village statutes by which they sought to order the external and internal affairs of their settlement according to Christ's precepts. In this manner, they hoped to guard its character as a community "built by the living God and a work of His almighty hand" (the Brotherly Union and Agreement). The result was to combine authority over spiritual life with authority over economic and family life. Their entire community rested on a Biblical basis and required a strong common faith as well as a subordination of individual interests to the needs of the Brethren as a whole.

As the number of people attracted to life with the Brethren rose in the late 1730s and the 1740s, they founded other communities in Germany and, eventually, in America. The two largest of those communities in America were Bethlehem, Pennsylvania, and Salem, North Carolina. Although the American settlements possessed their own local governing bodies, their decisions were subject to the approval of the central ruling body, which was based in Saxony during most of the period under study. This governmental structure that the Brethren brought with them makes them unique among the various sects that spread to America. I chose Salem as my particular focus because its first thirty years of existence as a full-fledged town took place during the Revolution and during the early period of the forming of a constitution. It literally grew up with the new nation.

The exploration of the struggle to maintain unity under divisive and difficult circumstances remains a part of the current story, but it has been linked to other issues. The study of Salem's first thirty years reveals the use of what its local leaders termed "the American freedom" as a weapon on the part of some of the Brethren (especially the American-born) against the authority of the Unity Elders Conference. This use of the term raised the question of exactly how the leadership and the "private" Brethren might have defined "American freedom." To answer this question, I wanted to see whether the behavior of the Salem Brethren was distinct from that of their German counterparts. This led to the larger issue of the challenge that eighteenth-century developments posed to the Brethren's Pietist worldview, as it became evident that the leadership in Salem and in Germany faced similar difficulties.

Because the dynamics of change were similar in the German and in the American *Ortsgemeinen,* this study reveals much about Germany and about America. In particular, it gives an intimate look at the complex cultural world that surrounded the Brethren in Saxony and in Silesia, and at the impact of revolution and reaction in that world. The American Brethren were distinct, however, when it came to the issue of authority and methods of defying it. The Brethren in North Carolina, particularly the youth, were more openly defiant; they generally opposed church control over practical, versus spiritual, concerns such as economic regulations and marriage, although the latter was a "hot" issue on both sides of the Atlantic. In the post-Revolutionary period, they called on "the American freedom" to justify resistance to the authority of the Salem Elders Conference and to the town ordinances over economic life. Those who did this associated this freedom primarily with individual control over professions and property, "the *American* freedom." This association contrasts with the more general and often negative references to freedom on the part of the German-based leadership.

Looking at the dynamics of American defiance helps one to understand the impact of the American Revolution on a non-Anglo-American group. It also gives insight into the process of shifting identity as the American Brethren moved toward an articulation of themselves as a distinctly American branch within the Unity. This process involved redefining the original ideal to fit American circumstances. The story of the Brethren generally reinforces Gordon Wood's emphasis on the radical nature of the American Revolution. It also underlines the power exerted by the frontier, at least on and in the minds of the European-born leadership.

The Revolution provided the American Brethren with a weapon against the dominance of the German central leadership, but the study of the relationship between the Salem Elders Conference and the Unity Elders Conference indicates that the process of immigration also aided in the development of a sense of distinction and, even, a measure of alienation. Difficulties in transportation and communication combined with expense made maintaining a bridge across the Atlantic very problematic. Although the American branch of the Unity did not achieve full independent status until the mid-nineteenth century, they were drifting away by the end of the eighteenth.

The comparison of late-eighteenth-century developments in the German and North Carolinian *Ortsgemeinen* also gives insight into the effect of English and German versions of the Enlightenment beyond strictly intellectual circles. This study thus contributes to the cultural/social history of the Enlightenment on both sides of the Atlantic. Although the Enlightenment and religious revivals are often seen as discrete movements within the eighteenth century, individuals involved in one could not ignore the other. The Brethren were certainly shaped by both. Admittedly, the Enlightenment, as with so many other movements, is very difficult to pin down. Recent studies of the Enlightenment have stressed its many-faceted nature, particularly regarding the attitude toward religion. I have not tried to define it too closely but have let the Brethren define it; they, after all, were caught in the middle of it. My interest is in what they perceived to be marks of the Enlightenment and what it meant to them. In general, the leadership in the later eighteenth century associated the Enlightenment with rebellion and religious skepticism, while the younger Brethren seem to have been drawn to its message of individual autonomy and creative expression. This statement reflects Dorinda Outram's definition of the Enlightenment as comprising a series of debates over issues such as reason, human nature, and freedom.[2] The Brethren's records also reinforce work done by Robert Darnton and others that suggests that much of what was considered "enlightenment" literature fell outside the realm of stately philosophical tomes.[3]

Looking at developments within the Unity throughout the eighteenth century highlights the complex nature of human relations. Historians often overrun this process in eagerness for a clear thesis. As J.G.A. Pocock said recently, historians can only count to two.[4] We insist that either this happened or the other, but we have trouble admitting that the truth probably lies somewhere in between. The story of the Brethren is full of paradoxes and tensions. It is not, for instance, the simple story of a conservative American leadership fighting a progressive membership. Many members continued to feel a strong attachment to the original ideal and to the community. In turn, the leadership shared a sense of otherness and distance from their German roots. Neither is it the story of an "oppressive" religious authority imposing a "repressive" culture on gallantly defiant individuals. Although, by the late eighteenth century, the majority of the central leadership was upper class and functioned under an aristocratic social ethos, the world that they created and defended had much to recommend it. This world included a worship that blended simplicity with a vibrant aesthetic, and an ideal that stressed unity over social status, with spiritual equality as the communal glue. All community members were to be united in a heart-centered attachment to Christ that provided love as the motivating force of social interaction. This ideal for Christian community confronted the reality of how difficult it was to transmit the effect of emotional religious experience to the second generation. A system with this experience as a base could and was viewed as a set of restrictive rules and regulations by those born into it. To these young members, the pull of new emotionally based movements, such as the Sturm und Drang, proved a strong rival to their heritage.

I have approached this study as a cultural history that focuses on religious life. It deals with the mental world of the Brethren, their ideals, their assumptions, and their perceptions, and how they expressed these in their actions. To this end, I have not focused on questions such as whether their definition of "the American freedom" was an accurate one. The fact that they perceived it as freeing them from European domination effectively put them on the road to independence. The voices that we hear are primarily those of the leadership, and the views are filtered through theirs. This is because the official records of the Brethren are very rich and because more private sources are largely unavailable for the eighteenth century. Of course, it also reflects the fact that, for the Brethren, "private" and "public" were not really distinct, at least within the *Ortsgemeinen;* an individual's inner world was bound up within that person's actions in and in relation to the community. Thus, autobiographies were intended for public edification, and letters were subject to scrutiny.

Basing a study on official documents need not be viewed as a weakness, however. In many ways, the members of the leadership, in their capacity as representatives and protectors of the Unity, were at the fulcrum of the meeting of "the world" with the "people of God." Often, they were also university-educated and, thus, sensitive, perhaps too sensitive, to contemporary intellectual developments. In addition, as David Sabean, Natalie Davis, and others have shown, it is possible to extract some understanding of the worldview of "ordinary folk" even from official records. This is particularly true for the Brethren because all the leadership were not upper-class, and they shared a unified set of ideals and assumptions that crossed boundaries of authority and subject. As noted earlier, all were subject to Christ.

The common thread in the tapestry is the view of the lot as representing the voice and, thus, the will of Christ as their "true head." The Brethren's use of the lot in almost all major decisions is a dramatic measure of their dedication to infusing their community with religious devotion. The controversy that arose over its use illustrates the inroads of the stress on reason and human responsibility that characterized much of eighteenth-century thought. Ultimately, the American Brethren threw down the gauntlet over its use in determining marriage proposals. Thus, it unites the themes of cultural change and transatlantic transformation.

With regard to the use of terms, I have chosen not to translate *Gemeine* because to translate it either as "community" or "congregation" does injustice to the very real way in which it was both. In general, I have used *Ortsgemeine* to refer to the actual physical settlements and *Gemeine* to refer to the inhabitants. After giving an initial translation for each, I have not translated within the body of the text the terms for the various offices within the Unity. I have distinguished between first and second generation on the basis of conversion to or birth into the Unity rather than in a strictly chronological sense, although these two most often coincide. Therefore, some people included in the spiritual "second generation" were actually third-generation members. I chose to do this because a distinction between spiritual rather than biological generations seemed most pertinent to this particular story. In addition, I have used the term "declension" in the sense familiar to scholars of Puritanism, to denote decline or decreasing intensity in piety, both real and perceived. Titles of the source documents are rendered in English in the notes with the German given in the bibliography.

Many of the documents in the archives of the Moravian Church of the Southern Province in Winston-Salem have been and are being translated. At present, this includes most of the minutes of the Elders Conference through 1847 (the minutes shift to English in 1856), the minutes of the *Aufseher Collegium*, the Single Sisters diary through 1842, the diary of the St. Philips Congregation (African American), and most of the minutes of the *Gemeine* Council. Unless otherwise noted, quotations given in the text are taken from the German original. All German quoted in the notes has been left in the original spelling.

Finally, I wish to note that this study scratches only the surface of the story of the Unity of the Brethren. Few religious communities have left such rich and relatively diverse sources. Scott Rohrer, a graduate student at the University of Virginia, is currently engaged in dissertation work on a community study of the agricultural *Gemeinen* in North Carolina, and Jon Sensbach has recently completed a comprehensive study of the Moravian slave community in North Carolina, but much work remains to be done on all of the settlements. The material exists, for example, for an analysis of changing economic attitudes, shifting marriage patterns, material culture, postbellum relations between black and white congregations, and so forth. Almost no work has been done on the Bethlehem community, although Beverly Smaby laid some excellent groundwork in her book on community dynamics and is currently working on an analysis of the Single Sisters Choir. Needless to say, the European settlements also offer tremendous possibilities for community and comparative studies. Two of the settlements in Germany were originally designed for specific ethnic groups: Niesky for the Czech members and Kleinwelke for the Wendish ones. Another (Neuwied) contained a large population of Huguenot refugees. I hope that my work and the work of others will provide an inspiration for future scholars. The world of the Brethren is a fascinating one, the spirit of which still lingers. After all, the bells of the *Gemeinesaal* in Herrnhut still call the community to a hymn sing [*Singstunde*] every Saturday evening, and literally thousands of people gather in the Salem square at sunrise every Easter.

Given the nature of this book as a story of change, generational conflict, the fear of loss of community, and the impact of new kinds of freedom, it is fitting that the research in Herrnhut, Germany, was born in August 1989 under the former German Democratic Republic and grew during the years following the fall of the Berlin Wall. I feel especially privileged to have known this little corner of Germany nestled between the Czech Republic and Poland both before and after "the change." The people I met that first August as a nervous foreigner, whose command of spoken German was rough at best, took me into their care: from the border guard who personally saw to it that I got the right ticket and the right train, to the couple who took me with them on a day trip to a health resort after a single evening's acquaintance. I was able to see daily life under the "old regime" in a way that few westerners had. In the years following, I have watched as new buildings have gone up and as old buildings have been restored; as restaurants, car dealerships, and megastores have appeared. Some of my friends and acquaintances have prospered in the new freedom. Others have experienced hard times and, just as their forebears did, have worried about loss of community and the growth of materialism. This book is very much the product of my experiences in Herrnhut and its environs, and of my love of the Upper Lusatian countryside.

Like many books, however, *Serving Two Masters* did not incubate solely in my head and heart. Throughout the various stages of writing, countless people (whom I will, nevertheless, try to count) have put their stamp on the work. First and foremost, of course, are those who saw me through the initial stages of research and the writing process. Chief among these is my mentor at the University of Virginia, H.C. Erik Midelfort. His patience with my early forays into German and into this topic made it possible for me to shape my ideas into something coherent. He also provided a source of encouragement through his interest in the Brethren and their practices, particularly the use of the lot. Carlos Eire also provided encouragement, a listening ear, and helpful criticism. I benefited, in addition, from the insightful comments of William Abbot and Steven Innes.

This book has certainly been enriched by communications with my fellow scholars of the Moravians. Jon Sensbach and I shared research time in the archives in Winston-Salem, and I deeply appreciate his input. Daniel Thorp, Craig Atwood, and, more recently, Scott Rohrer have all shared drafts of their work, as well as their ideas about the Brethren. Beverly Smaby was my earliest contact among the Moravian scholars, although I did not meet her until many years later. She has been very supportive. Other "Moravianists" who have been of great help are Johanna M. Lewis, through many phone conversations; Katherine Faul-Eze; Aaron Fogelman; and Peter Vogt.

Colleagues in early modern history and colonial American history have put their stamp on this book as well, some directly, others indirectly. Jodi Bilinkoff read a draft of some chapters and spent a long lunch hour trying to persuade me to amend the title (she lost, I won). Greg Roeber also read chapter drafts and shared his wide knowledge of the translation of German culture to America. I am additionally grateful to the two anonymous readers for the *Journal of the History of Ideas,* whose comments on my article about the lot helped to improve chapter 4. Various commentators on papers given over the years have sharpened my arguments. I think in particular of William Monter, Thomas Robisheaux, and Richard Gawthrop. Vernon Nelson, director of the archives in Bethlehem, taught the German script seminar in which I first learned to decipher the beautiful but often maddening gothic script. Others who helped with ideas and encouragement probably have no notion that they did so. These include the participants in the "Peopling America" conference sponsored by the German Historical Institute: particularly Marianne Wokeck, Mack Walker, and Hans Medick; also Bernard Bailyn, Steven Ozment, and Natalie Davis. Several colleagues at Grand Valley State University provided encouraging support during the revision process, especially Gretchen Galbraith, Jim Goode, and Cliff Welch.

No research project such as this could have come to completion without the assistance of archives and other institutions. Over many years now, I have tried the patience of the staff at the Moravian Archives of the Southern Province in Winston-Salem, and they have proven unfailingly helpful. I thank archive director Daniel Crews and support staff Grace Robinson and Richard Starbuck for their time, for their willingness to listen to my ideas, and for their sharing of their insights as members of the Moravian Church. The staff at the Unity Archives in Herrnhut has been equally helpful over the years; they even invited me to partake in their tea breaks. I thank in particular former archive director Inge Baldauf and former assistant archivist Renate Bötner, as well as current archivist Paul Peucker. My greatest debt is to the Unity of the Brethren in Germany, who provided me with room and board for my initial research period in 1989. Their generosity during a time when they had little to give will remain in my memory always. Members of the Unity in both East and West Germany helped me to procure a work visa and guided me through the GDR bureaucracy. The staff of the Christian David House, where I stayed then and in subsequent summers, provided an atmosphere of friendship and community. I wish to thank, in particular, Karin and Eberhard Clemens and their family. Grand Valley State University provided me with a summer fellowship and stipend that allowed me to make two trips to Germany, and our departmental office coordinator, Michelle Duram, offered friendship and unflagging technological aid and comfort. In the later stages of revision, I have benefited from office space and support given by Old Salem Inc., and by the Museum of Early Southern Decorative Arts. I wish to thank, in particular, Gene Capps, John Larson, and Paula Locklair.

Aside from the support of institutions, friends and family have aided in the writing of *Serving Two Masters*. Members of the Herrnhut community have extended their hospitality and friendship over the years, especially Sieglinde Köhn, Mechthild and Dietrich Lehmann, and Brother and Sister Winter. David Appleby, Lynda Coon, Jena Gaines, Janis Gibbs, Kathy Haldane Grenier, Ellen Litwicki, Peter Potter, and Beth Schweiger have been the sources of numerous conversations and encouragement in earlier stages and beyond. Ellen Whitener provided me a place to stay in Charlottesville when I was sweating through the initial stages of revision. Amy Rominger gave me a "down-to-earth" reading of the introduction. My sisters and nephews were a welcome distraction and a refuge. Finally, and most important, my parents Sebastian C. and Nancy W. Sommer have given me unfailing emotional and financial support throughout the whole process. In many ways, this is their book.

Introduction

IN THE BEGINNING

The Moravian Brethren, who are known in Europe as the Renewed Unity of the Brethren, first settled on the estate of Count Nicholas Ludwig von Zinzendorf in Upper Lusatia in eastern Saxony in 1722. They began as a gathering of peasant and artisan exiles from Bohemia and Moravia. The 1720s and 1730s saw the formation of a community, the internal regulations of which, ideally at least, centered on establishing a simple, Christlike pattern of life. During the 1730s and 1740s, the number of people attracted to life with the Brethren grew and came to include a number of nobles. By the close of the century, settlements were spread throughout Europe and had been planted in America as well.

The Ancient Unity: A Model for Piety

To understand the eighteenth-century Brethren, we need to look at what they were trying to renew. The Moravians trace their ecclesiastical ancestry to a group known as the Unitas Fratrum, or Bohemian Brethren, which was established in Bohemia in the fifteenth century. The Unitas was one of several religious dissident groups that formed in the wake of the execution of Jan Hus for heresy in 1415. The Moravian Brethren called themselves the Renewed Unitas Fratrum, and Moravian historians consistently begin their histories with the Hussite movement. John Holmes, writing in 1825, described this early background of the Renewed Brethren as being "the main spring which originated, matured, and still preserves to the Church of the Brethren much of primitive Christianity."[1] Despite the breakup of the Church of the Bohemian Brethren during the Thirty Years' War, which makes tracing a direct line between the old and the new Unity quite difficult, clear similarities between the two exist. These appear most particularly in their emphasis on community, simplicity, and conduct, but also in their desire to adhere to certain specific New Testament standards.

Fifteenth-century Bohemia was plagued by religious dissension. Two distinct groups emerged from the smoke raised by the burning of Jan Hus in 1415. The more conservative group, known as the Calixtines, or Utraquists, desired only that the Communion cup be restored to the laity and that the service again be conducted in the Bohemian tongue. The Taborites' views were more radical and included the rejection of images, purgatory, and auricular confession as well as an insistence on strict church discipline. This group also split between those of a more violently radical stamp and those who generally disapproved of resorting to arms. The Ancient Unity probably arose from the latter of these two branches, although the more traditional histories merely refer to the founders as the "real Hussites."[2] The Brethren formed their initial community on the advice of Archbishop Rockyzan, who secured them asylum in Lititz on the border of Silesia and Moravia.[3] This settlement, begun in 1453, was led by Gregory, Rockyzan's nephew, who advocated keeping the church free from political activity and supported pacifism. Their ministers initially came from the Calixtines, but, eventually, the community chose them from within their own ranks.[4] This development enabled them to be more independent in their doctrine.

The Ancient Unity as a whole resembles the Renewed Unity particularly in the ideal of conduct. The Brethren of the Ancient Unity were to be "humble, retiring, temperate, magnanimous, long-suffering, loving, full of pity and kindness, meek, pure, modest, peaceable, desirous only of the right, compliant, willing, and ready for every good action."[5] They initially disapproved of any occupation requiring a great deal of contact with the "outside" world, favoring agriculture, fishing, and the basic crafts. Aside from a general emphasis on conduct marked by purity and love, the Ancient Unity initially specified particular points of conduct that they held to be necessary for a true Christian. These included the refusal to bear arms and the opposition to the death penalty. They experienced the most hardship, however, as a result of their refusal to take oaths. This stance, as well as their pacifism, arose from a literal interpretation of Matthew 5:33–37.

The Moravian Brethren followed them in the basic refusal to take oaths, but doing so was never grounds for expulsion as it was in the early years of the Ancient Unity. In his commentary on the Augsburg Confession, Zinzendorf argued that Christ's admonition against oaths applied only to oaths made in private conversation. However, he also viewed the refusal of oaths as spiritually advantageous because it removed Brethren from eligibility for high office and giving evidence in court, both of which might entangle Unity members within "the world."[6] In the settlement towns of the Renewed Unity, the pressure to take oaths was considerably lessened by the fact that these communities were self-governing. Therefore, holding local office did not involve oaths, as it did not require exercising authority over or being under the direct authority of non-Brethren. The circumstances of the American Revolution, which involved oaths of loyalty, altered this situation for the Brethren in the American settlements.

One final practice common to the Ancient and to the Renewed Unity was the use of the lot in making important decisions. This practice implied a dependence on God as the ultimate source of guidance in major decisions. The lot was the sole means used to choose the first elders in 1467. It had also been used earlier in the decision to break with the Utraquist Church in 1465. Interestingly, in this practice, the Moravian Brethren appear to have been more "radical" than were the Ancient Unity. The histories make no mention of the Czech Brethren using the lot in connection with marriage, as did the Renewed Unity.

Persecution of Brethren was renewed during the Thirty Years' War. They were scattered and driven underground in the seventeenth century, at which point the records of individual congregations in Bohemia and Moravia disappear. The episcopal succession and the seed of the faith were kept alive, however, by Jan Amos Comenius, the last independent bishop of the Ancient Unity. He managed to find asylum in England, where he recorded the precepts of the Brethren in his *Ratio Disciplinae*. Zinzendorf and the band of exiles from Bohemia and Moravia, who designated themselves the Renewed Unity, found a copy of this work in 1727 and rejoiced that the regulations that they had drawn up before the discovery of the *Ratio* resembled it very closely. With the death of Comenius in 1671, the Unity ceased to exist as a recognizably independent body. Comenius provided for the continuation of the episcopacy by ordaining Daniel Jablonsky, who also served as a minister of the Reformed Church. Thus, Jablonsky carried on the succession but kept it hidden; he did not perform any of the episcopal duties openly, but he kept watch over the underground congregations scattered through Bohemia and Moravia.

Zinzendorf and the Renewed Unity

The Unity of the Brethren was "renewed" in the early eighteenth century under the protection and guidance of Count Nicholas Ludwig von Zinzendorf. Making a direct connection between the Renewed Unity and the Ancient Unity is difficult. The Ancient Unity contained several distinct groups within its bounds. The largest of these consisted of a number of German-speaking Waldensians who emigrated from Brandenburg to Fulneck and Landskron and joined the Unity in 1480. One historian of the Unity argued that the initial settlers of Herrnhut were descended from this group.[8] Another traces the two core groups of settlers to a fellowship led by Samuel Schneider. Samuel's grandfather, Martin, was a native of Zauchtenthal, one of the Moravian centers of the Unity and was a contemporary of Comenius. The fellowship headed by Samuel included Melchior Kunz, Andreas Beyer, Matthias Stach, Johann and David Zeisberger, the Jäschke and Neißer families, and the Grasman and Nitschmann families.[9] Many of these people played a leading role in the early years of the Herrnhut community, and their descendants held prominent offices in the Renewed Unity.

The first group of emigrants from Bohemia settled on Zinzendorf's estate at Berthelsdorf in 1722. This group consisted primarily of the Neißer and Jäschke families, who were related by marriage. Some question exists as to whether these people were, in fact, descendants of the Brethren. But there is "no doubt" that the second group, which came in 1724, was connected to the Ancient Unity.[10] This group, made up of the Nitschmann and Zeisberger families, included the men who insisted on preserving the heritage of the Ancient Unity. In addition to these, Martin Linner, one of the first elders, is also cited as a direct descendant of the Ancient Unity.[11] The fact remains that the dispersal of the Unity under persecution and the century that separates the Ancient Unity from its reincarnation combine to cloud efforts to establish a direct line of descent. The task proves even more difficult because the men and women who settled in Herrnhut came from approximately twenty places in Bohemia and eighteen places in Moravia.[12]

The Renewed Unity contained an internal tension from its beginnings due in part to the background and influence of Zinzendorf. Aside from his personal impact on the character of the Renewed Unity, Zinzendorf's contacts in society drew the Brethren into the waters of aristocratic patronage. This factor, which encouraged growth and prosperity, also threatened to stain their pure and simple way of life. It also focused a beacon on their situation vis-à-vis the established church. Throughout their formative years, the Moravian Brethren came under suspicion of being a separatist movement. Despite Zinzendorf's vehement insistence that they were and should remain part of the Lutheran Church, his equally strong defense of their "peculiar discipline and practice" made it impossible for them to retain status as members of the Lutheran Church. Zinzendorf himself was of one mind only in his devotion to Christ. In his personality and in his social and political opinions, he was torn between the influence of his aristocratic heritage and his religious ideals.

Zinzendorf traced his descent from the old Austrian noble line of Zinzendorf-Pottendorf. His grandfather, Maximilian Erasmus, chose to convert to Protestantism and, as a result, was forced to emigrate, settling in Oderburg in Franconia in 1661. The main branch of the family remained Catholic, however, which may account for Zinzendorf's relatively open attitude toward Catholics. Zinzendorf's aunts married into the families of Ortenburg, Polheim, and Castell. His father, Georg Ludwig, married Zinzendorf's mother, Charlotte Justine von Gersdorf, as his second wife. Georg Ludwig had a son by his first wife, so Nicholas Ludwig did not inherit the headship of the family. This may have made him more vulnerable to attack from nobles who held more prominent positions.[13] Nevertheless, his heritage on both sides was beyond reproach, as the Gersdorfs were also of high standing. Charlotte Justine's father was prefect of Upper Lusatia, and Zinzendorf clearly possessed a sense of his heritage and his place in the world. The portraits that hung in his rooms during his studies at Wittenberg, for instance, contained a large number of contemporary rulers of Europe and members of the nobility.[14]

Zinzendorf grew up in an atmosphere of learning and piety. His father died in 1700, when the count was only six weeks old. His grandmother, with whom he lived after his mother's remarriage in 1704, wrote poems in German and in Latin, read Greek and Hebrew, and wrote hymns.[15] Jakob Spener stood godfather at Zinzendorf's baptism. Indeed, both his grandmother and his aunt, Henrietta von Gersdorf, were involved in the Pietist movement as friends and patrons of Spener and August Hermann Francke. His mother's second husband, Dubislaw Gneomar von Natzmer, was also a Pietist. One of Zinzendorf's biographers remarked that the influence of Zinzendorf's mother has been underemphasized.[16] While it is true that Zinzendorf saw little of her after her remarriage took her to the Prussian court, the two did correspond regularly, and the fact that, only a year before his death at age sixty, Zinzendorf withheld news of his marriage to Anna Nitschmann for fear of upsetting his mother says much about her impact on his life.[17]

The difficulties in Zinzendorf's nature surfaced early. In his youth, he was often "irascible, violent, and impetuous," and his mother said of him, "He is like tinder."[18] He became attached to Jesus and His ideal of humility, however, before the age of ten. Over the years, his intensely intimate attachment to Christ matured but did not lessen. On the occasion of his first Communion, Zinzendorf wrote a hymn that contains this stanza: "Happy, thrice happy hour of grace! I've seen, by faith, my Savior's face. He did himself to me impart, and made a cov'nant with my heart."[19] Zinzendorf said, regarding his years at Wittenberg, "My mind inclined continually toward the cross of Christ. My conversation always turned to that subject and since the theology of the cross was my favorite theme . . . subjects not related to that I treated superficially."[20] Personal devotion to Christ can be described as the linchpin of all Zinzendorf's activities[21] and puts him squarely within the framework of Pietist religiosity.

Owing largely to his grandmother's Pietism, he was sent to Halle to study under the watchful eye of August Hermann Francke, but his years at Halle were not pleasant. He had trouble with his classmates, who seem to have found the oil-and-water mixture of his high birth and his piety unpalatable.[22] Francke's establishment was aimed primarily at providing educational opportunities for less privileged students, and Zinzendorf was initially the only imperial count at Halle.[23] In his studies, the young count did well in Greek and excelled in French but did poorly in Hebrew.[24] In addition to academic work, Zinzendorf absorbed much of Halle's piety, which was shaped by Francke. Specifically, this consisted of an emphasis on the need for an identifiable personal conversion to Christ, a focus on upright Christian conduct, and the vision of Christian piety as an active force in the world.

After his studies at Halle, Zinzendorf's maternal uncle, who served as his guardian, sent him to Wittenberg to study law and to prepare to take his place in the administration of the Saxon court. Interestingly, Zinzendorf's religious convictions led him to take a step of which the Ancient Unity would have fully approved. Instead of the usual formula, his matriculation oath read, "I Ludwig Count von Zinzendorf do not swear but promise."[25] At Wittenberg, Zinzendorf was exposed to the moral philosophers of the early Enlightenment. His studies included Bayle, Voltaire, Descartes, Spinoza, Leibnitz, and Defoe. He also became interested in certain contemporary Catholic mystics such as Fenelon and Madame Guyon.[26] His studies may have strengthened his emphasis on the emotional tie to Christ because he believed that morality was an insufficient indication of true conversion. An incident during his years at Wittenberg reveals the extent of Zinzendorf's extravagant emotional nature. When his great-uncle, Baron von Friesen, died, Zinzendorf made elaborate plans for mourning him that included black clothing and symbols of mourning draped on the furniture and windows of his rooms. He was only deterred by his mother's succinct observation that such a display would be ridiculous.[27] The young count's interest in more mystical piety and a more ecumenical vision of the church than that held by Francke increased during his postmatriculation grand tour in 1721.[28]

Zinzendorf's stress on the importance of a personal relationship with Christ is particularly important because it became characteristic of the Renewed Unity as a whole. Zinzendorf's love for Christ led him to set high ideals for himself, which, given his flamboyant nature, he had difficulty fulfilling. The struggle between nature and spirit marked his social opinions most clearly. Some of his remarks indicate that he desired that the Brethren possess a true equality in Christ; indeed, he seems to have considered the "lower social orders" superior in spirit. In one of his more radically unorthodox statements, he declared, "I believe that our Savior himself spoke broad dialect. He may perhaps have used many peasant phrases in which we now seek to find something totally different since we do not understand the idioms of the apprentice boys of Nazareth."[29] Since he made this remark after he had been the leader of the Brethren for many years, it might be viewed as a result of his long intimacy with the predominately artisan community. Even in the very early years of the community, however, many Pietist nobles complained of the lack of attention paid to differences of social rank among the Brethren, particularly on the part of the count.[30] In 1730, just three years after he became the active leader of the community, Zinzendorf wrote to his wife, "I finally heard from Superintendent Hilleger of Saalfels the true root of the animosity against me. None other, he said, than that you [Zinzendorf] would act as though your rank did not matter."[31] Zinzendorf described Martin Dober, the master potter, in almost reverential tones: "At nine o'clock a visiting count, nobleman, or professor, found him barefoot in his workshop. . . . They sat down before the potter's wheel and listened to the voice of the priest."[32] It should be noted, however, that Dober was able to read both Latin and Hebrew, which made him a somewhat unusual potter.

Despite this idealization of the working man, Zinzendorf remained a noble in many of his basic attitudes. Evidence of this abounds. One of his statements runs as follows: "The natural caste remains as it is. If one wishes to make a gentleman out of someone who is born to be a peasant one inflicts upon him a mask with donkey's ears."[33] These are scarcely the words of an egalitarian. In his biography of August Gottlieb Spangenberg, who guided the Renewed Unity after Zinzendorf's death, Levin Reichel speculated that Zinzendorf used the familiar "du" with Spangenberg because he suspected some nobility in Spangenberg's family.[34] Although this remains speculative, it does not seem unlikely for a man who insisted that his daughter's fiancé, who was of humble origin, be adopted by Baron Friedrich von Watteville before the marriage could take place. During negotiations in London for recognition of the Unity as an ancient episcopal church (and, therefore, not dissenting), Zinzendorf strained the already weak financial status of the Unity because he felt that his suit to Parliament on behalf of the Brethren was more likely to prosper if the nobles, whose support he was seeking, were entertained in a suitably lordly state.[35] This, then, is a sketch of the man whose influence shaped much of the development of the Renewed Unity until his death in 1760.

The Road to Community

When the first immigrants arrived in Saxony from Moravia and Czechoslovakia in 1722, Zinzendorf intended only to open his estate to Protestant refugees from imperial lands and had no notion of heading a unique Christian community. Indeed, during the first few years, it must have seemed unlikely that there would ever be enough cohesion to produce any shape. The first settlers in Herrnhut were not of a single confession. Eventually, the community did unite, but, initially, disputes arose among them "upon subjects which did not . . . belong to the fundamental doctrine of salvation by Christ" such as the use of the wafer in Communion, the nature of confession, and the form of the liturgy.[36] The confessional variety of the community is well illustrated by a remark made by Christian David, a prominent member of the group of exiles, regarding the Communion service of August 13, 1727: "It is truly a miracle of God that out of so many kinds and sects as Catholic, Lutheran, Reformed, Separatist, Gichtelian, and the like we could have been melted into one."[37]

Two developments brought order to the community. The first was Count Zinzendorf's decision to take an active hand in the ordering of Herrnhut, in the course of which he yielded to the demands of the Nitschmanns regarding the retention of the practices of the Bohemian Brethren. This action resulted in two documents that were issued on May 12, 1727: the Manorial Injunctions and Prohibitions; and the Brotherly Union and Agreement, also referred to as the statutes. The Manorial Injunctions applied to the entire settlement and served as the village constitution. As such, it bore the signature of all the inhabitants. The Brotherly Union served to embody the spiritual ideals of the Ancient Unity and, thus, to satisfy the Nitschmanns and those of like mind. Subscription to it was, therefore, voluntary. Zinzendorf resisted drawing up this second document, as he did not want to endanger the immigrants' status as members of the Lutheran Confession. The Nitschmanns and their party, however, threatened to separate altogether from Lutheranism and from Herrnhut. The count, fearing such separation most of all, agreed to allow them to draw up the Brotherly Union. His general ecumenicism probably made it easier for him to appreciate the immigrants' argument that such discipline was not incompatible with Lutheranism. These documents provided the foundation stones for the religious settlements, or *Ortsgemeinen* (what I refer to as "baptized towns"), that gave the Unity its unique character.

The statutes were designed to avoid specific statements of doctrine. Indeed, given the religious diversity of the young community, one can well understand the Brethren's much-noted tendency to emphasize conduct over doctrine. Zinzendorf's report of the publication of the statutes indicates the depth of his desire for harmony and the power that he began to exercise in the community: "In the afternoon he [Zinzendorf] published the statutes in Herrnhut and claimed the handshake from each inhabitant. They were very surprised that they saw the abovementioned young people as well as the remaining separatists give the handshake, after the Lord Count had spoken for over three hours with a greatly moved heart of the evils of separation and the purpose of the statutes."[38] Whatever their religious background, the settlers appear to have possessed a common desire to live according to New Testament standards of conduct. In this, if not in all specific points, they did resemble the Ancient Unity.

It is possible that the founding of Herrnhut as a new settlement actually facilitated the renewal of the regulations of the Unity. Its location within the precinct of an established town might have severely limited the freedom to develop a community bound by Biblical standards.[39] From May 12, 1727 on, Herrnhut clearly was intended to serve as much more than simply a new village that might become like any other, despite its origins. The opening article of the Brotherly Union reads as follows: "It shall be forever remembered by the inhabitants of Herrnhut that it was built on the grace of the living God, that it is a work of his own hand, yet not properly intended to be a new town, but only an establishment erected for the Brethren and for the Brethren's sake."[40] This statement justified the institution of regulations based on the assumption of a shared faith in Christ and a desire to walk according to His word as laid out in the Gospel. Yet it also threw down a considerable challenge to the Brethren. By the very act of drawing up regulations and instituting a government, they created the potential for becoming a town. The fact that a great many of the settlers were artisans increased the likelihood that Herrnhut would move in this direction.

The Manorial Injunctions and the Brotherly Union provided the grounds for the practical unification of Herrnhut. A second development brought a union of spirit. On August 5, 1727, Zinzendorf and a group of the Brethren held a prayer meeting on a hill, the Hutberg, just outside Herrnhut. This meeting initiated a week of great spiritual awakening and culminated in the Communion service of August 13, which gave rise to Christian David's observation regarding God's power to unite diverse peoples. Zinzendorf reported that, at one point during the service, the congregation prostrated themselves before the Lord and, at the same time, began to weep and sing "Here I Lay My Sins before Thee."[41] This period of revival established the piety of the Renewed Unity as a blend of concern for Christian morality with a strong emotional attachment to Christ. Zinzendorf undoubtedly encouraged the latter. After 1727, Pierre Bayle was the only philosopher that Zinzendorf continued to study, for Zinzendorf appreciated Bayle's skepticism regarding the place of reason in religion.[42] It seems likely that it was the emotional element that allowed the distinct structure of the Brethren to succeed as well as it did. It also made the Brethren vulnerable to change as their children and their grandchildren grew to adulthood.

Forming the Ideal

THE DEVELOPMENT OF
THE *ORTSGEMEINE*

While the village community of early modern Europe was to some extent a religious community, its secular aspects—financial and political— and Zinzendorf's concept of the ideal for Christian living—"to live right godly"— would appear to clash. In the formulation of the Moravian *Gemeine*, most especially of the *Ortsgemeine*, however, they became closely intertwined. Although the ground for this development was clearly prepared in the statutes signed in 1727, the concept of the *Ortsgemeine* did not reach full bloom until the 1740s and 1750s. These years also saw the foundation and development of the majority of the German settlements.

From its beginning, the frequent dilemma of Christians to be "in the world but not of the world" faced not only the individuals within the *Gemeine*, but the *Ortsgemeine* as a body. These settlements had both to serve as a model of the heavenly city and to function smoothly as an earthly city. This double vision made some stumbling inevitable.

As the *Ortsgemeine* took shape, many of its basic characteristics and institutions reflected secular models. Even in this respect, however, the *Ortsgemeine* was peculiar. Herrnhut and most of the other settlements mixed the characteristics of village and a town. In size it was closer to a village, ranging from around two hundred people to around a thousand. Size as well as the spiritual ideal that defined it made the community a close-knit one (for good and for ill) similar to a village, where privacy was rare. In addition, the early governing institutions had a village template.

The economic and cultural life of the settlements, however, developed much closer to that of a town. The economic base of an *Ortsgemeine* was not agricultural, but rather artisanal and commercial. Herrnhut received much of its agricultural supply from Berthelsdorf because the count had allotted little room in the former for fields. Zinzendorf discouraged members of the *Gemeine* from taking up farming; he believed that the evangelical purpose of the Unity was best served by periodic changes within the population of the *Ortsgemeinen* to prevent them from becoming mere "towns" as a result of a fixed and settled population. He thus favored the more mobile occupation of an artisan over that of a farmer for inhabitants of the *Ortsgemeinen*.[1] This more "urban" economic life meant that the inhabitants were often located on or near major trade routes. In addition, the settlements were usually plotted around a central square. This mixture of village and town characteristics makes it understandable that Herrnhut, for instance, was and still is referred to as a *Städtchen* or "little town."

The Creation of the "Baptized Town"

When Zinzendorf and the exiles from Bohemia renewed the Unity of the Brethren in 1727, its membership consisted solely of those people gathered on Zinzendorf's estate at Berthelsdorf. Under these circumstances, the *Gemeine* of

Engraving by L.F. Schmuz and Laurin of Herrnhut in the late eighteenth century. *Courtesy of the Wachovia Historical Society, Winston-Salem, North Carolina.*

the Unity was limited to a number of the inhabitants of Herrnhut and Berthelsdorf. After the count's exile from Upper Lusatia in 1736, he formed a group of members of the Unity who traveled with him and were charged with spreading the Gospel wherever they happened to be.[2] This group, which he designated as the *Pilgergemeine,* carried out its mission with great success, and the number of people associated with the Unity became larger and geographically diverse. The *Gemeine,* then, was no longer confined to one place but was scattered throughout Europe and America. During the same period, several other settlement villages like Herrnhut sprang up under the patronage of various German nobles and rulers.[3] The planting of these *Ortsgemeinen* gave the Unity its unique shape, and its unique headaches.

The Unity did not create its settlements in isolation from the world around it. The *Ortsgemeine* received its general structure from two primary influences: German Pietism and the European manorial village community. While these influences may seem oppositional, they actually complemented each other in the creation of the "baptized towns." Pietism stressed the need for the Christian faith to be an active faith. This included the expectation of proper moral conduct on the part of the believer.[4] Offshoots of these two concerns were charity work and an interest in education. The Pietists also encouraged the formation of small fellowship groups, or conventicles, for the purpose of mutual edification. This idea found most full expression in Philipp Jakob Spener's idea of erecting *ecclesiolae in ecclesia,* or a number of small "churches" (or "cells") within the overarching structure of the local parish churches. Pietist nobles took a particular interest in Spener's system and often attempted to implement it on their estates. One such fellowship, begun on the manor of Ebersdorf by Count Heinrich X Reuß and his wife, Erdmuthe Benigna, had a marked influence on Zinzendorf.[5]

The Reuß family deliberately sought to draw pious people to their service. A manuscript history of Ebersdorf captures the sense of protective exclusivism that the estate fostered in this period: "There now arose in Ebersdorf a manor entirely removed from the common vanity of the world, in which, on the contrary, true godliness was zealously pursued."[6] It is worth noting that the status and manorial authority of the Reuß family allowed them to promote and protect their pocket of piety. The Ebersdorf *ecclesiola* was centered in the castle but maintained an official connection with the pastor of the manorial village of Friesau until 1720, when Zinzendorf's father-in-law, Heinrich XXIX, succeeded to the lordship. He definitively separated the castle *Gemeine* from the village *Gemeine.* It is important to note, however, as did Zinzendorf himself, that the Reuß *ecclesiola* did not include any outward institutional structure of its own, beyond possessing its own pastor.[7] It was also clearly confined to the Ebersdorf court, and the Reuß family did not seek at that time to establish a new village.

Manifestations of Pietism, the drive for education and charity work (best embodied in Francke's establishment at Halle), and the conventicle influenced the early development of Herrnhut. Zinzendorf originally intended to build a community on his estate based on the Halle model, which offered educational opportunities and provided practical needs such as healthcare to the neighboring villages. By 1724, he had begun to build a *Landschule* as well as a pharmacy and a bookstore.[8] In part, he intended these to help support the new settlement, but the immigrants needed more immediate means. During the years when the count was an absentee landlord, his steward, Johann Georg Heitz, established Herrnhut as a self-contained village and artisan settlement.[9] In the same period, the pastor, Johann Andreas Rothe, began organizing the "awakened" of Herrnhut into a fellowship with special officers (*Ämter*) under his leadership as elder.[10] Zinzendorf thus built on the groundwork laid by Heitz and Rothe as well as on his own Pietist interests.

The admixture of village community, Pietist conventicle, and the renewed Unity, which became the *Ortsgemeine,* was already evident in the formation of the Herrnhut statutes. Writing in 1728, Zinzendorf described how the two documents, the Manorial Obligations and Prohibitions and the Brotherly Union and Agreement, came into being: "On this [May 12] was the payment of homage in Upper Berthelsdorf . . . and I wanted to use this opportunity to take all the inhabitants of Herrnhut at one time into [my] care . . . and to lay before their eyes their spiritual as well as physical obligations through certain regulations which are usually established in all newly built places."[11] The underlying unity of these two concerns, the physical and the spiritual order, is highlighted by the fact that what became two separate documents originated as one document divided into two groups of points by marginal notes in Zinzendorf's hand.[12]

The two documents did preserve a differentiation between the inhabitants who simply ascribed to the Obligations and Prohibitions, and those who also subscribed to the Brotherly Union and thus were members of the *Gemeine.* It is clear in this, as in other instances, that Zinzendorf's ideal of Christian unity was strictly voluntary. He most certainly did not want to impose the expectations of faith on those who had none. The life of the *Gemeine* member was supposed to revolve around a heartfelt devotion to Christ (typical of Pietistic faith) and to one another. At this point in time, the count was still thinking in terms of a special conventicle in which the exiles could exercise the discipline that they believed to be integral to their faith. By acceding to their desire to retain their "special constitution," Zinzendorf avoided the greater evil of separation. The Herrnhut Obligations and Prohibitions generally followed the pattern of other village ordinances that regulated economic relations, the physical maintenance of the village, and, often, the behavior of the inhabitants. Yet, in some aspects, the Obligations departed from the usual village order and pointed to the later development of the *Ortsgemeine* proper. Zinzendorf freed the Herrnhut inhabitants "for all time" from their feudal obligations, although not from monetary payments amounting to one *Thaler Schützgeld* and one *Thaler Grundzins* for each house.[13] More significant was the village government in which the elders acted, in essence, as village elders and church elders. Initially, they held powers that outreached those of most village elders, who acted in the name of the assembly as assistants to the village head.[14] The Herrnhut elders, however, had the final say over all matters except criminal justice. Indeed, of the six articles added to the Obligations when they were reissued in 1728, three clarified and emphasized the powers of the elders.

In addition, some of the Obligations resonate with biblical undertones and appear to stand in direct opposition to David Sabean's picture of the ordinary village community. Sabean maintained that community dynamics are such that "community exists where not just love but frustration and anger exist."[15] In reality, of course, this is quite true, but the Herrnhut statutes held to another standard: "No quarrel in Herrnhut should last longer than eight days. Also no complaint should be lodged unless it will not entangle property (and indeed must be lodged within these eight days)" (article 20). "He who attempts to lodge a formal legal complaint in the *Gemeine* should stay here no longer" (article 21). "All cheating and overcharging of his neighbor . . . should be viewed as infamy" (article 22). One additional article indicated an awareness of potential difficulties peculiar to a community with otherworldly standards: "No one should expect proofs of love and good deeds which are unjust and hard" (article 34).

The statutes also included the prohibition of such elements of popular culture as the hawking of medicines, "dancing bears, acrobats, fortune-telling booths, conjuring tricks or some other mountebank [*Gaukler*] or seller of curiosities" (article 25). This type of attack on popular culture was not uncommon by the eighteenth century.[16] Less usual, however, was the prohibition of dancing, feasts, the abundant eating and beer drinking at the celebration of baptisms and funerals, and of the "common games among the inhabitants . . . Whosoever has the desire thereto, however, should depart from Herrnhut" (article 13). The prohibition of these entertainments reflected the Pietist concern with upright moral conduct. Village and town celebrations could provide many occasions for sinning.

It appears, then, that in many ways the division between village community and conventicle was blurred even at its inception, despite the fact that Zinzendorf did differentiate between the members of the *Gemeine* who had bound themselves to the Brotherly Union and those who stood solely under the Obligations. The relationship became ever closer after November 8, 1728, when Zinzendorf allowed the Brotherly Union to lapse because it had come to be viewed as a new "Confession" by the imperial authorities. In its place, the Obligations were revised and reissued with six appended articles that included one designed to ensure the continued drive for conversion within Herrnhut. In addition, the exiles were guaranteed the right "to remain undisturbed in their present simple constitution." In specific, they retained the right of discipline and evangelism within the community.

With the revision of the statutes, Zinzendorf came a step closer to the "mixture" that he sought to avoid. Between 1728 and 1769, the expectations regarding the piety of the inhabitants of a village created around and for the *Gemeine* underwent some significant alterations. The most critical developments in the creation of a sense of exclusivity and the gradual disintegration of the distinction between village and *Gemeine* came in the 1730s and 1740s. As early as 1730, in fact, the *Gemeine* Council conflated the two. During a discussion of trade regulation, council members described the *Ort* as being "for Brethren and inner fellowship."[17]

The desire to protect themselves from government persecution provided much of the impetus for the change. The Saxon government was particularly concerned with the Moravian exiles and never became fully reconciled to their "peculiar constitution," at least not as long as Zinzendorf remained in direct supervision of them. On August 29, 1735, the count split the *Gemeine* at Herrnhut into two parts: the Moravian exiles, who were to be kept ready to seek another refuge if necessary, and all other inhabitants. What is important to note here is that although the non-Moravian members of the *Gemeine* were explicitly given the choice as to "whether they would stand under the constitution of the Brethren or not," most of them chose to do so.[18] Thus, this "new *Gemeine*" remained largely fictional.

Although this change dealt only with the makeup of the Gemeine and not of the village (hereafter referred to as the *Ort*), Christian David's "Description and concise report of Herrnhut," written in 1735, sheds some light on the increasing importance of the *Ort* in the thinking of the Unity:

> Although it is certainly true that all children of God already have a single way, Jesus the crucified, yet it is also true that strong and weak need to secure themselves on this way with good boundaries that they do not wander to the right and to the left and go astray. Secondly, it is

necessary that the children of God live together in one place [*Ort*] also have one kind of rule . . . and third, [they] are a good means of help and necessary guidance [*Handleitung*] to lead on this way those who do not yet travel on the path of life but are already asking after it. And therefore it was the purpose of our entire arrangement, that we might have for ourselves the same kind of ordinances, boundaries, rules, and house-discipline, according to the mind [*Sinn*] of Christ, for the general use.[19]

Christian David's expectations of the *Ort* came very close to Jerome Blum's description of the village community because they included house-discipline and mutual aid. Yet a significant difference existed. The primary goal of the *Ortsgemeine* was to develop people "according to the mind of Christ." This was the primary raison d'etre for the ordinances of the *Gemeine*, which regulated its physical as well as its spiritual life.

The closing of the Zinzendorfian *Gemeine* proceeded apace after 1735, particularly in the years following the count's exile from Saxony in 1736 for allegedly encouraging those tenants who were inclined toward pietism to abandon their lords in favor of Herrnhut. On July 1, 1737, the government in Dresden issued a Conventicle Patent that forbade conventicles in Upper Lusatia and prohibited members of other parishes from visiting Herrnhut. The *Ort* was now closed indeed, at least to those from the immediate area. Then, on August 7 of the same year, Herrnhut and Berthelsdorf received a *Reskript* permitting them "their present institutions and discipline."[20] This action emphasized the distinctiveness of the Brethren.

In the meantime, Herrnhut had been growing at a considerable rate. By 1738, it numbered approximately eight hundred inhabitants.[21] Zinzendorf, who was always wary of large groups, sought to solve the population problem and the difficulties with the exiles in one stroke. In 1737, he wrote, "Our primary intention is to build a new closed place for thirty to forty families from Herrnhut in the lordship of Isenburg or at some other place in the Wetterau."[22] This seems to be the count's first reference to an *Ortsgemeine* as "closed." The *Gemeine* at Herrnhaag ultimately grew larger even than Herrnhut. Thus, "closed" came essentially to designate the requirement that those accepted for habitation in the *Ort* also be seeking a spiritual home. Certainly, by the 1740s, petitions for habitation very frequently included expressions of the petitioner's desire to save his or her soul, and many were sent from the *Ort* for lack of conversion.[23]

The change in Zinzendorf's attitude toward Berthelsdorf and Herrnhut also reveals the increasing spiritual standard to which the *Ortsgemeine* was held.

By 1736, Zinzendorf had already turned responsibility for his estates over to administrators and confined his interest regarding the inhabitants of Berthelsdorf to the "awakened," while the remainder continued under the usual "moral-social" relations.[24] Of considerably more importance is Zinzendorf's description of Herrnhut's government, which he gave in his 1742 history of Herrnhut. The count said that although he retained his position as *Gutsherr* of the upper and lower judicial venue of Berthelsdorf, with relation to Herrnhut he had given all his rights over to the Savior. In theory, he had made over his feudal rights to Christ. In so doing, he had bound himself "not to spoil this place with any ordered upper and lower judicial venue, but rather to leave it in suitable subordination to the Berthelsdorfian middle justice and on the other hand to make [it] *ipso facto* a Theocracy through an apostolic *Gemeine* court [*Gemeingericht*], in which one exercised no other right than that of love and truth."[25] This seems to be one of Zinzendorf's earliest uses of the term "theocracy" in connection with the government of Herrnhut. It is also worth noting that, by 1757, the count remarked that he would not live in Berthelsdorf anymore "since there are the most execrable people there with whom nothing can be done."[26] It is difficult to imagine what else he could have expected because the Brethren frequently used Berthelsdorf as a "dumping ground" for their "disorderly people." The image of Christ as feudal lord of the *Gemeine* surfaced very strongly in a speech given by Zinzendorf at the Synod of 1749. He began with a litany of the difficulties faced by the Brethren and their patience throughout: "They [the world] think if they could bring us around [to give up their peculiar institutions], then they would have brought us all around . . . however the mighty patron [*Schirmherr*] of this constitution, the great protector and advocate of these Anatolian churches [*Ecclesiae Anatolicae*] and Slavonic Union [*Unitas Sclavonicae*] is the Savior himself."[27] In this same speech, he also referred to the "villages of God."

In the issues of daily life, the *Ortsgemeine* functioned much like other eighteenth-century German village/town communities. It regulated trade, maintained the physical order and appearance of the settlement, cared for its poor, oversaw public morals, and shared ownership of some basic businesses such as the general store, tannery, grain mill, and tavern. Not surprisingly, however, it viewed itself in all these activities as infused with the spirit of the Savior, some sense of which is evident in the fact that it termed its common fund the *Diacony*. This ideal held true particularly after the concept of the *Ortsgemeine* was developed during the 1730s and 1740s. In 1757, David Cranz described it in this fashion: "In communal life, or in civil life and household affairs, they are rustic [*ländlich*] [and] moral. They avoid all distinction."[28] This stress on simplicity and morality was bound up with Zinzendorf's stress on the importance of a "relationship with the Savior" as opposed to the "life of faith." A relationship could become cold or indifferent.[29] The emphasis on a living faith created the ideal of an organic dynamic in which the conduct of a member took a backseat to the member's "heart's situation." It was not so much what one did but how one did it. The Brethren expressed this idea quite well in the minutes of their *Gemeine* Council when they observed, "We indeed do everything as it is done in the world, not, however, as it does [them] but as is meet for a member of the body of Jesus."[30] Of course, the evaluation of the members' spiritual "walk" took into account inner disposition and outward action.

How the blend of religious concerns and practical action expressed itself in the daily life of the *Ortsgemeine* is well illustrated in its economic regulations. Basically, the mind-set of the Brethren caused them to maintain a somewhat medieval attitude toward money. They deplored the pursuing of individual profit and charging more than the "fair price" for an item. In addition, they remained wary of mercantile business and industry, although they allowed for the pursuit of such when practical necessity dictated it. In essence, they equated practical necessity with the good of the *Gemeine* and viewed self-interest as one of the greatest offenses to the Savior and the *Gemeine*. In part, at least, their circumspection stemmed from their concern for the reputation of the Unity as it became more well known. In 1734, the *Gemeine* Council stated "that in buying and selling here and in other places they should act wisely as proper to Christians and members of a true *Gemeine* of God. Thereby the *Gemeine* will in no manner fall under slanderous judgement."[31] Once again, the standard to which the Brethren were held was not that of their status as members of a secular community, but as members of an eternal *Gemeine*.

To a degree, the inhabitants of all villages in the early modern period were interdependent, but, in the *Ortsgemeine*, this interdependence formed one of their central tenets. As mentioned, the *Aufseher Collegium* functioned as a collective guild. While an awareness of the responsibility of the artisan or merchant to the *Gemeine* might reasonably be expected of those who worked in the businesses owned by the Diacony, the Brethren extended this ideal to every individual. In 1746, the *Gemeine* Council declared that every Brother who had his own household and business "will see to it that nothing occurs on that account against the interest of the whole, [and] that his own outward circumstances contribute to the common good. [When] the whole *Gemeine* does well, then each member does well."[32] It is worth noting that the council may have had in mind the image of the body and its members. While this image occurs in Scripture, secular governments also frequently used it when they wanted to emphasize the need for order and subordination. The Brethren, in fact, often expressed themselves in terms of the need for order, but they often accompanied this with a desire for purity, which seems a more clearly spiritual concept.

The sense of the *Gemeine* as a whole and the *Ortsgemeine*, in particular, as standing under the rule of Christ continued to develop in the years following Zinzendorf's death in 1760. The report from the Synod of 1764 indicates that the Unity had begun to view the model *Ortsgemeine* as a "city on a hill" and as a place under the special governance of the Savior. This was not entirely new because the term itself had been applied to the settlement of Niesky in 1742, but the model had been more thoroughly developed by the 1760s.[33] The report also reveals the link between this concept and the use of the lot in decision making. The section dealing with theocracy began quite succinctly: "We are a people that stand under the immediate government of our head and lord, Jesus Christ, and thus [are] neither a Republic, nor Aristocracy, nor Monarchy, but a Theocracy."[34] The report then discussed what this meant for the Brethren and differentiated between the term and the matter itself. While the term might be dispensed with because it had caused some difficulties, the matter could not because it involved the divine: "Of the matter itself, we can allow nothing else to happen but that [it] must remain as long as the Savior maintains His *Gemeine;* we understand nothing else through this than the immediate government of the Savior in the *Gemeinen,* which proves itself through the lot in doubtful circumstances and keeps the course [*Gang*] of the *Gemeinen* and their leadership out of human hands."[35] This is a fairly dramatic statement of the intimacy between Christ and the *Gemeine*, which went beyond the purely spiritual. The Brethren viewed the use of the lot system to make or ratify decisions as a means of manifesting Christ's will for His *Gemeine* in a physical way. Clearly, the Unity took Christ's role as "supreme head" quite seriously.

The synod report also addressed the place of the *Ortsgemeine* within the "plan" of the Unity. Things had changed since Christian David described it solely as a refuge for the pious:

> The *Ortsgemeinen* are places that the Savior himself has chosen, on which a peculiar grace certainly rests. [This is] a phenomenon of the eighteenth century, which had indeed never before occurred as far as one can tell from history . . . They should give off a witness to the world that is more effective than so many sermons . . . They are establishments which are brought together to the end that the Holy Spirit has a free hand so that each inhabitant becomes a child of God, and . . . the opportunity for temptation is cut off and prevented, and where the youth obtain an impression of the Savior from their first years on.

This, the report declared, was what distinguished a *Gemeinort* from "Religious *Gemeinen.*"[36]

Three important themes for the *Ortsgemeine* surfaced in this section of the report: the special nature of the *Gemeine,* the role of the *Ortsgemeine* as witness to the world, and its role as protector of the faithful. By 1764, the *Ortsgemeine* had received a mission that the Unity believed came directly from the Lord. They frequently referred to the *Gemeine* as being a people gathered from the world, as did the Anabaptists. Unlike the Anabaptists, however, the Brethren developed a strong missionary impetus that made it particularly difficult for them to keep the wolf of the world from their door. The *Ortsgemeine,* then, had a threefold task that they were to carry out under the leadership of the Savior: they were to be concerned for their appearance in the world, to be a refuge for their inhabitants, and, finally, to be a spiritual incubator for those born into their midst. This would have been a daunting task under the best of circumstances. What it did was to lay the basis for conflict between the three ideals.

In shaping the *Ortsgemeine,* Zinzendorf often adapted familiar structures such as the village ordinances. The synods continued this practice in the years after his death.Despite their intense preoccupation with the spiritual, the Brethren were a practical people who realized that to accomplish their threefold mission, they needed the goodwill of the worldly authorities. They also needed to be able to resort to legal force themselves, when necessary; but exercised this only through the specified representatives and only on behalf of the *Gemeine,* not of the individual. This resulted in the further unification of secular and spiritual government with regard to the *Gemeine* ordinances. The Synod of 1769 put it this way: "It is necessary that the *Gemeine* have statutes which the judicial authorities themselves sign and confirm. In such a manner the court authorities [*Gerichts Herrschaft*] can have the full use of their judicial office in matters of public order [*Policy Sachen*]."[37] This statement meant that the regulations of the *Gemeine* would carry legal force recognized by the secular government. The synod made clear that this power was severely limited and was only to be used for matters in which the discipline of the *Gemeine* was not sufficient. Judicial authority was never to replace spiritual authority but was to work in tandem with it. Offenders could be "relaxed to the secular arm" (although the Brethren never used this phrase) if their behavior warranted it. In addition, the Unity took pains to ensure that the judicial authorities were also members of the *Gemeine* wherever possible.

One final observation needs to be made regarding the concept of the *Ortsgemeine* as it stood by 1769. While the 1740s had witnessed an increasing sense of exclusivity, the Synod of 1769 appeared to leave the door ajar while maintaining the view of the *Gemeine* as a peculiar community. The report's description of the *Gemeine observed* that while it "should really consist purely of such souls who have found grace in Jesus blood," it was "at one in the same time an asylum or commonwealth [*Freystatt*] for those who because of the ascendancy of godlessness in the world can no longer reside or exist in their places, and so assemble themselves under the wings of the *Gemeine*."[38] This view implies that the synod saw the *Gemeine* and its settlements as a place of general refuge, likely because of the series of wars that had been fought on the European and the American shores in the first half of the century. During these wars, many *had* fled to the various settlements for safety. Neudietendorf, in particular, housed a large number of Huguenot refugees. Here again is an example of how the Brethren blended practical necessity with their spiritual ideal. The accommodation allowed them to prosper, but the mixture tended to separate when heated.

Governing "God's People"

The governmental structure of the Unity borrowed from the ecclesiastical and the secular realms. As might be expected given the shape of the *Ortsgemeine*, the government served to regulate the church and the community. Although different offices were designated to care for spiritual and worldly matters, it proved almost impossible to separate the two spheres. At any rate, the Synod of 1764 declared that "the Savior will not have the Unity Directorate separated in consideration of inward and outward matters."[39] Thus, it is not surprising that some tension existed between practical needs and spiritual ideals.

The structure of the government of the Brethren, like the concept of the *Ortsgemeine*, developed over time in response to circumstances. This makes following its history rather complicated, especially because the synods tended to shift the names given to the various offices. Nevertheless, the basic areas of responsibility that made up the local and general government of the Unity changed relatively little. The terms themselves can help illuminate the traditions on which the leadership drew in forming their government.

The development of the governmental structure cannot be fully understood without some understanding of the status of Zinzendorf and other aristocratic members as feudal lords. Many of the terms used for the offices in the *Gemeine*, at one time or another, came out of the manorial structure. Although the dynamics of the relationship between lord and tenant were changing, the structure itself was still very much in place in most of Germany. Zinzendorf used his position in shaping Herrnhut's local government, which became the model for all settlements (toward the end of his life, the count referred to it as the "mother-place"). It should be noted, however, that for the most part, the manorial yoke sat lightly on the members of the *Gemeine*. In this case, religious standards tempered authority. Indeed, the Unity benefited financially from Zinzendorf's position as feudal lord. Zinzendorf's estates provided "the most important security" in the 1750s during the Unity's most critical period of debt.[40] After the count's death in 1760, the estates became the possession of the Unity itself and were held in trust by his daughter and her husband. They thus continued to provide income for the Unity, which then stood in the position of lord of the manor.[41]

Prior to the issuance of the 1727 statutes, Pastor Rothe had organized the members of the *Gemeine* into a fellowship with various offices that were probably based on New Testament examples. These offices consisted of overseer, admonisher, teacher, servant, and attender on the sick.[42] Rothe designated himself as elder. We have no description of the function of these offices under Rothe, but the terms "overseer" [*Aufseher*], "teacher" [*Lehrer*], and "servant" [*Diener*] continued to be used to designate local officials in the Unity throughout the eighteenth century. Rothe's position as elder was clearly ecclesiastical. When Herrnhut and the *Gemeine* were formally organized in 1727, however, the office of elder changed, and Rothe was not among those chosen to hold it. In the nature of this change, one can plainly see the interplay of the profane and the sacred. Chief authority over local matters rested in the hands of a group of elders. This setup strongly suggests a New Testament model, but a council of leading citizens (usually larger landholders), sometimes designated as elders, was a common element of village government in early modern Europe, so it would have been a familiar form.[43] These particular elders were distinguished by their greater involvement in spiritual matters and by the greater authority granted to them by Zinzendorf.[44] While he may have had church elders rather than village elders or councillors in mind, their authority clearly extended beyond spiritual matters. Article 47 of the Herrnhut statutes stated, "The Elders have oversight over all these points, [i.e., the previous articles] as generally over the entire *Ort* and all inhabitants."

Twelve elders may have proven a bit unwieldy, however nice the symbolism, and, on May 20, 1728, four of them were designated through the lot as chief elders.[45] At this point, Zinzendorf became "warden" [*Vorsteher*] and Johannes von Watteville, his adjunct.[46] It is noteworthy that in his earliest history of Herrnhut, Zinzendorf referred to the four chief elders as "superintendents," rather than as "elders." This reference may have been an attempt to explain their authority in accordance with the common structure of local government, because the superintendent of a community typically stood in immediate authority over the elders.[47] Not one of the four held any "worldly" rank, but they and their descendants sat in the top ranks of the government of the Unity for the next century, as did the von Wattevilles. Gradually the number of elders was reduced to one, and their duties increasingly focused on spiritual affairs. In 1741, the chief eldership fell to Christ after Leonard Dober resigned. The lot consistently rejected all candidates for his replacement until the Brethren were inspired to propose that the Savior fill the vacancy. This suggestion received the approval of the lot (that is to say, the Savior approved his own candidacy). This development intensified the use of the lot and the sense of the *Gemeine* as a peculiar people. Zinzendorf continued in his office of superintendent, however. Although the office of elder per se was no longer filled after 1741, holders of all the other major offices were also designated as elders and made up the Elders Conference, which was the main local governing body until 1801. Although this body, in theory, occupied itself primarily with spiritual matters, in practice, it held final authority in all local decisions except where it was subordinate to the Unity Elders Conference.

The second major local governing body developed as a result of the "spiritualisation" of the eldership and the attempt to enforce justice within the *Gemeine* without setting up a formal court. At the inception of Herrnhut, the village had no independent judicial authority. Zinzendorf stressed that the elders "exercise only the voluntary jurisdiction of the statutes as long as his [Zinzendorf's] lordship permits, but all disputes and [granting of] favors [concessions, privileges, etc.] shall belong to the Berthelsdorf court."[48] The "Worldly Direction of the Place of Herrnhut" of April 1728 repeated this same stricture: "All civil matters depend on the Elders until they run to disobedience. If [the inhabitants] show disobedience towards [the Elders] however, they belong under the Berthelsdorf justice [*Gerichtsbarkeit*]."[49] The dependence of Herrnhut on the Berthelsdorf court never changed. It should be noted, however, that either Zinzendorf or his administrators exercised ultimate jurisdiction over the court. In this way, the Unity retained some control over the action of the court while keeping itself pure from the stain of worldly law.

The relatively rapid growth of Herrnhut undoubtedly put a strain on the elders, particularly given all the disputes that might arise in the process of establishing a new village. Because the Unity forbade the Brethren to engage in lawsuits, the elders' power of arbitration became very important and probably quite time-consuming, particularly for immigrant artisans and farmers untrained in the law. On April 25, 1729, the four chief elders, Zinzendorf, and some of the other elders "decided after heartfelt prayer and for many important reasons to get rid of the Elders Conference's power of arbitration [*Schiedrichterschaft*] completely and to appoint a few upright and respected men who should undertake these matters so that they [the elders] might even more fully retain brotherly love, and their souls might act with even better earnestness, watch-fulness, and supplication for help."[50] Zinzendorf's secretary and Johannes von Watteville were proposed for this new office, but it is an indication of the depth of the religious commitment of Zinzendorf as well as that of the Unity that the office went to David Nitschmann, the wagoner, and Michael Kloz, when *they* received the approbation of the lot.[51] The men present at the meet-ing designated Nitschmann and Kloz as syndics. Again, this was the familiar office of town clerk, but the Brethren gave it a different twist in accordance with their values. Writing to the Saxon Ministry in February 1732, Zinzendorf said of the Herrnhut syndics, "There is hereby only this difference, that, be-cause everything in Herrnhut proceeds Christlike, simply, and cordially, people of that kind have no name and salary, much less full judicial power etc. but only selective [powers] according to the condition [*Befinden*] of their gifts."[52]

Difficulties within the community continued despite syndics. Evidence points to a possible need for the participation of men who carried a higher rank, because, in January 1734, Secretary Friedrich and the senior territorial judge, Herr Marche, were appointed to meet weekly with the syndics and the newly created vice-judge [*Vizerichter*] to hear all complaints. At this point, Herrnhut had all the trappings of a regular court, with the notable exception of the authority to pass sentence. In February 1734, this pseudocourt received its final form. Zinzendorf's announcement of this development reveals the diffi-culty involved in holding a human community to divine standards:

> Because with some ill-bred people in the *Gemeine* mere love does not
> help, but sternness [should] also be used, and [because] one can here
> *join the spiritual priesthood to the magisterial office* because authority is
> also Christian, we would act here according to I Corinthians 6 and use
> [authority] for the improvement of souls who do not respect the spiri-
> tual workers and their activity. Therefore all matters which do not
> belong to the realm of God and could become an offense, should be
> settled quickly by certain men selected from the *Gemeine* and be dealt
> with severely by them according to the occasion [emphasis mine].[53]

It was more than likely no accident that Johannes von Watteville and Secretary Friedrich were elected to this new body, which was designated as the College of Judges [*Richter Collegium*]. The remaining members were Johann Gottfried Bezold and Michael Linner (a weaver). The use of Scripture in this passage exemplifies the increasing mingling of the spiritual and the practical arenas in the government of the *Gemeine* even as the two were being separated in administration.

The College of Judges received authority over all the outward ordering of the village, including the reception of new settlers, oversight of the economic situation of the inhabitants, wage and price control, building, sale of houses, and so forth. Most of the responsibilities of the College of Judges were not unusual to village government, although they were not generally all held by one body.[54] While the College itself held no power of punishment, it seems to have had relatively little hesitation in handing offenders over to the court, which may account for Zinzendorf's designation of *Gemeine* justice as a "*pretrial.*" It also had no qualms in recommending imprisonment and even corporal punishment when deemed necessary. Its activity declined in the late 1730s, however, and discipline shifted away from physical punishment.

The increasing number of trades in Herrnhut occasioned the formation of a special Tradesmasters Conference, which, under the supervision of a member of the College of Judges, took much of the responsibility for economic affairs away from the College as a whole. In essence, this conference and, later, the *Aufseher Collegium* functioned as a collective guild and brought the *Ortsgemeine* closer to the town model. By the later eighteenth century, the *Aufseher Collegium* functioned in the duties previously accorded to the College of Judges. Thus the *Aufseher Collegium* became the second most important governing body in the settlements. When the *Aufseher Collegium* came into this position, however, the more stringent means of discipline (which included flogging) were no longer in use, and, thus, the Brethren had indeed a College of Overseers rather than a College of Judges.[55]

The *Ortsgemeine* also retained the use of the village assembly as a unit of local government. The structure of this body within the *Gemeine* appears to have followed the pattern of "worldly" assemblies. It originally consisted of all adult communicants, but, in the late eighteenth century, it was reduced to a smaller body of elected and ex officio members. The fact that the same change occurred in much of Europe during approximately the same time period indicates an awareness of and an attunement to contemporary developments on the part of the guiding hands of the Unity.[56] The restriction of voting rights to communicants, however, emphasizes the more eternal perspective of the Brethren. It also could mean that even in their most "democratic" body; the decisions were made by a relatively small number of inhabitants because the Brethren used the lot to determine when one could be accepted for membership and when one could go through candidature and confirmation.

Although much of the government of the *Ortsgemeine* took place in conferences and committees, individual offices also existed. As a group, those people who filled these offices were referred to as "workers" or "servants" [*Arbeiter* and *Diener*]. The most important of these individuals were the *Oeconomus* and the

Vorsteher (warden), usually referred to after 1769 as the *Gemein-Helfer* and the *Gemein-Diener*, respectively.[57] A deputy often assisted them in their duties. The offices of warden and of *Oeconomus* predated their use within the Unity and again show the adoption of established administrative terms. The *Oeconomus*, or *Helfer*, rather than the warden, stood at the head of the *Ortsgemeine*. Although he and the warden each represented the individual *Gemeine* within the Unity and to the outside world, the *Helfer* (helper) had the final authority. The office appears to have been created in part to help expedite the keeping of order and to foster piety. The count recognized that government by weekly conference could be obstructive in cases where one or two men could handle matters. He referred to the *Helfer* as one who heard everything in his *Ort* and reprimanded those who needed it.[58] By at least 1757, the authority of these offices was firmly in place. After a visitation, David Cranz described the *Oeconomus* as one in charge of carrying out the vision of the *Gemeine* and as one whose counsel should be taken; he said further that "what he oppos[ed] ought to remain undone."[59]

The duties of the *Diener* consisted primarily of those things involved in expediting the daily running of the *Ortsgemeine*. His role was more that of an administrator than that of a governor or counselor. He kept a check on the finances of the various common businesses and saw to it that the physical aspects of the *Ort* ran smoothly. This job included such tasks as ordering the repair or building of fences and overseeing the construction of buildings.

As the Unity grew in size and established more *Ortsgemeinen*, including some outside of Germany, it developed a central ruling body with special offices. For dealing with secular affairs, Zinzendorf created the position of *Senior Civiles* or civil elder. In the description of this office, we can see the same concern for the legitimation of the government of the Unity in the eyes of the world as was evident in the creation of the College of Judges. The count intended the position of civil elder for those Brothers "who are especially suitable for representing the *Brüdergemeine* in State affairs through juridical training or community position [as nobles] or through *both*."[60] These men, along with the bishops, made up the top rank of the central governing body. In a sense, their authority was a more intense version of that of the *Gemein-Helfer* (*Oeconomus*). Within the *Gemeine* to which they belonged, the civil elder, rather than the *Helfer*, headed the government. Such was the case in Salem, where Friedrich von Marschall directed the *Ortsgemeine*.

In his account of the Brethren, written in 1757, David Cranz described the civil elders as magistrates and spoke of them as belonging to the district court [*Vogtshof*], which also was a term common to secular government. The *Vogt* generally stood between the local government and the overlord. His authority, however, derived from the overlord, and he served as the overlord's representative. For the Brethren, this model probably made perfect sense in ideal, with Christ as feudal lord of the *Gemeine,* and in reality, with the preponderant influence held by Zinzendorf and his inner circle. This inner circle can effectively be identified with the *Vogtshof.*

In 1745, the same year in which the Brethren created the office of civil elder, they also "renewed" the ecclesiastical offices of *Acoluthe* (Acolyte) and *Diaconus* (Deacon) from the ancient Unity. The office of bishop had been renewed earlier in 1735. Although these were strictly ecclesiastical offices within the ancient Unity, such was not the case in the renewed Unity. The position of acolyte, a preparation for priesthood under the original Unity, became "a sort of candidature for office within the *Gemeine.*"[61] The office thus provided a means for consecrating even those offices that in theory dealt with practical concerns. The office of deacon involved more extensive responsibilities in its renewed form than it did originally. The deacon helped the preacher in *all* matters, including the administration of Communion, and could, in fact, administer Communion on his own. Only very rarely did anyone hold a major office within the *Ortsgemeine* without also being consecrated as an acolyte or a deacon.

From the very beginning of the creation of special offices in the *Gemeine,* women held their own. Ironically, this resulted from the extreme caution of the Brethren regarding the mixing of the sexes and from the concept of what work was properly "male" and what "female." Speaking of the servants [*Diener*] in 1731, Christian David said, "Since, however, the Sisters are entirely different from the Brothers in special duties and obligations, they also have their particular offices instituted among themselves just as do the Brothers, partly to avoid the appearance of evil, partly to be more edified among themselves."[62] A sermon by Zinzendorf, in which he spoke of the female character and metaphysical makeup, laid out the limits of female authority but made a very revealing assumption. The count said that when "the Scripture calls the female person a weak worktool, it means by this that she cannot think as broadly, deeply, and continuously as the Brothers. Therefore one finds many fewer among you than among us who have the gift of governing."[63] In this speech, Zinzendorf reiterated the common conception of women as intellectually weak, yet he assumed that God *did* grant women "the gift of ruling" even if not on a par with men.

Despite their tendency to borrow "worldly" concepts, the Brethren stood apart from the world in allowing women to hold authority within the church. They also stood apart in their use of the lot in order to be assured that the Savior was indeed head of the *Gemeine.* All major administrative and spiritual decisions within the Unity as a whole and the individual *Ortsgemeinen* were always subject to the greater authority of the lot.

The Brethren began early on to develop a system of local government for their "baptized towns." In the early years of the Unity, however, no central government for the Unity existed outside of the office of chief elder and the will of Zinzendorf. As long as only a few towns existed, there was no immediate need for any more elaborate means of organization. The first changes in this situation came in the early 1740s. When the count went to America in the fall of 1741 to visit the fledgling settlement in Pennsylvania, it was necessary to provide for the continued oversight of the work of the Brethren in Europe. At a conference held in London in September 1741, Chief Elder Leonard Dober resigned his office, and Christ was designated as chief elder.[64] Clearly, however, for the purposes of practical administration, some human provision was necessary, and, to this end, the Brethren set up a general conference of several prominent members of the Unity. Although the exact size and makeup cannot be determined from the information available, this conference was the first step toward the creation of a permanent central unit of government.

During Zinzendorf's absence in America, the activity of the Brethren in Europe increased under the leadership of those who favored a more distinctive identity for the Unity (i.e., distinct from the Lutheran Church). This period saw the foundation of several new settlements throughout the German territories. The Brethren grew in number so that, by 1743, 20,974 people were listed as being in "close fellowship" with the Unity.[65] On his return in the spring of 1743, Zinzendorf protested vigorously against this attempt to expand the Unity since he feared that it would jeopardize the Brethren's standing within the Lutheran Church (the count always maintained that the Brethren were in no way "separatists"). He could not turn back the clock, however, or stem the tide of growth. Frederick the Great had granted the Brethren independent status within his territories in exchange for the establishment of four settlement towns in Silesia. Despite Zinzendorf's best efforts Frederick refused to reverse his decision. The count did succeed in reestablishing his own authority. He abrogated the powers of the general conference, and the other leaders of the Brethren formally guaranteed him unlimited authority.[66]

This situation did not last more than a decade. The continued growth of the Unity; its large-scale building projects in Herrnhaag, Herrnhut, and Bethlehem; and the large establishment Zinzendorf set up in London at Lindsey House, combined to create great financial and administrative strain. Under these circumstances, one-man rule, particularly by one so financially naive as Zinzendorf, simply was not practical. Thus, in 1754, after the Unity barely avoided bankruptcy, the count agreed to accept an administrative board consisting of eight men, including five fellow noblemen. These eight men, however, continued to answer to Zinzendorf rather than to the Unity as a whole.[67]

The conferential system of government became permanent after Zinzendorf's death in 1760. It also gradually became more bureaucratic and compartmentalized. From 1760 to 1764, government continued to rest in a small advisory board. The Synod of 1764 established the basic outlines of the future Unity government. They determined that the body as a whole should be governed by synod with a synodal administrative board holding the responsibility for running the unity between synod meetings. The synods themselves were made up of the current members of the board, those whom the members called to the meeting from the various *Gemeinen,* and one person elected by each *Gemeine* to represent its interests. The Synod of 1764, then, established three basically autonomous units of administration that would hold authority in the name of the synod until the next meeting.[68] The Synod of 1769 overhauled this system, as overlapping areas of responsibility had created confusion. It established one central body of thirteen men and designated it as the Unity Elders Conference. This body, in turn, was divided into three departments: the Unity *Aufseher Collegium,* which oversaw civil matters; the Unity *Helfer Collegium,* which oversaw spiritual life; and the Unity *Vorsteher Collegium,* which held financial responsibility.[69] The structure of government established at the Synod of 1769 remained unchanged throughout the eighteenth century with the exception of the addition of a Unity Missions Department late in the century.

The responsibilities for oversight taken on by the UEC were not inconsiderable. "Baptizing" a town proved to be no easy task. Keeping order often conflicted with the ideal of Christian forgiveness and love emphasized by Zinzendorf. This tension permeated all of the governmental structures developed by the Brethren. In the social structure developed for the *Ortsgemeine,* the Brethren sought to mitigate this tension by emphasizing the union of the *Gemeine* as a family; the discipline necessary for order could thus be viewed as parental. At the same time, they created a system designed to prevent the occasion for discipline.

The Choir System

The subordination of the individual to the whole that was so important to the *Ortsgemeine* needs to be viewed within the context of the *Gemeine* as nurturer and refuge. The Synod of 1769 described the *Aufseher Collegium* in this way: "The *Gemeine,* according to the rule of the apostles, has elected prudent men who are fathers of the Brethren, carry out their affairs, judge between Brother and Brother, and guard it from harm and misfortune."[70] In a very real sense, the *Gemeine* played the role of a family to its members. One of the most striking ways in which this manifested itself was through the development of the Choir system, whereby the members were separated into support/fellowship groups according to life status and sex. The Choir system grew out of the organization of the members into *Bands*, or small fellowship groups, in early 1728. These appear to have divided naturally by gender, but, at approximately the same time, groups called *Classes* also arose. *Classes* were consciously divided by gender and by age, and their meetings focused special attention on the matters most pertinent to their age and sex.[71]

This concept of fellowship along lines of age and sex was combined with a physical separation when a group of young men decided to leave houses "where [there are] either single females or wives whose husbands are seldom at home" and to live in one place for the sake of mutual edification. They hoped, thus, to avoid "suspicion and evil appearance" as well as "unnecessary thoughts" on the part of the single people. By late October, the records show that any extramarital association between the two sexes was forbidden.[72]

The number of Brothers attracted to this mutual living arrangement grew rapidly, and on May 7, 1739, all the Single Brothers in the *Gemeine* at Herrnhut decided to build their own house and to work under one roof. This house was to be dedicated "solely to the work of the Savior" and became known as the Single Brothers House.[73] Soon thereafter, they pooled their financial resources and began to conduct their trades for the benefit of the common fund or Single Brothers *Diacony*. The increasing separation of the *Gemeine* from the world also affected the Single Brothers. In late December 1740, the decision was made that single men who were Brothers should always stay in the Single Brothers House, while visitors and new arrivals would be housed in the Herrnhut tavern.[74] As with the structure of the *Ortsgemeine*, the development of the Single Brothers House probably also had a secular model. German towns frequently provided a special hostel to house journeymen while they worked in the town.[75]

The Single Sisters Choir developed in a similar manner. Eighteen single Sisters made a "covenant" on May 4, 1730, "to be entirely the Savior's, not to fix themselves in the single state but to yield everything to the Savior and the Elders and have no other will and choice."[76] The rest of the single Sisters soon followed, and, by October 1740, they had purchased their own house where they could live as one.

The married Brethren never lived in a single dwelling, with the exception of those in Bethlehem, Pennsylvania, who lived in a dormitory until 1760. Despite the fact that they lacked a physical unity, the Married Brethren still met in their Choir for devotion, sat together in church, and, finally, were buried, not with their genealogical family, but with their Choir, or spiritual family. For the purposes of devotion, the Married Choir was divided into the Married

Brothers and the Married Sisters; this meant that husbands and wives were not buried together, nor, of course, were children buried with their parents.[77]

Perhaps the most significant aspect of the Choir system was the shape it took among the children. They too had their own Choirs, which corresponded to their life cycle. They stayed in the Little Boys and Little Girls Choirs (often called simply the Children's Choir) until age twelve, when they joined the Older Boys and Older Girls Choirs. They remained in these Choirs until approximately age eighteen. Although no Children's Choir house existed per se, from the 1730s until 1760, all children entered the *Anstalt* at a very early age (usually age two); they lived there until age twelve, at which time they entered the Sisters' or Brothers' House.[78] Even after the responsibility for the rearing of children was returned to them, many parents continued to place their children in the *Anstalt* when called to another *Ortsgemeine* or when in dire financial straits. The government of the *Ortsgemeine* could also remove children from their families when the situation was such as to put them "at risk," either physically or spiritually. In addition, apprentices most often lived in the Single Brothers House, even when their masters did not.

Thus, the *Gemeine* served, in reality, as the family for those children reared in the *Anstalt* and, in ideal, for those raised by their parents. It was no accident that the Synod of 1769 applied the image of family to the Single Brothers Choir when referring to their Choir government: "In so far as the Single Brothers' Choirhouses are to be viewed as a family in the *Gemeine,* so do the Warden [and] other superiors represent the Housefathers of this family."[79] The "warden and other superiors" spoken of in this quotation probably referred to the warden and other leaders of the Single Brothers Choir rather than to the officials responsible for the *Gemeine* as a whole. Each Choir had its own warden [*Vorsteher* or *Diener*] and *Helfer,* who exercised the same responsibilities within the Choir that the *Gemeine Diener* and *Gemeine Helfer* exercised within the town. In this way, Choir government mirrored that of the *Ortsgemeine.*

By 1770, the Unity of the Brethren had created an ideal for living by which it essentially "baptized" the secular village community. This ideal placed ordinary human dynamics within the context of a divine standard. In addition, it developed a governmental structure that was hierarchical and interdependent. During this same period, the number of Brethren grew considerably through new members and through the birth of a second generation. This growth, combined with the Brethren's desire to spread the Gospel and their reputation as productive tenants, led them to found settlements throughout Europe and, by the 1740s, in America as well. Their settlement in Pennsylvania was founded for the sole purpose of evangelizing the natives and the neighbors. The motives behind the venture that began in North Carolina in the

1750s, however, were more complex, although clearly the product of events of the preceding years. The Brethren appear to have looked to this settlement as a refuge after the verbal attacks that they suffered in the 1740s and as a possible source of much needed revenue to pay off the debt incurred during this same decade. It is also possible that Zinzendorf felt that the communities in Pennsylvania had grown too large, particularly after they had to absorb many of the Brethren from Herrnhaag after that *Gemeine* was dispersed.[80] Thus, the Brethren founded their North Carolina venture with Salem as its center. This *Gemeine*, however, was separated from her parent *Gemeine* by an ocean and from the "first days" by almost half a century. Under these circumstances, the Brethren in North Carolina sought to perpetuate their discipline and reproduce their ideal.

2

Order in the Wilderness

THE PLANTING OF THE IDEAL

Looking at the development of the concept of the *Ortsgemeine* and of Unity government provides a basic picture of the blend of secular and sacred that characterized this early modern community. It also underscores the Germanic and feudal heritage of these settlements that ultimately spread outside of the European continent. The ideal dynamics of the *Ortsgemeine* are more

Ludwig G. von Redeken's 1788 watercolor of the town of Salem. *Courtesy of the Unity Archives, Herrnhut.*

fully revealed, however, by a portrait of an individual settlement. The ordinances that governed the *Gemeine* were identical for the most part, and they all shared the same rhythm of devotion. Thus, a study of the structure of one settlement can help to illuminate the structure of the others. For the purpose of this portrait, we will focus on Salem.

Planning Paradise

The area that the Brethren came to call the Wachau, or Wachovia, lies in the piedmont region of North Carolina within sight on a clear day of the foothills of the Appalachian Mountains. The Brethren had great plans for the Wachau settlement, of which Salem was to be the crown jewel. Their vision for this settlement, however, came from men largely unfamiliar with the North Carolina backcountry. As outlined in the previous chapter, the ideal for the *Ortsgemeine* called for a high degree of devotion to the Savior and to the community, while much of its structure had been modeled on the secular structures of early modern Germany. In the specific plans, ordinances, and devotional life set out for Salem, the Brethren sought to reproduce this ideal in the wilderness of North Carolina.

When the Salem *Gemeine* finally became a separate entity from the original *Gemeine* of Bethabara in late 1771 and early 1772, the settlement in the Wachau had been in existence for nineteen years. In many ways, however, Salem can be viewed as a fresh start. Certainly, a great deal of thought went into its construction and into the role it was to play within the Wachau. In addition, the years before Salem's official foundation saw relatively little deviation from the standards of the Unity on the part of its members. Nevertheless, certain adjustments to American reality had to be made even in these first years.

Many signs exist of the idealism with which the Unity approached its venture into the southern backcountry. The Brethren had two primary goals for this project: They wanted a refuge for their members where they would not encounter the hostility that had been directed at the Unity in the late 1740s and early 1750s, and they hoped to achieve a measure of financial success to help alleviate the large debt incurred in the 1740s. Thus, they needed a place that was isolated but that had potential for growth. They also wanted to secure a large block of land that would enable them to control the settlement pattern. In this way, they could choose their neighbors and leave a "buffer zone" around their *Ortsgemeine*. Lord Granville's land in North Carolina appeared perfectly suited for this purpose.[1] It seems very likely that the Brethren would have been familiar with a published report on North Carolina that included a German edition. The author wrote, "It must be confessed that the most noble and sweetest part of this country is not inhabited by any but the savages; and a great deal of the richest part thereof has no inhabitants but the beasts of the wilderness . . . backwards, near the mountains, you meet with the richest soil, a sweet thin air, dry roads, pleasantly small murmuring streams, and several beneficial productions and species, which are unknown in the European world."[2] Such a description must have made the Wachau area (so named for an Austrian estate held by Zinzendorf's family) seem a paradise, as the Brethren later referred to it. By the 1750s, it did contain some European settlers but, as yet, only a few. While leaving a great deal of empty land available, the immigration provided solid signs of growth potential. The Unity secured one hundred thousand acres, thirty thousand of which were reserved for the use of the Unity; the remaining seventy thousand were put into a land company for which the Brethren solicited investors.[3] The Brethren hoped to bring in additional funds through this company, but they were disappointed.

The Unity's plan for the settlement itself was very deliberate in shape. It called for a central town to serve as the trade center, buffered by villages and family farms that would stand under the supervision of the town. Historian Mack Walker has pointed out that the interdependent relationship between towns as trade centers and villages as agricultural centers was frequently found in those areas of early modern Germany where towns held greater autonomy from territorial rulers. He also pointed to a continual rivalry between the towns and the villages in which the towns, in particular, guarded their role as chief provider of finished goods. Walker observed that as a means of preserving the economic identity of what he designated as "hometowns," the citizens "had constantly to guard the line dividing accepted rural activity from peasant groundrabbitry."[4] The Brethren made no distinction between "peasants" and "artisans" but rather between those Brethren called to life in an agricultural village and those called to life in the town. However, the leadership did fight to maintain a line between the proper spheres of village and town activity. The Unity's plan was altered somewhat by Bishop Spangenberg, who objected to a large number of family farms, because most of the Brethren had little farming experience and needed support. Thus, in 1756, three years after the first group arrived, the Unity adopted Spangenberg's preferred plan of agricultural villages surrounding the central town of Salem.[5] This arrangement was the first of its kind in the history of the Unity and, ultimately, posed some difficulties. Although the villages and the town were all to be *Ortsgemeinen*, with their attendant special standing in the eyes of the Brethren, the villages were on an essentially unequal footing with the town. Thus, they were held to the same high standards without sharing the same privileges. In addition, the *Ortsgemeine* as developed in the 1730s and 1740s was geared toward an artisanal way of life, not an agricultural one.

The men most likely responsible for laying out the settlement were all European, and at least six were of noble or upper-middle-class background.[6] Only Zinzendorf and Spangenberg had been to America, and only the latter had seen North Carolina. The influence of their background surfaces in the almost "hot house" nature of the vision that they had for the Wachau. In the early stages of planning, their discussions included plans for the settlement of nobles.[7] Although a few nobles did live in the Wachau at one time or another, they were never distinguished as such from the rest of the population. The lack of nobles within the community may well have played a role, however, in the lack of deference toward the leadership that plagued the Wachau Brethren in later years.

Evidence of the idealized nature of the settlement and the element of upper-class influence is found in Zinzendorf's original plan for Salem, or Unitas, as he then called it.[8] It is the only known attempt to put a Vitruvian radical concentric plan on American soil. The city, for such it was intended to be, was to cover 380 acres, with a 15–acre octagonal space at its heart. This space was to contain the *Gemeinsaal* (church) surrounded by six Choir houses (two of which essentially functioned as boys' and girls' boarding schools), a *Gemeinlogis* (inn), and a *Gemeingericht* (courthouse). From this, eight tree-lined streets radiated, with 160 houses flanking them. The interior design for these houses was to be drawn up by Siegmund von Gersdorf. Eight lanes, also tree-lined, ran between the streets, and an inner circular street ran outside of the central open space, connecting all the others. The entire plan thus centered on the *Saal* and the Choir houses, and all life, in turn, radiated from them.[9] In this way, the Brethren gave physical expression to their spiritual ideal. It is worth noting that the circle was bisected by the "road to the great highway," which fitted the dual goal of isolation and contact. It was thus not an entirely self-contained city.

Zinzendorf had a tendency to overdream in his plans for other Unity settlements, and this was most clearly the case with his plan for Salem. Spangenberg allowed that the plan was "certainly very pretty" but questioned the wisdom of drawing it up before the site had been chosen. Christian Gottlieb Reuter, the Brother responsible for surveying the Wachau, objected that the plan was impractical for the piedmont area, which had "no square mile . . . in which there are not at least twenty to thirty hills and dales."[10] He further pointed out that the circular plan entailed the use and clearing of far more land than did the normal grid pattern and, thus, also more expense. Reuter did not confine his objections to such mundane matters, however. True to the "baptized"

Reuter's 1773 map of Wachovia. *Courtesy of the Moravian Archives, Winston-Salem, North Carolina.*

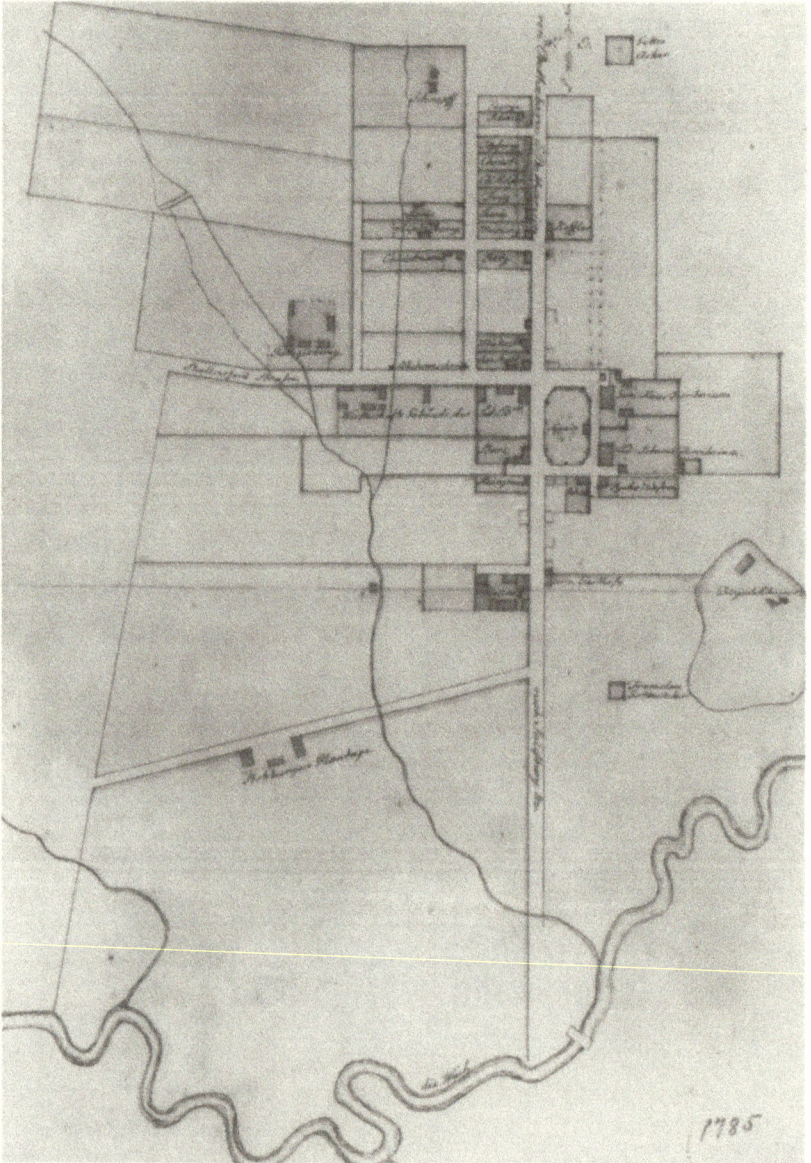

The town plan of Salem as of 1785. Note that the Single Brothers House, the Single Sisters House, the *Gemeine* House, and the community store are located around the square. *Courtesy of the Moravian Archives, Winston-Salem, North Carolina.*

nature of the *Ortsgemeine,* he complained that because the plan was not twelve-sided like the city of God in Revelation nor laid on an east-west axis, it gave "no spiritual sensation." In 1765, after Zinzendorf's death, a more modest grid form officially replaced the circular one as the plan for Salem. Had Zinzendorf's plan been carried out, it would have resulted in a city unprecedented in colonial North Carolina, which boasted, as of 1775, a scant dozen towns inhabited by less than five thousand people.[11]

The grandeur of the Unity leadership's plans for the Wachau is also evident in its economic plans. The Unity expected to develop a flourishing export business in silk, wine, olives, and grain. In the late 1750s, the leadership began the attempt to implement this scheme only to abandon one product after the other. The mulberry trees, silkworms, and olive seeds were imported from southern France by Henry Cossart, one of the early investors, but the records contain no references to silk being produced, and the olive seeds failed to germinate. The export of wheat proved to be more successful, but the settlement was too far inland to make much of a profit. The Unity did finally establish a profitable export in deerskins, an item native to the backcountry and in plentiful supply.[12]

A third area in which the Brethren's idealism surfaced was in their plans for the settlement pattern of the Wachau. Although they desired their *Ortsgemeinen* to be closed settlements, they needed to have people nearby to generate commerce and to obtain enough income to pay off their purchase. They originally intended to allow only for the lease, not the sale, of land in the thirty thousand acres reserved to the Unity so to ensure their control over their neighbors. In 1764, however, Friedrich Wilhelm von Marschall, who had charge of the settlement as *Senior Civiles,* wrote to the Unity leadership that he was doubtful whether many people could be found who would be willing to rent when land was so readily available for purchase. He admitted that it might not be wise to encourage the settlement of people who would not be subject to *Gemeine* regulations, but he believed that they could be settled at a distance "where they could not easily be in the way of the new establishment (i.e., Salem)."[13] This plan did not take into account two things: the rapid population growth in the backcountry, particularly after the Revolution; and the nature of North Carolina society, which was not amenable to control. Social activity consisted primarily of drinking bouts, shooting matches, and "frequent bouts of boxing and gouging," and the level of deference to authority was generally low.[14] This place was hardly a setting for paradise.

In 1756, Spangenberg enunciated the high expectations that the Unity leadership had for their North Carolina settlement when he said, "The Savior's heart will be blessed by you and your light will be seen far and wide, for you are a city built upon a hill."[15] He applied these hopes to the individual members in a statement that he made in 1759 regarding those going to the Wachau: "They shall always know that they belong to a pilgrim folk, and therefore never settle themselves so that the Savior cannot have them as soon as he needs them."[16] Yet, in 1760, among his objections to dismantling the communal economy in Bethlehem, Spangenberg included the fact that more land and opportunity existed in America than in Europe for a family to become "rich and content" and, thus, less committed to the Savior and to the *Gemeine*.[17] Indeed, recent studies have revealed how central the acquisition and protection of land became to the Brethren's fellow German immigrants.[18] This situation may well have been one reason, besides the desire to retain control, that the Unity allowed for only the lease of land with the three *Ortsgemeinen*. The area outside of these, however, including the territory that encompassed the *Landgemeinen*, was open for sale, and, as we will see in the next chapter, Spangenberg's fears proved justified.

Despite Spangenberg's worries, the years of the communal economy in Bethabara were relatively quiet. In fact, over the first nineteen years of the Wachau settlement, an average of one person in every two years was expelled as opposed to an average of approximately three times as many during the following thirty years.[19] This relative quiet more than likely resulted from the fact that the earliest inhabitants and the majority of adult inhabitants who came later were first-generation European-born. For many of them, their religious intensity and attachment to the *Gemeine* had been forged or strengthened during the period of intense piety, excitement, and growth in the 1740s, and their roots were solidly German. By 1771, however, the situation had changed with the addition of a number of American-born adolescents and young adults who arrived in the years after 1765. By the end of 1771, for instance, of the forty-two Single Brothers, twenty were native-born Americans.[20]

Before 1772, other changes occurred that challenged the maintenance of order and ideal. The Unity plan called for the founding of a village that would have a communal economy until a sufficient economic base could be built and the central *Ortsgemeine* completed. The Unity founded the village of Bethabara to this end in 1753, but, during the French and Indian War, a number of German and English refugees took shelter in the Bethabara fort. In 1759, the local leadership created a second village, Bethania, to house some Unity colonists and the refugees. In Bethania, the inhabitants leased their own land from the beginning and worked for themselves. Probably because of the presence of Unity members among this group, the entire village was designated as an *Ortsgemeine*, and all residents were required to sign leases in which they submitted to the Unity government, regardless of whether they were actually members of the *Gemeine*. This mixture of members and nonmembers in a single village stood as a radical departure from the concept of the *Ortsgemeine* in its fully developed form. Despite the fact that the village strongly resembled the original arrangement in Herrnhut, which had contained members and nonmembers in its early years, Zinzendorf wrote back trouncing Spangenberg for having allowed such a "mixed" settlement.[21] The settlement, however, was not entirely mixed; the original members were placed in the lower portion of the village, and the newcomers, in the upper. In addition, those in the "upper village" were eventually received into full membership in the *Gemeine*. It is well worth noting, though, that the upper village consistently pushed at the bounds of the Unity regulations and that the Wachau leadership often despaired of Bethania as a whole.

By 1772, two additional groups of immigrants had settled on Unity land. In 1769, twenty-eight people arrived from a German settlement in Broadbay, Maine. They had been persuaded to move to the Wachau by Georg Soelle, a prominent Unity missionary. In 1770, nine more families joined them, also from Broadbay. During these same years, another group of settlers living near the Southfork River, to whom the Brethren preached regularly, were organized into a formal Diaspora Society, whereby they enjoyed ministry from the Brethren but were not counted as full members. This arrangement had originally been devised by the Unity as a means for allowing people to have fellowship with the Brethren without leaving their own denomination. In 1772, both of these groups were transferred to the status of *Landgemeinen,* which allowed those Diaspora Society members who wished to, and were approved by the lot, to come into full membership and to be guided by a Brotherly Agreement. Unlike an *Ortsgemeine,* however, members of a *Landgemeine* were subject only to spiritual and moral regulations and remained free to conduct their civic life independently. The Synod of 1764 defined *Land* and *Stadt Gemeinen* as those *Gemeinen* "which indeed have their inner *Gemeine* and church constitution, but in civil constitution they are the same as the other inhabitants of their town or country."[22] With regard to spiritual and moral matters, the *Landgemeinen,* like Bethabara and Bethania, stood under the authority of the Salem Elders Conference. Conversely, the leadership in Salem held a certain responsibility for the care and education of their *Landgemeine* members. By 1772, then, the Wachau consisted of a central trade-oriented *Ortsgemeine* surrounded by and tied to two agriculture-oriented *Ortsgemeinen,* and two *Landgemeinen* made up of members who lived on scattered farms.[23] Salem may, indeed, have been a closed artisan community of which much was expected, but it could not function in isolation from those less-guarded settlements around it.

The Salem Ordinances

The Salem Brotherly Agreement and Contract set the standards by which the town was to be ordered. It thus reveals much about the mind-set with which the Brethren approached town life. As with the plan for the Wachau, the standards were high. Like the earliest version drawn up for Herrnhut, the ordinances [*Ordnungen*] encompassed the life of the spirit and the life of the flesh. They also reflected the development that the concept of the *Ortsgemeine* had undergone since 1727. The life of the flesh was assumed to be thoroughly permeated and guided by the life of the spirit, with Christ as the head of the *Gemeine* and its government. The ordinances served to provide a measure by which to discipline human weakness, but they were drawn up for a people in whom the Holy Spirit worked toward sanctification and to whom the Holy Spirit gave continual strength to resist evil. This resulted in the call for a delicate balance of cooperation between members of the *Gemeine* and for subordination to each other and to their governing bodies. All activity was to be governed by the spirit of brotherly love. The ordinances held no room for renegade individualism and little room for conflict. In addition, all ties of family and friendship were subordinated to the good of the *Gemeine* and to devotion to the Savior. For the Brethren, civil order, piety, and unity stood inextricably bound.

Salem came into full being in stages. Its communicants were separated from those of Bethabara in the fall of 1771, and its government was completely organized by April 1772. Salem did not receive its new ordinances until 1773, however. The ordinances were drawn up in response to a general recommendation from the Synod of 1769 that all *Gemeinen* establish a new set of statutes. As a template, the synod sent a copy of the ordinances that had been drawn up for Herrnhut. These ordinances were to be revised according to the particular circumstances of each *Gemeine*.[24] In general, the Salem ordinances followed the German model very closely. Evidence from the land leases for the *Ortsgemeinen* indicates that the ordinances held legal status. A provision in the lease specified that the ordinances were to be regarded as being "verbally inserted" into the lease.[25] All masters of trades, heads of households [*Hausväter*], employers, and the Single Sisters curator were required to assent by signature, while all other residents were to assent by a handclasp, as had been done in 1727. The residents not only heard and/or read the ordinances when they assented to them, but they were also reminded of them at least annually through a public reading.

Physically, the document consisted of an introduction, seven sections, and a conclusion. The section headings mirrored the various section headings in the synod reports, and much material was taken from the reports almost verbatim, particularly in the section on *Gemeine* government. The remaining sections treated, in order, the relation of the *Gemeine* to religion, the relation of the *Gemeine* to secular government, the relation of the *Gemeine* and its officials to each other, the relation of the individual members to the *Gemeine,* the relation of *Gemeine* members to each other, and the regulation of the handicrafts. In this manner, all aspects of human relations and civil order were carefully covered. The concluding paragraph was a statement of the submission of the assentors to direction and discipline by the *Gemeine* government in all matters.

The opening sentence made crystal clear the ground from which the ordinances proceeded: "Therefore through the grace of our Lord Jesus Christ various members of the United Protestant Church of the Brethren have already settled in the province of North Carolina . . . nineteen years ago in order to live together in the same in true fellowship of faith and brotherly love under the protection of our heavenly father and the spiritual direction [*Gnadenleitung*] of the Holy Spirit."[26] This statement encompassed the spiritual government that they intended and the communal fellowship that they held to be its base. It also retained an echo of the feudal terminology on which the *Ortsgemeine* system had been built that emerges in its specification that the inhabitants were to live under the "protection" [*Schutz*] of God, just as tenants lived under the "protection" of their overlord. This opening section, then, turned to the reasons for the establishment of the ordinances: "And since because of human weakness this salutary [*heilsam*] intention cannot be attained without ordinances established on and generally observant of the teaching of Jesus and His Apostles, and also suited in every way to the circumstances of the town, it has been decided to draw together *Gemeine* ordinances . . . as that to which the entire *Gemeine* in Salem . . . confesses and freely agrees upon . . . before our dear Lord and Savior."[27] In this manner, as in earlier years, the Brethren retained a sense of voluntarism while establishing the bounds of order. Their freedom was a negative freedom whereby they voluntarily yielded up their individual interests for the sake of the *Gemeine* and of the Savior. The difficulty in this view was that the *Ortsgemeinen* were no longer primarily a gathering place for new converts but rather a nursery for the offspring of the members. Thus, many were subsumed under the ordinances who had not necessarily freely chosen to submit to them.

The centrality of adherence and submission to Christ and to His *Gemeine* in government, in family life, and in work was driven home again and again in the ordinances. In speaking of the order of *Gemeine* government, the ordinances said: "In all outward order in the *Gemeine* we have to see foremost that the living knowledge of Jesus Christ be planted in the hearts of the *Gemeine* members for the promotion of the godly life and conduct, whereby they may recognize how useful and beneficial good discipline and order is, and what sort of loss it would be if it did not exist."[28] Nothing can express more explicitly the extent to which maintaining order in the *Gemeine* depended on an experiential piety. Zinzendorf believed that the gratitude of the believer toward the Savior provided the ground of moral behavior. One particularly telling example of this belief occurred in a sermon in which Zinzendorf juxtaposed the Old Testament "thou shalt" with the New Testament "I am allowed."[29] By implication, rebellion against "good discipline and order" indicated the lack of a true conversion and, thus, might jeopardize one's right to be counted among "God's people."

The specific branches and offices of government served as the means by which the ordinances of the *Gemeine* could be carried out. In this way, the *Gemeine* reinforced the final goal of promoting the "true fellowship of faith and brotherly love," and its activities and decisions had a spiritual dimension even in "earthly" affairs. The ordinances emphasized this point when they referred to the *Aufseher Collegium* as being formed according to I Corinthians 6:5: "Is there no wise man among you? no not one that shall be able to judge between his brethren?" The governing bodies were further expected "to seek not what is theirs but what is of the Lord."[30] The officials were responsible to the Savior for the welfare of the *Gemeine,* and the "private" members were responsible to the Savior for obedience to the ordinances and support of the officials. The whole functioned, in ideal, not from any sense of legalistic obligation, but from a freely rendered and joyous gratitude to Christ as Savior.

Perhaps the most dramatic example of how the demand for complete devotion to the Savior and to the *Gemeine* overrode all other concerns lies in the area of family relations and in the separation of the sexes. The relationships between family members and between women and men are two of the most essential bonds human beings have with one another. In the mentality of the Brethren, however, the very strength of these bonds could make them a threat to the greater spiritual and even physical well-being of the individual and of the *Gemeine.* The Brethren were not unique in their attempt to prevent the "unseemly" mixing of the sexes. For instance, legislation issued by the counts of Hohenlohe in the late sixteenth century forbade wedding dances because they allowed young people of both sexes to mix freely and contract secret engagements, while legislation issued in sixteenth- and seventeenth-century southwest Germany sought to control or suppress the mixing of the sexes at spinning bees.[31] The counts of Hohenlohe, however, were primarily concerned with reinforcing parental authority over marriage, and the action against the spinning bees aimed to reduce illegitimate births. The Brethren had a larger agenda and, consequently, extended their walls of separation far beyond the occasional wedding celebration or work gathering.

Article 4 of the section dealing with the relation of the *Gemeine* members to the *Gemeine* reads: "We recognize the *Gemeine* ordinance regarding the separation of the sexes, which is to be immutably held in seemly order and decency, as one of the most important and profitable for the prevention of all spiritual corruption [*Seelen-Schadens*] and injury of the glory of Christ among us."[32] Every aspect of the relation between the sexes, including but, by no means, limited to marriage, came under the regulating hand of the *Gemeine* government in order to preserve the spiritual safety of the members and to prevent any diminution of the glory of their Lord. The concern with sexual relations is quite understandable at a time when the men of a household often seduced female servants and when illegitimate births were becoming an increasing problem in western Europe. The Unity's spiritual concerns very frequently had a basis in earthly circumstances. The Brethren conceded the power of sexual attraction when they specified that these regulations did not arise from any special holiness but, rather, from an awareness of human sinfulness. Gratitude to God could only take one so far. The article went on to state that, therefore, the Brethren "held firmly that all unnecessary private association [*Umgang*] between single persons of both sexes [be] prudently avoided and be permitted under no pretext of any sort." This separation was to be carried out in the family circle with regard not only to the servants, but also to siblings. Young children were to be "kept under constant prudent supervision and never left alone with one another, so that all opportunity for curiosity and temptation may be prevented as much as possible."[33] The extent to which separation of the sexes was extended to siblings in Salem is evident from the many admonitions from the Elders Conference that brothers and sisters should curtail visiting with each other as much as possible and that they should never meet at the Single Sisters or Single Brothers House.

As mentioned in the previous chapter, the *Gemeine* served as the true family of its members. The article on parental duties stated the following as the first of its "maxims" [*Grundsätze*]: "Our married members blessed by God with children must never forget that their children are the property of Jesus . . . [and] that they thus are to raise them for the Lord alone."[34] A second article drew this emphasis on children as the literal "property" [*Eigenthum*] of the Savior to its logical but somewhat radical conclusion: "If it should arise . . . that children cannot be reasonably left together without danger to their souls, a change or transfer of one or the other children must consequently be recommended; the parents thus have justly to consent to such out of love and loyalty to their children."[35] Ties to the biological family were never to stand in the way of sanctification or of the health of the *Gemeine* family.

This power of intervention in domestic affairs resembles aspects of the modern child-welfare system and makes the Brethren appear to be "ahead of their times." As with much of their ideal, however, it had contemporary roots. Practices such as the charivari were aimed at holding individuals and their families to the village norm of social behavior regardless of individual desires. Not surprisingly, the manorial system provided a closer model. German philosophe Christian Garve spoke of the moral authority of the lord as follows: "He can punish drunkenness, he can punish gross indecency, he can punish deceit or physical violence. He can intervene in the internal affairs of the family, in the economic and marital affairs of the peasants, in the relations between parents and children, relatives and neighbors."[36] For the inhabitants of the *Ortsgemeine*, Christ was their lord in ideal, and, in most cases on the continent, members of the leadership were their lords in reality.

The overriding importance of the good of the *Gemeine* affected the family in more mundane areas as well. Article 6 of the section concerning handicrafts made it clear that the final voice in determining apprenticeship did not lie with the parents. Parents were simply to report on their children's capabilities, strengths, and inclinations so that suitable trades might be selected for them. Perhaps of even more importance were the restrictions on property inheritance. In order to preserve the *Ortsgemeine* as a "pure" town, no one was allowed to possess a house or lease land unless that person was a member and received permission from the *Aufseher Collegium* and the lot. As a consequence, no one was allowed to sell a house or lease to anyone other than someone with said approval, "nor can [the person] bequeath that possession to his children or other kinsmen if the same are not likewise recognized as *Gemeine* members and judged capable of the possession of the same."[37] With this article, the Brethren incorporated one of the elements most basic to the early modern family under the aegis of the *Gemeine* government. The article gave particular urgency to the desire to maintain children within the *Gemeine*. Most basically, however, it indicated the extent to which life in the *Ortsgemeine* was directed toward the Savior and toward the *Gemeine*.

The same directedness pervaded the Brethren's attitude toward work and toward the economy. In the opening article on trades, the ordinances stated that the Brethren were always to acknowledge employment and economic success as God's gift. They were further to ask for grace that the desire for wealth would never replace the service of their neighbor as the motive behind their work. Not surprisingly, this mind-set held no room for individualistic free-enterprise capitalism. Journeymen were specifically forbidden to contract with a master "according to their own choice"; they were to follow the instructions of the *Aufseher Collegium* concerning who they did business with. Prices were not to be haggled over, nor to exceed the "true value" [*wahren Werth*] of the product. In addition, a master tradesman was not to attempt to undercut another's prices and, thus, draw his clientele; the tradesman was, rather, to strive to produce wares worthy of their price.[38] In all these matters, the Brethren continued to function according to standards that stretched back into the Middle Ages but were becoming obsolete.

The high level of hope and expectation for order and behavior in the *Ortsgemeine* gave particular poignancy to how the Brethren reacted to deviations from the ideal. Although they shared with the Calvinists an emphasis on sanctification and an interest in discipline, they did not share their generally low expectations of human behavior. In the eyes of the Brethren, the strength of a heart devoted to the Savior was a mighty strength.

The ordinances were revised once before 1801. In 1786, it was deemed necessary to do so; changing circumstances had made several points no longer correct or proper. This revision did nothing to alter the ideal, however. The changes dealt almost exclusively with minor points of administration and with the statements regarding political allegiance (which had to be changed for obvious reasons).[39] For the most part, even the wording remained identical to that of 1773.

The Rhythm of Devotion

"Those who had been offended with one another, fell around each other's necks and joined together . . . Then the *Gemeine* fell down before God and began to weep and sing . . . and we went home again . . . pretty much out of ourselves. We spent this and the following day in a quiet and amiable contentment and learned love."[40] Thus the Herrnhut Diary described the Communion of August 13, 1727, whereby the exiles in Herrnhut first became a truly united *Gemeine* under Zinzendorf's leadership. This passage illustrates quite well the closeness of the union between devotional life and community that existed from the very inception of the *Ortsgemeine*. Devotional life formed a support system for the *Gemeine* ordinances by reinforcing ties to the Savior and to the *Gemeine*. The rhythm of devotion renewed flagging spirits and constantly reminded the Brethren of the larger family of which they were part and of God's special relationship with the *Gemeine*. Exclusion from the liturgies, communions, and festivals that made up the large part of devotional life meant, in a sense, being cut off from one's family. Ironically, it also meant being cut off from the very system by which the wandering individual was encouraged to rejoice in his submission to the Savior and to His *Gemeine*. Thus, despite its overall strength, the importance of devotional life had an Achilles' heel. So, too, did the centrality of emotion within the system.

Peter Burke's influential study of popular culture in early modern Europe includes a discussion of the creation of an alternative "Christian culture" as part of an attack on popular culture in the sixteenth and seventeenth centuries. He tied this cultural creation to a larger movement for behavioral and spiritual reform. In many ways, the Brethren provide an example of this process in the eighteenth century. Their devotional life served as a support system for the regulation of the community. But Burke's use of the image of the carnival figure of Lent (an old woman) suggests that the alternative culture was a colorless, joyless one.[41] The culture of holiness created by the Brethren does not fit this picture.

Emotion and aesthetics each played an important role within the devotional cycle that colored the Brethren's world. Evidence from the Bethlehem, Pennsylvania, *Gemeine* diary, for instance, points to the use of art, such as paintings of Christ's passion and portraits of the "first fruits" of missionary efforts, in worship.[42] Although the membership was largely artisan and middle-class, the leadership was heavily aristocratic; the result was a unique combination of baroque lavishness and simplicity in the material and spiritual culture of the Brethren.[43] One concrete example of this is the sconces used by the Brethren in their *Gemeinesaal* in Bethabara. The *Saal* itself is quite small and plain, and the sconces are made of tin. They are shaped in such a way, however, that when the candle is lit they throw the shadow of a butterfly on the wall of the *Saal*.

In line with Pietist thought, the Brethren emphasized the heart as the seat of response to Christ.[44] Zinzendorf believed that a true understanding of man's justification through Christ's sacrifice could enable man to become a true disciple of Christ and to live as such. For the count, a true understanding produced an intense thankfulness in the sinner. This thankfulness partook of love and of gratitude and was centered in the heart. Speaking of the divine work in the heart of a sinner, Zinzendorf said that the image of the crucifix is painted by the Holy Spirit "in there like a fresco if the heart is soft from need, affliction, and misery."[45] This heart image provided the fuel that kept the flame of gratitude alive. It found its highest expression and stimulation in monthly Communion, which celebrated Christ's sacrifice.

For Zinzendorf, however, this devotion could never be confined to the individual. As he constantly maintained, there could be no faith without fellowship. The development of the *Ortsgemeine* in the form of the "baptized town" with its fellowship of citizens gave an added dimension to the role of devotion in the *Gemeine*. Zinzendorf referred to communal devotion as the means by which various earthly interests were maintained in brotherly love. The sacrament of Communion had traditionally been associated with communal harmony (or lack thereof, signified by nonattendance), but the Brethren extended their resources.[46] The establishment of special times set aside for devotion allowed members of the *Gemeine* to unite together in spirit away from the distractions and pressures of daily living.[47] At the same time, it provided a means of emphasizing that greater unity that could heal any rifts among the members that might arise during the course of business or while running a household. A passage from the Synod Report of 1775 on the role of singing within the *Gemeine* epitomizes this blending of individuals within the whole: "It is also a part of the external beauty in the meetings, which at the same time has an influence on the heart, that therein many sing and perform music as if they were only one, and thus besides binding the hearts to a single purpose, also directs the necessary attention of each single individual upon the whole."[48] Significantly, singing played a major part in the various worship services of the Brethren. The kiss of peace and the foot-washing ceremony [*Pedelavium*] also served as community builders. These rituals were shared only among those of the same sex.[49]

The devotional rhythm of the *Gemeine* operated on three levels. On one level were the festivals that celebrated life in the *Gemeine* as a whole. These included thirteen days that commemorated the anniversaries of important events in the history of the Unity.[50] In addition to these anniversary celebrations, the *Gemeine* gathered weekly for the *Gemeinstunde* (literally, "congregation hour"), in which the *Gemeinnachrichten* (newsletters)[51] were read, and for the *Singstunde,* in which hymns were woven together around a selected devotional theme. This weaving of hymns was often done spontaneously, with various members picking up the thread. Once a year, the *Gemeine* held a *Gemeintag* (congregation day), at which time members were received and recognized. The Brethren marked the end of the year by reading the *Memorabilia,* an account of the year's most notable events within the local *Gemeine,* including statistics on births, deaths, marriages, arrivals, and departures. The celebration of other special days, such as funerals and weddings, usually included the Love Feast. This was (and is) a ritual in which the Brethren sang hymns and shared a common refreshment, usually coffee and a sweet bread. This ceremony was also referred to by the Greek term *Agapen* and took its origin from the New Testament references to the practice of believers sharing meals in fellowship. Other celebrations might include the *Bundeskelch* (or *Lobkelch*), which functioned as a sort of unofficial Communion. In this ceremony, the Brethren shared a draught of unconsecrated wine from a common cup and pledged their faith anew. The Brethren also celebrated Christmas and Easter, but strictly as holy days. The Easter celebration began with a sunrise service in which the *Gemeine* processed from the church to the cemetery accompanied by hymns played antiphonally on brass instruments. In addition to these specific occasions, the

Brethren also met for public reading from the Scripture or from the devotional writings of the Unity leadership, including Cranz's *History of the Brethren;* for liturgies; for sermons; and for monthly Communion.

A second level of devotional activity took place within the Choirs that formed the social structure of any *Ortsgemeine*. In many ways, the rhythm of Choir devotion echoed that of the *Gemeine*. Each Choir had its own anniversary celebrations, including the first official gathering of that particular Choir and, in the case of the Single Brothers and Single Sisters, the completion of their Choir buildings. In fact, the Salem Choirs marked the beginning of their "year" on the month in which their Choir house reached completion. In addition, each Choir had its own festival day. This festival was the highlight of the Choir year. The entire schedule of events for the *Gemeine* that day centered on the celebrating Choir. A description of the schedule for the day gives some idea of its "special" nature. The Choir would be awakened to chorales written especially for them. They then dressed in their best clothes (the women would often wear white) and gathered for a morning *Singstunde*. They next attended the children's devotions, at which they were celebrated in special verses, and shared the noon meal with the *Gemeine* officials. In the afternoon, new members were received in a distinctive ceremony in which those entering the Choir received consecration by the laying on of hands and the kiss of peace. This ceremony probably partook of the significance of a rite of passage. Certainly, this was true in the case of the female Choirs, in which a change of Choir also entailed a change of dress. The women wore the visible symbol of their Choir status in the form of varying colors of ribbon on their caps and dress lacings.[52] Afterward, the Choir had a Love Feast. At the *Gemeinstunde,* they were congratulated and prayed for by the entire *Gemeine*. The day climaxed and closed with the celebration of Communion within the Choir. Aside from such exceptional times of celebration, each Choir had brief morning and evening devotions that consisted of the reading of the daily text, hymn singing, and a short prayer. In all of this activity, individuals identified with their Choirs in symbol and in ritual. The festival occasions also served as an outlet for an emotional renewal of faith and as aesthetic enjoyment embodied in the special music and clothing.

The third level of devotional life centered on the individual members but emphasized their ties to the whole. Permission to reside in an *Ortsgemeine* did not carry with it admission into the *Gemeine* as a member. This privilege was granted by lot whether the individual was a newcomer or born into the *Gemeine*. Nor did membership automatically qualify one for Communion. This, too, was granted by lot in two stages: candidacy and confirmation. This admission by stages undoubtedly heightened the anticipation of participation.

The belief that the lot was the true voice of the Savior added to the sense of privilege in being given His spiritual stamp of approval. Those participating in Communion for the first time were recognized publicly, and the *Gemeine* sang verses in their honor. Many of the devotional meetings were confined to communicants, as was the ability to vote and hold office within the *Gemeine*. In reality, full membership in the *Gemeine* came only with admission to Communion. The individual also experienced death, or "went home," as they termed it, within the fellowship of the *Gemeine*. No member died alone but "went home" accompanied by the soft sound of hymns sung at their bedside. This practice may have been developed as an acceptable replacement for the common village deathwatch or wake prohibited by the Brotherly Agreement of 1727.

The rhythm of devotion thus surrounded the individual from earliest childhood to the end of life on several interconnecting levels. At each level, *Gemeine*, Choir, and individual, the bonds of fellowship and dedication to the Savior and to His people were stressed. This process of continual reminders of the history and purpose of the *Gemeine* became increasingly important as the second generation grew to adulthood. It provided a means of incorporating them into the *Gemeine* and helping them to experience its history in imagination, although they had not experienced it in reality. The Brethren added two devotional events specifically aimed at problems posed by the second generation. In 1783, they instituted a regular children's *Anbeten* or prayer service, to which only those nominated by their Choir leader were admitted. Then, in 1789, as a result of fear of declension, they established what was basically a coming-of-age spiritual test. When members turned twenty-one, they were questioned by the *Gemeinhelfer* as to "their mind towards the *Gemeine*." The nature of the questions indicates that this was an attempt on the part of the Brethren to ensure that their young people understood the requirements of life in an *Ortsgemeine*.

Knowledge of the ordering of devotional days within the *Gemeine* does not necessarily reveal the actual impact that these events had in the lives of the members, nor the strong emotions that accompanied it. Evidence indicates, however, something of the role played by these events in stimulating piety.

The event most central to the Brethren was Holy Communion, in which they shared the Body and Blood of their true Lord. One member of the Salem *Gemeine* said of her First Communion, "For many months after, I had such a longing for the Lord's Supper that I could not wait patiently from one month to the other."[53] In a letter written to his son, Benjamin LaTrobe described his first Communion in the following manner:

I hardly knew whether I was still in the body and felt myself indeed unworthy of being admitted into the fellowship of such a family of God on earth. The Lord gave me at that time that most desirable of all gifts, a broken and contrite spirit . . . and when . . . the congregation rose and with united voices sung that hymn Praise be given to Christ, our souls' beloved etc., the effect on me was such that I thought myself transported among the saints in bliss, joining in the song of the redeemed. . . . The organ was played with such incomparable simplicity and attention to the subject that it was as if he had the art of making inanimate matter speak the language of devotion. I hardly knew my way out of the chapel.[54]

Aside from illuminating the sensuous aspect of worship, this description illustrates how closely personal piety was bound up with corporate worship in the *Gemeine* ideal. The references to being "out of the self" that begin and end the narrative emphasize the emotional ecstasy that gave shape to their piety and the extent to which the individual gave himself to worship. The reference to receiving a "broken and contrite spirit" further emphasizes this aspect of "yieldedness." Other services also quickened the spirit of many *Gemeine* members. Friedrich von Marschall told of attending his first Love Feast in Herrnhut, "during which I felt a clear call to the service of the Savior (hitherto I had thought only of salvation. . . . I spent the night in tears and left with a heart forgiven and blessedly convinced of my call to grace through Jesus' wounds . . . feeling weak and small as a new-born child."[55] Here, again, participation in devotion aroused a sense of dedication and "yieldedness."

Nor was it the first generation only on whom the rhythm of devotion had an effect. Maria Praetzel, a Pennsylvania-born member of the Salem Elders Conference, remarked, "I felt the Savior's grace wooing my heart . . . especially at the children's festivals," and Carl L. Meinung spoke of the special "seizing of [his] heart" at the elders festival.[56] The second-generation descriptions are less detailed, however, than those of the first generation.

Various devotional aids could serve to overcome personal dissatisfaction and to bring a member back into the fold before severe measures were needed. Gottlieb Strehle "fell away" from piety and was excluded from Communion. He testified that he was unable to discover the reason until he heard the *Lebenslauf* of David Zeisberger, which brought him to the understanding "that I had sinned against Him because I had grumbled over the position [as a worker in the Single Brothers kitchen] in which I found myself through His leading. I asked Him for forgiveness and received the same to my comfort."[57] In another case, American-born Christina Dixon Biwighaus told of experiencing an increasing spiritual indifference and discontent within the *Gemeine* until she considered leaving, but her experience in a *Singstunde* renewed her devotion: "In a *Singstunde* I became so alarmed that I did not know where to turn, for it seemed to me that all the verses were directed at me." This "alarm" led her to speak of her trouble to another Sister and, in turn, to receive the assurance of Christ's love.[58]

The System of Discipline

The *Ortsgemeine* was a "little town" as well as a spiritual refuge, so some method of keeping order was necessary. This was the function of discipline. Given the nature of the *Ortsgemeine,* church discipline and community discipline were inextricably bound together. If devotion to the *Gemeine* and to the Savior failed to maintain the members in the order prescribed by the ordinances, the system of discipline provided a means for bringing the member back into the fold or for weeding out those who did not fit in. The Brethren based their procedure on that outlined in the New Testament. According to the Synod of 1775, as a first step, the head of the Choir would speak with the erring Brother or Sister. After this, the Choir *Helfer* and the *Gemeine Helfer* would admonish the person. If this, too, proved unfruitful, the matter would be remanded to the Elders Conference, if it was deemed an essentially spiritual or moral offense (one of *Herzensgang*), or to the *Aufseher Collegium,* if it was an offense against the ordinances. In the final step, if public exclusion or expulsion was thought necessary, the matter was taken before the *Gemeine* Council.[59]

Sometimes the Brethren would attach to the order of expulsion the express declaration of the removal of all *Gemeine* privileges. These privileges included protection from legal action on the part of the Brethren; exemption from military service and quartering; and, in the case of some of the settlements, exemption from manorial service. The member thus expelled would become a "stranger." The governing bodies could also recommend such "worldly" measures as arrest or corporal punishment.[60] As the Unity grew and the second and third generations appeared, forces from within and from without led to the gradual "softening" of disciplinary action. By 1770, the most common form of discipline was exclusion from Communion. Thus, for the maintenance of the *Gemeine* ideal, the Brethren became increasingly dependent on voluntary cooperation and on intensity of devotion on the part of their members.

In practice, the process of discipline was not really systematic. The Brethren kept no separate record of the disciplinary process but incorporated it into the minutes of the Elders Conference and of the *Aufseher Collegium.* Unlike the consistory courts that oversaw church discipline in the Reformed Church, no one body dealt with all disciplinary infractions. The *Aufseher Collegium* usually handled the process of admonition but made no decision as to punishment, although it could recommend certain actions. Decisions regarding disciplinary action were reserved to the Elders Conference, which usually consulted the lot on cases of exclusion or expulsion from the *Gemeine* but did not always do so. Only very rarely, however, was a Brother readmitted to Communion without the lot, and never to the *Gemeine*. Decisions on exclusion from Communion were usually made during pre-Communion "speakings" between the Choir *Helfer* and the Choir *Helfer's* charges. The purpose of these sessions was to determine whether any impediment to the enjoyment of Communion with the Savior and with the *Gemeine* existed. The results were not recorded because the Brethren were very concerned that they remain confidential. Nor does any guideline for them appear to exist. We can gain some sense for what transpired in the speakings from an entry in the minutes of the Elders Conference for 1778, where it was noted that, in the speakings, the Brethren were reminded "about various observed defects and likewise about good deeds done. We can hope for love and trust toward one another."[61] The speakings served as another means of encouraging adherence to the ideal, with the ultimate goal of a *Gemeine* united in "love and trust." The Brethren emphasized this unity, particularly with regard to Communion, to the extent that they canceled Communion in Salem (with the approval of the lot) three times in the period from 1771 to 1801 when they felt the trust of the *Gemeine* to be too disrupted for a proper celebration.

Profiles in Leadership

To gain a true understanding of the dynamics of the Salem *Gemeine* and its relationship with the central ruling body, it is important to be acquainted with some of the individuals who made up the leadership. An analysis of the backgrounds and history of the original members of the Salem Elders Conference reveals a closely knit group with very strong ties to the early leadership of the Unity. In addition, all of these first leaders of Salem were first-generation Brethren whose ideals had been formulated in Europe.

The four members who played the most vital role in guiding the *Gemeine* were Hedwig Elisabeth and Friedrich Wilhelm von Marschall, and Gertraut and Johann Michael Graff.[62] The von Marschalls and the Graffs were involved with the establishment of the Brethren in North Carolina from its beginning. Of the two couples, the von Marschalls wielded the most influence. The Graffs appear to have served as "vice-governors," and their responsibilities increased after the von Marschalls' departure for the general synod in Europe in February 1775. This increased authority proved to be of longer duration than was expected. The revolution in America delayed the return of the von Marschalls until February 1779. Because of their predominance in government, the lives of these four deserve special attention. When taken as a unit, the biographies (hereafter referred to as *Leben*) of the von Marschalls and of the Graffs show strong common patterns. To begin with, they were close in age. Johann Michael Graff, born in 1714, was the oldest. Friedrich Wilhelm Marschall (he didn't use the "von" in America)[63] and Gertraut Graff were born in the same year, 1721, and Hedwig Elisabeth Marschall followed close behind in 1724. The Marschalls were well educated, as was common by the eighteenth century among German aristocrats. Both had private tutors, and Brother Marschall attended the academy at Jena. Brother Graff attended the gymnasium at Schleussing and then the academy at Jena. His father was mayor of Heyna, he should, therefore, be counted among those of middling social rank. Unfortunately, no information is available on Sister Graff's education, but her parents were farmers, so it is unlikely that she received more than basic instruction in reading and writing.

The primary tie between these four leaders of the Wachau lies in the course of their relationship with and career within the Renewed Unity. All became acquainted with the Brethren at an early age. They joined the Unity during its period of greatest spiritual excitement, when the ideal of the *Ortsgemeine* was in the process of being firmly formulated. Sister Marschall's father, Georg Abraham von Schweinitz, was an early friend of the Brethren through his acquaintance with Zinzendorf. A visit from Zinzendorf when Sister Marschall was five made a deep impression on her. In 1737, at age thirteen, she moved with her father to Herrnhut and shortly thereafter had a conversion experience. Brother Graff first met with the Brethren in 1737 while at Jena, and, by 1738, he moved into the Single Brothers House and was converted. That year also saw Sister Graff's first meeting with Zinzendorf and Brother Marschall's first visit to Herrnhut, where he was converted.

All four, then, converted and were received into various *Gemeinen* within three years of each other. They also all had ties to the original *Gemeine* at Herrnhut and to the *Pilgergemeine,* which was Zinzendorf's during his years of exile from Saxony. Some contact between the Marschalls and the Graffs undoubtedly occurred before they ended up in North Carolina. Brother and Sister Graff were at Marienborn in 1739, as was Sister Marschall, while Brother Marschall and Brother Graff each went to Herrnhaag in late 1739. In 1740, the strands of their lives were clearly united, if only temporarily, at the Synod of Gotha. At this synod, they each received offices in the Unity, and the Graffs were married. Afterward, the lives of the two couples diverged until 1761, when the Marschalls first came to America, where the Graffs had been stationed in Pennsylvania since 1751.

Aside from the common time period of their acquaintance with the Brethren and aside from their conversions, their lives exhibit a similar pattern in their relationships with the early leaders of the Unity. All were, at one point, members either of Zinzendorf's household, of his wife's household, or of that of his son, Christian Renatus. In fact, Zinzendorf officially adopted Sister Marschall in 1741, and, from 1741 to 1745, she traveled in the company of her new mother, Countess von Zinzendorf. In addition, during her childhood, Sister Marschall had met many of the Brethren, including Friedrich von Watteville, who had charge of Herrnhut for many years. Brother Marschall made his first visit to Herrnhut in the company of then Chief Elder Martin Dober; was tutor to Zinzendorf's son, Christian Renatus, from 1739 to 1740; traveled in Bishop Spangenberg's company in 1744; and was sent to London as a member of Renatus's household in 1748.

Although they were not as intimate, the Graffs had close contact with the Zinzendorfs and with other prominent members of the Unity. Johannes von Watteville, who later became Zinzendorf's son-in-law and who was a prominent member of the UEC, and Johann Nitschmann, the son of one of the first immigrants to Herrnhut, who was also a member of the UEC, introduced Brother Graff to the Brethren when he was at Jena. Then, at the Synod of Gotha, Brother Graff and his wife were placed in Zinzendorf's household, and she was put in charge of the count's infant daughter, Liesel, a task that she deemed "important and pleasant." Indeed, Sister Graff's relationship with the Zinzendorf household began in 1739 when she entered the countess' service after meeting Zinzendorf while walking from Büdingen to Marienborn. The count gave special orders that she was to be received at Marienborn and wrote from Holland "that as the Savior had given [her] to him," he expected her to be there on his return.[64] Sister Marschall's *Leben* also contains several instances of the deep impression that Zinzendorf made on her. Clearly, both women felt a strong measure of devotion to him and to his family. In addition, the count personally officiated at the weddings of the Graffs and of the Marschalls.

The Marschalls and the Graffs may have dominated the Salem Elders Conference, but the conference did have five other original members. Anna Maria Krause and Anna Maria Quest served as leaders of the Single Sisters Choir until their retirements in 1786. Paulus Tiersch came to Salem in 1771 as preacher, and his wife served on the conference with him, as was customary among the Brethren. Richard Utley was sent to the Wachau in 1766 as preacher to the English, but, in 1771, he was installed as interim *Gemeinhelfer*. His wife was eligible to sit on the Elders Conference, but the members decided against her (no note was made of why).

The lives of Krause, Quest, Utley, and Tiersch show some similar patterns to those of the Marschalls and the Graffs, although, with the exception of Tiersch's, their *Leben* are not as detailed. The social backgrounds of these members were somewhat diverse: one came from burgher stock, one from a farming family, and another was an artisan. Their common ties overshadow their social differences, however. With the exception of Tiersch, they all converted and joined the Brethren in the early 1740s, close on the heels of the Marschalls and the Graffs. All held office in the service of the Brethren soon after being received into the *Gemeine*. All spent time at either Herrnhaag or Herrnhut, both of which served as centers of the intense piety that marked the Unity's formative years (although the nature of piety in Herrnhaag was somewhat more undisciplined during the Sifting Period). In fact, the Utleys and Sister Krause were in Herrnhaag in the same year, while the Marschalls, Sister Quest, and Brother Tiersch all served in Herrnhut from 1758 to 1760. It is more than likely, then, that these Brethren knew each other before their service in America. There is no question that they were all well acquainted with the *Gemeine* ideal as it was set up under Zinzendorf. In addition, for Sister Marschall, Brother Tiersch, Sister Quest, and Sister Krause, the adherence to the *Gemeine* cost them conflict with family and, in Tiersch's case, with his worldly career. Thus, these early leaders of Salem formed a strong bridge to the European origins of the Brethren through their experience with the Unity in its early years and through their relationships with the "founding fathers." The backgrounds of those officials sent later from Europe indicate an attempt on the part of the UEC to maintain this general profile. By century's end, however, those sent had no personal experience of the early years of the Unity.

This gives us a portrait of the Salem leadership; but what of the men who sat at the helm of the Unity? Giving a similarly detailed analysis of the twenty-eight members who served on the UEC during the period from 1771 to 1801 would be extremely convoluted and take up far too many pages. We can, however, get a revealing overview of this body.[65] In many ways, a profile of the UEC resembles that of the Salem Elders Conference. Most striking is the numerical dominance of first-generation members. During the period in question, only seven members were second-generation, and, of these, one was the child of immigrants from the Ancient Unity. At least ten of the members were either part of Zinzendorf's inner circle themselves or close to those who were. Thirteen also experienced the expansion and spiritual excitement that characterized the Unity in the 1740s. Thus, a large proportion of those who guided the Unity during the late eighteenth century had experienced the spirit of its early years. Fourteen also had served in local *Gemeine* government before joining the UEC.

The profile of the UEC, however, also illustrates the leadership's connection to the larger world of European government and society. An analysis of their social origins reveals a body that certainly did not conform to the stereotypical artisan world of so many sectarian groups. Nor did it conform to the profile of the majority of the Unity membership. Of the twenty-eight who served during the period in question, ten were nobles, although Johannes von Watteville was not born noble but was adopted by a baron before marrying Zinzendorf's daughter. An additional seven came from the upper burgher class (prominent merchants, lawyers, high church officials), and, indeed, two of them married into the nobility. Eight were from clerical families, and only two were peasants or artisans. Nine also had a university education, most often from Jena or Leipzig. An additional two had private tutors when young but did not attend university, and four attended the Unity seminary at Barby. Finally, nine members had either represented the Unity at various royal courts of Europe or had served as provincial administrators. Only two, however, had any experience working in America.

When the Unity built Salem in the wilderness of North Carolina, it had great expectations of this settlement, both material and spiritual. Salem's physical layout and administration were carefully planned, and it was undergirded with a system of ordinances, devotion, and discipline designed to instill and maintain an ideal of dedication to the Savior and to the *Gemeine*. For the most part, this ideal remained largely unchanged throughout the first thirty years of Salem's existence. The plan and the system, however, were based on an ideal developed in Germany during a period of intense religious excitement. The very step of systemizing what was essentially an organic movement created a certain tension. The very high standards required of inhabitants of an *Ortsgemeine* aggravated this tension, particularly as an increasing number of them were born into their position as "God's people" and did not choose it themselves. Moreover, the men who planned this settlement had little or no experience of life in the North Carolina backcountry. Under these circumstances, the Brethren positioned themselves for an uphill battle in their attempt to keep the reality in line with the ideal, not only in Salem, but also in the German *Ortsgemeine*.

3

Battling Chaos

DISCIPLINE AND DECLENSION IN THE *ORTSGEMEINE*

The Brethren built their *Ortsgemeine* on high ideals and surrounded it with a wall of discipline and devotion intended to protect it from the world and from human weakness. To create an ideal for Christian living is one thing; to maintain it is quite another. As the massive research on the Puritans has shown, passing on a way of life and a mind-set based on religious faith poses a serious problem. To retain the next generation, the faith must adapt; the "halfway covenant" of the Puritans is an example of this. At the same time, adaption can and often does alter the form of faith significantly. The Brethren faced this same difficulty and faced it in the eighteenth-century environment of rising consumerism and prosperity; an emphasis on reason, at least among the educated; and a growing emphasis on romantic love as a primary motivator for marriage. All of these things could threaten the *Gemeine* ideal, particularly if the spiritual dedication of the members weakened. The freezing of the ideal and consequent systemizing of devotion clashed with an inborn membership that was increasingly restless within the boundaries of their world and that was vulnerable to outside influence. This restlessness manifested itself similarly in Germany and in North Carolina and illustrates the inroads of the "modern" world into the *Gemeine* and its culture of holiness.

The Question of Declension

On September 5, 1786, the following statement was recorded in the minutes of the *Gemeine* Council: "The Brethren have already often been urgently reminded . . . not to forget that the Savior calls us to be His witnessing people [*Zeugenvolk*] and therefore we were obligated to purify ourselves from all work of the flesh and of reason [*Vernuft*] and from what could hinder His intention with us in any way. We must, however, state with shame and sorrow that despite such repeated admonitions and warnings, much that belongs to the luxury and lust of this life, and to the worldly and fleshly mind, still remains in the conduct of an increasing number of local inhabitants."[1] By the time of the meeting of this *Gemeine* Council, the Salem leadership clearly believed that something had gone wrong with the *Gemeine*. This text hints strongly at the failure of the devotional cycle and of the power of material and physical desires to distract the Brethren from their calling as God's people. In other words, Salem had become the victim of declension. The Salem elders were not alone, however. Their sense of the sorry state of devotion in their *Gemeine* was echoed in the minutes of the UEC with regard to the whole of the Unity.

When discussing declension, the question arises of whether it was real or perceived. Much ink (or toner) has been spilled over this issue among scholars of the Puritans. Some historians have pointed out that evidence suggests that religious values continued to play an important role in New England life and that claims of declension were exaggerated; what occurred was change, not decline. The research of other historians indicates a rejection of the way of life of the earlier Puritans by their descendants.[2] The key to understanding this debate lies in exploring the attitude toward change. Declension among the Brethren seems to have been the product of a shift in attitude from above and from below. Within the context of the *Ortsgemeine*, change was good only when it resulted in a more Christlike community. By the later eighteenth century, the leadership became increasingly wary about doctrinal and behavioral deviation, and focused on the retention of those born within the *Gemeine*. Consequently, the leadership viewed change largely in negative terms and increasingly systemized devotional life in the communities. At the same time, the laity appear to have had growing difficulty in their spiritual experience, to have had a greater inclination toward their biological family, and to have been more susceptible to the lure of the world outside. This does not necessarily mean that the laity (or even the second generation) were becoming irreligious. They simply seem to have been discontent with treading the path worn down by their elders. One generation's "decline" was another generation's move forward.

Aside from the hand-wringing declarations of the UEC and the Salem Elders Conference, evidence of difficulties within the Unity can be found in a study of the pattern of discipline, in particular the figures for expulsion and exclusion from the *Gemeine*. One might argue that a rise in these figures reveals only an increasing determination on the part of the leadership to enforce discipline. The records throw doubt on this argument, however, by indicating many instances of probation granted to offenders. This suggests that the leadership was never really eager to use the ban, although exclusion from communion was another matter.

If we take Herrnhut as an example, we find that, from 1773 through 1801, 132 people were expelled out of a population that averaged around 900. The most dramatic jump came in the 1780s, when the number of expulsions quadrupled by the end of the decade. The average number expelled per year peaked in the late 1790s. The figures for Salem show a similar increase, although the rise is less steady and the increase is less dramatic. Over the same span of years, thirty-eight people were expelled out of a population averaging around two hundred. This rate is actually higher than that for Herrnhut and may reflect the fact that members expelled from Salem were more likely to keep their feet economically due to less economic restriction than existed in Germany; thus, the leadership felt less compunction about exercising the ban. The numbers did rise over this period, with the greatest jump in the 1790s. The numbers for this decade were double those of the previous one.

If we include the people excluded but not actually expelled from the Salem *Gemeine*, the numbers show a more dramatic increase, particularly from the 1770s to the 1780s. During this period, the number expelled more than doubled, while the adolescent and adult populations rose by only 50 percent.[3] As the figures for both *Gemeinen* indicate, the 1780s and the 1790s were troubled decades for the Unity on both sides of the Atlantic.

Other evidence can put some flesh on these bones. In Herrnhut, of the eighty cases in which the cause for expulsion can be determined, twenty-nine fell into the area of sexual sins; twenty-six fell under "bad conduct," which could include frequenting taverns, fighting, cursing, and so forth; eight were labor problems; eight were for drinking; four were for theft; three were for lying; and two were Single Brethren who had a "harmful connection" the exact nature of which is difficult to determine.[4] In Salem, a cause can be determined for thirty-seven cases. Of these, nineteen involved sexual misconduct; eight involved wild behavior, including drinking; and four were for disobedience to the instructions of the *Aufseher Collegium*. In addition, one member was expelled for beating his apprentice and another probably for introducing "bad books" into the *Gemeine*. The minutes of the Salem *Aufseher Collegium* also give insight into the pattern of disorder in this *Gemeine*. The amount of detail included in the minutes dropped off toward the end of the century, so the picture they yield is admittedly a rough one. In general, though, complaints of drinking; the bad influence of outsiders, or "strangers"; disobedience to the ordinances; and the desire for economic profit increased in the late 1780s, in some cases dramatically. These problems then leveled off and remained relatively steady through the 1790s.

The pattern of change in attendance at Communion in Salem also suggests a type of declension. If the records for Communion attendance are broken down by decade, the figures show an average increase of between ten and fifteen persons each decade who either abstained or were excluded from Communion. The figures thus rose from one out of every ten persons to approximately one out of every five persons. By the 1790s, between 20 and 25 percent of those persons eligible for Communion were not participating in this most important expression of devotion to the Savior and to the *Gemeine*.

Aside from the rise in the numbers absent from Communion, scattered hints exist of a general inattention to devotion, particularly among the young people. In 1780, the Elders Conference stated, "It is considered a shocking state of affairs when parents do not hold table prayers at meals with their families."[5] Three years later, the Single Brothers *Helfer* observed, "The Brothers who do not want to go to morning devotions should at least have so much respect for the same that they do not rise during them and disturb them with heavy stomping and rumbling around."[6] By the late 1780s, the difficulties were not confined to the Choir house. "It was noted that many Brothers roam about in the countryside during the Sunday meetings, which is altogether contrary to the Christian faith and also altogether against our house ordinances."[7] This same entry also noted the neglect of communicant and Choir meetings. The extent to which youthful indifference seemed to have progressed surfaced in the *Gemeine* meetings themselves. In August 1797, the *Aufseher Collegium* observed, "Some of the people are laughing or talking during the *Gemeine* meetings and we thought a public warning about this would be wise."[8] In that same year, the Elders Conference remarked the following regarding those Single Brothers who were of an age (twenty-one) to be questioned as to "their mind toward the Savior and the *Gemeine*": "The subjects on the Brothers' side . . . are almost all of the sort that we thought with embarrassment about whether we should wait awhile longer until we could hope for a better effect for them from the Speakings."[9] At this point, the Salem leadership seems to have sensed the increasing ineffectiveness of the devotional cycle when faced with intransigent youth.

The leadership (local and UEC) cited similar signs of devotional decline in Herrnhut, although not until the troubled 1790s. In 1792, the Herrnhut Elders Conference admonished several young Single Brothers for frequenting a nearby tavern [*Dorfschenke*] during the *Gemeinestunde* (devotional hour). The report for a visitation in 1793 noted that more Single Brethren were abstaining from Communion and that over twenty had skipped the foot-washing service that preceded their Choir festival.[10] Given the importance placed on special devotional days, not to mention the pressures exerted by a visitation from the UEC, this indication of creeping indifference is telling. More important, the increasing tone of frustration on the part of the leadership would have widened the gap between them and the wayward youth. The observation of slackening devotion in Herrnhut occurred in a decade marked by entries in the records such as this: "Because some Single Brothers go into the bush by moonlight and shoot with pistols, it must be generally announced in the Brothers House that they stop it and get rid of their firearms"; and, a few months later: "Since some young Single Brothers on a sleigh ride offended against the regulations for public order by shooting and therefore came under manorial punishment, the *Collegium* found it necessary to notify the Single Brothers who still have firearms to give up or get rid of them, so also the whips."[11] Salem had its pistol problems, too, though of a slightly different order. In 1782, the Elders Conference found it necessary to note that the practice of pistol-toting Brothers accosting others on the street was grounds for expulsion.[12]

The basic similarity between the patterns of discipline in Herrnhut and in Salem is striking given the difficulty of communication (letters generally took at least six months between Germany and North Carolina) and the differing environments. Two things should be noted that help to explain it. The first point has to do with devotional life. A comparison of the *Lebensläufe* of the first- and second-generation members reveals a significant difference in their conversion narratives for the European- and for the American-born Brethren. In specific, the point of conversion of first-generation Brethren emerges quite clearly, while the second-generation narrative expresses many more spiritual peaks and valleys (especially valleys), making the actual point of conversion fuzzy. This fuzziness may be the result of Zinzendorf's implication that children born into the *Gemeine* needed only to grow into their grace rather than to receive it; but it also strongly suggests a basic spiritual uncertainty among the second generation similar to that of second- and third-generation New England Puritans.[13] The *Leben* exist only for those who died within the fold, but we might expect that the uncertainty was as bad or worse for those Unity children who were expelled. In general, the *Leben* give a good indication of the difficulties involved in transferring experiential piety across generations.

The second point that explains the similarity in discipline patterns relates to outward rather than to inward circumstances. The periods of greatest difficulty within Herrnhut and Salem correspond to upheavals in their respective environments. These upheavals occurred at relatively the same time in both places. In Salem, we see two distinct periods of increased trouble: one during the war of independence in the late 1770s and early 1780s, the other in the late 1780s to mid-1790s. In 1781, Salem played "host" to rebel and royal forces successively. Various references in the minutes of the ruling bodies indicate that despite, and, perhaps, because of, their less-than-brotherly nature, these men exercised a fascination on the youth of Salem. In one instance, the leadership admonished the young boys not to consort with the soldiers (the boys were apparently curious about military life). In another, it admonished the Brethren, in general, not to seek out news of the battles.[14] The ill effects that this martial influence had are indicated by such references as the admonition against threatening people with pistols and the exclusion of a Brother from Communion after he got drunk with some officers in the tavern.[15]

The second period of increased trouble coincided with the increase in references to strangers employed in Salem and with a general rise in population in the North Carolina backcountry. Although economic necessity often forced the leadership to allow the employment of strangers, it was reluctant to do so in large measure because of the fear that the strangers might have a bad influence on the inhabitants of the *Ortsgemeine*. The records reveal that the Brethren did consort with these potentially "dangerous" outsiders. In 1787, the Single Brothers diarist recorded the following: "In the late evening drunken people came into the town who accosted many Brothers in our house and sought out quarrels. Some of our Brothers were guilty in this since they have many dealings with them."[16] In 1795, the *Aufseher Collegium* remarked that the younger Brothers and the boys were "very much inclined to take up a connection with such strangers" (i.e., the outsider journeymen), and, by 1797, it placed the burden of guilt for the problem primarily on the shoulders of the youth because they sought out the friendship of the disruptive strangers.[17] Clearly, the youth of Salem found the company of those other than the Lord's people increasingly congenial and increasingly available.

Evidence suggests that this was also true of the young people in Herrnhut. Certainly, the records of the 1790s contain a large number of references to the lure that life in the neighboring villages held for them. However, there were other impetuses to disorder during this period. Among the laments of "unregulated" and "deviant" behavior is a brief remark about the proper venue for publishing a governmental proclamation regarding "tumult and insurrection."[18] This remark refers to the regulations issued in early 1791 after a series of peasant uprisings in Saxony following the news of the French Revolution and the attendant spread of radical political ideas. Although activity in Upper Lusatia was limited, the man whose writings inspired the revolt had been raised in the "pietist, Herrnhuter sense." In addition, signs of radicalism surfaced again in 1794 when a placard bearing the symbols of revolution accompanied by revolutionary verses appeared on the door of the Rathaus in Zittau.[19] Intriguingly, the UEC minutes contain almost no discussion of these uprisings, nor of the Revolution, nor do they indicate a connection between the upheavals outside the *Gemeine* and those within it.[20] Nevertheless, it seems unlikely that the confluence was purely coincidental.

Patterns of expulsion and Communion attendance along with anecdotal evidence from the records of the ruling bodies reveal a growing problem with adherence to the spiritual and moral standards of the *Gemeine* that faced the leadership in Europe as well as in North Carolina. Evidence from the German *Gemeinen* and from Salem shows that, to a large degree, this declension from the ideal involved a struggle over a shift in loyalties. The ideal of life in the baptized town called for the primary focus of the individual to be on the Savior and on the *Gemeine,* with all else subordinate to it. During the late eighteenth century, the Brethren confronted the harsh reality of the pull exerted by the biological family and by the lure of sex. The economic and emotional demands of the family and the desire for earthly (or earthy) intimacy proved powerful rivals for the loyalty of *Gemeine* members. Cultural developments in the eighteenth century, specifically the rise of sentimentalism regarding family ties and the Sturm und Drang celebration of passion, intensified this rivalry.

The Pull of Family

As we have seen, the *Gemeinen* came to be viewed as spiritual incubators, particularly for those born into their midst. The Synod of 1764 expressed this view in its definition of the *Ortsgemeinen* as places where "the opportunity for temptation is cut off and prevented, and where the youth obtain an impression of the Savior from their first years on."[21] For the Unity, the community as a whole served as nurturer and refuge charged with the task of providing a proper environment for the work of the Holy Spirit. In a very real sense, the *Gemeine* played the role of a family to its members. In this respect, it resembled a monastic community in which the abbot was literally viewed as "father," just as the Brethren described the members of the *Aufseher Collegium* as "fathers of the Brethren." The monastic community, however, eliminated the family from its ranks, at least as a recognizable unit. The Brethren did not. They chose, rather, to incorporate it as one type of family among others (i.e., the *Gemeine* and the Choir) and to place it in a subordinate role to them.

The ruling bodies of the *Gemeinen,* vested with the task of caring for the community, exercised ultimate control over its children. Although they worked in close consultation with parents, the *Aufseher Collegium* determined the children's vocations, and the Elders Conference determined their marital fate as well as their fitness to become full members of the *Gemeine.* Of course, the Savior, speaking through the lot, had the final voice. This subordination of parental authority seems odd in a period in which parental and, specifically, paternal authority was generally reinforced by state and religious authorities, but the *Gemeine* ordinances illuminate the thinking behind it with their description of children as the "property" of the Savior. The proprietorial view of children, combined with the concern for their spiritual welfare, justified the provision in the ordinances for intervention into domestic affairs. The provisions included one for the physical removal of children from the household when deemed necessary. As noted earlier, the right of intervention mirrored similar rights of lordship under manorial law.

It became particularly important to delineate the responsibilities and limitations of parental authority after 1760, when it became the exception, rather than the rule, to turn children over to the *Anstalten* to be raised. This move increased the importance of the biological family in raising children for the Savior, but it also increased its potential as a rival. The minutes of the Salem ruling bodies are replete with instructions on proper child rearing, and they held a growing number of special conferences with parents to discuss this issue. The Salem leadership and the UEC continually reminded parents of the great importance of their influence on their children; yet, an element of suspicion lurked beneath the surface, and the leadership often limited contact between parents and children. This ambiguity in attitude toward the family reflects the multifaceted identity of members of the *Gemeine*. An individual member was, first and foremost, the possession of the Savior. The individual was also a member of the baptized town however, and, as such, a Sister or Brother to all other members, a member of a Choir, and finally, a member of a biological family with the attendant identity of husband, wife, father, mother, son, daughter. In the last quarter of the eighteenth century, these identities conflicted with each other, with the biological family often winning. During the same period, family ties, that historically had been of economic and social importance, became sentimentalized under the influence of Rousseau and others. Evidence from Salem and Germany reveals that parents articulated a concern for the feelings of their children in addition to an economic need in their opposition to *Gemeine* intervention in family affairs.

The fact that the Salem leadership felt the need to continually admonish brothers and sisters to limit their visits with one another indicates the difficulty of subordinating family bonds. It is in the realm of *Gemeine* discipline, however, that the conflicting loyalties become most clear. The pattern of exclusion from Communion in Salem indicates the pull of the biological family. The records allow for a full analysis of this only for the 1780s; this is the only decade in which the minutes of the Elders Conference list all the individuals abstaining or excluded from Communion. These years show a pattern worth noting. From 1782 through 1786, the number of siblings sharing exclusion or abstention rose steadily every year from two in 1782 to eleven in 1786. After 1786, the number held steady until 1789, when it dropped back to five. In that year, however, at least two of these siblings moved out of Salem, which accounts for some of the drop. Although we cannot be certain that either family loyalty or sibling influence was behind this pattern, at least two known examples indicate that they may well have been. In 1788, Christoph Loesch was excluded from Communion for protesting his brother's exclusion from the *Gemeine*, and, in 1795 Christoph Buttner suffered the same fate for the same offense.[22]

Family ties also interfered with the exercise of discipline in the *Gemeine*. This interference resulted from the leadership's recognition of the interdependence of family members and from resistance on the part of the parents. By 1760, the government of the Unity proved increasingly inclined to use leniency with married people and with children born into the *Gemeine*. Ironically, this leniency was fueled by the ideal itself. The concept of the *Gemeine* as parent had a special reality from the 1730s to 1760. During this period, all children entered a common nursery or *Anstalt* (usually at age two) and lived there until they entered the Single Brothers or Single Sisters House at age twelve.[23] Thus, as supervisors of this institution, the *Gemeine* leadership had a large share of responsibility for raising children born during this time. This situation contributed to the softening of discipline. For example, in 1761, the Herrnhut Elders Conference yielded to one father's protest over his young son's expulsion, observing that he could be let off with a warning "since he had been raised in the institution from his second year on."[24] One of the leaders of Salem voiced the same view in a letter written to the UEC in 1775: "There is less doubt when we send an artisan who has come out of the world back [into it], than a child who has grown up among us [and] whose parents have given him over to us."[25]

The acknowledged interdependence of its members also made the biological family a special problem for maintaining discipline in the *Gemeine*. In addition to the basic concern for the effect of the removal of one member of a family on the remaining members, the German *Gemeinen* faced particular problems. Transfers from one settlement to another could be complicated because of varying local economic regulations and emigration laws, and economic opportunities were more limited for those expelled from the protective blanket of the Unity.[26] Thus, parents and the local leadership were acutely concerned with the consequences of removing "disorderly" Brethren. Yet, leniency also posed a danger.

Some examples from the German settlements illustrate this dilemma. In 1784, the Niesky Elders Conference asked the UEC what to do with a young man who had sneaked off to the "big city" of Görlitz and gone drinking (among other things). Although, in the end, it advised the Niesky authorities to send him away, the UEC expressed reluctance to do so because the young man's help was necessary to his old father.[27] The Gnadenberg Elders Conference made a similar observation when it feared that expelling a young man who had given "public offense" would be too hard on his parents. The Elders Conference also remarked on its inability to arrange a transfer to another *Gemeine*.[28] The next year the Gnadenfrei Elders Conference agreed to allow Brother Hentschel, for his father's sake, to continue teaching in the town school despite the fact that young Hentschel refused to pledge his obedience to the town ordinances.[29]

Although they faced fewer obstacles to expulsion, the Salem leadership also proved reluctant to expel family members, particularly the heads of households. The case of Abraham Loesch provides an example of compromise in discipline for the sake of the family. Loesch had come under discipline several times previously and finally stepped over the line when he disciplined his apprentice too harshly. The Elders Conference regretted the need to expel him but stated that it had had patience with him thus far "only for the sake of his family." This same concern led the Elders Conference to allow him to settle near Salem despite its severe hesitation. The elders decided that it would be "too difficult" to refuse because his outward circumstances had been made critical by the loss of his right to reside in Salem.[30] Thus, although expelled from the *Ortsgemeine,* Loesch was not removed from the area. The Elders Conference cited the same reason for their persistent patience with one of Salem's chronic drinkers and debtors. "The main reason it is so difficult for us to give him notice regarding his residence with us," the elders remarked, "has always been his wife and children, on whom we cannot think without the greatest compassion."[31] This reluctance on the part of the Salem Elders Conference to expel members who had a family is confirmed by the fact that, from 1771 through 1801, only two family men were expelled, including Loesch.[32]

In the cases cited above, the *Gemeine* or Unity leadership took the initiative in softening discipline in the name of family ties. More often, the initiative came from the family members themselves. The records of the Salem *Gemeine* yield several examples of parental resistance to discipline, some quite emphatic. In 1783, the Jacob Blums protested so vigorously over the Elders Conference's decision to turn their son over to the justice of the peace for punishment that the elders feared that their protective attitude would cause the "blessing of discipline" to be lost on their son.[33] The Charles Holders objected so strongly when the Elders Conference instructed them to place their young daughter in the Choir house because of disciplinary problems that the leadership abandoned the idea.[34] In another case, the Elders Conference advised Traugott Bagge that it might be "useful and necessary" to transfer his son out of the Wachau, perhaps even to a European *Gemeine*. The elders noted, however, that, when told this, Bagge appeared to be blind to the "danger" his son faced at home.[35]

The Herrnhut records also reveal parental resistance. A similar stand on the part of authorities there resulted in a sharp argument in which the aggrieved father appears to have claimed that the *Gemeine* authorities were partial in their discipline.[36] Foot-dragging on the part of parents surfaced in Herrnhut as well. In 1791, the *Gemeine* authorities reported that the son of the knife smith had been punished for theft; they remarked that his father had often been told that it would be good for his children to be placed in another *Gemeine* but that he had been unable to agree to this.[37] In at least one instance, parents fought expulsion with worldly weapons. When Franz Büttner of Gnadenberg became "carnally" involved with a stranger woman and was consequently expelled, his parents insisted on a legal investigation of the matter. The legal action was unsuccessful, and the UEC commented that Büttner's parents should be taken to task for their "bad childrearing."[38]

It is difficult to know to what extent parental resistance to *Gemeine* discipline sprang from simple economic grounds and to what extent emotion fertilized the soil. Evidence exists, however, that suggests that a strong emotional bond between parent and child overrode dedication to the *Gemeine*. In 1773, Andreas Schober of Pennsylvania wrote to Marschall trouncing him for apprenticing Schober's son without his father's permission "and to a profession that perhaps is opposed to his temperament."[39] This certainly is a case of resistance to *Gemeine* authority over the family, but what is particularly striking is that Schober specifically objected that his son's happiness had not been properly considered. In Herrnhut, a Brother Enderlein agreed to bring back his young son, who had run away after committing petty theft, on the condition that the boy not be punished.[40] In another case, the Neuwied Elders Conference had to threaten Sister Elsasser with public exclusion in order to persuade her to put her youngest daughter in the Choir house. They remarked that, according to the "ordinances given by the Savior himself," it was unacceptable for "such a grown girl" to stay in a house where "Single Brothers and natural [i.e., stranger] men" were employed. A later note in the records suggests that the girl's reluctance to leave home was the source of her mother's resistance to the Elders Conference.[41] On a more general level, the UEC bemoaned the lack of response to their admonitions regarding proper discipline in child rearing.[42]

The Lure of Sex

The threat from the strength of family ties was closely related to an even greater challenge faced by the Brethren. Shortly after several young members of the Single Choirs married and set up housekeeping in Salem, the Elders Conference declared, "In connection with these new marriages, it was earnestly recommended that the single Brethren [*Geschwister*] refrain from *unnecessary visits* to the families, especially the newly married Brethren. These ought rather to visit their friends in their respective Choirhouses" (emphasis theirs).[43] Visits between friends and siblings could and did eat away at the wall of separation of the sexes and, hence, allowed temptation to slip in. Using the pretext of a visit to a family member to make the acquaintance of the opposite sex must have been quite a temptation in a society structured to prevent any means of contact between single men and single women.

The temptation was undoubtedly especially strong among the second generation. Although the separation of the sexes had arisen voluntarily out of concern for spiritual edification and physical protection, it had become institutionalized and involuntary. Marriage, according to the *Gemeine* ideal, was to be viewed as a union of warriors for the Savior, a union that would foster the Savior's cause. On a practical level, marriage was usually seen as a necessary foundation for establishing an independent business. In neither case, however, did personal inclination play a role in the choice of a partner. Proposed partners and time of marriage were both controlled by the Elders Conference in consultation with the *Aufseher Collegium* and, in the case of younger Brethren, with the parents. No marriage proposal, however, took place without the approval of the lot, which could result in delayed marriage or even in the inability to find suitable partners.

Given this situation, it is no wonder that the breakdown of offenses for which Salem and Herrnhut inhabitants were expelled shows a heavy preponderance in the category of sexual misconduct. More specifically, the fact that the pattern of clandestine courtships and elopements in Salem shows a steady increase throughout the mid-1780s and 1790s (from two cases in the 1770s, to seven in the 1780s, and ten in the 1790s) argues that the youth came to view marriage as a matter of personal choice.[44] Evidence from the German *Gemeinen* reinforces this picture and hints, too, at the role played by "bad books" in fostering the desire for romance.

Maintaining the separation of the sexes was no easy task, particularly when many of the Brethren seem to have been less than cooperative. According to the UEC, some Brethren came up with a rather ingenious, although fruitless, argument against it. In a discussion of the problem with economic dissatisfaction among *Gemeine* members, the UEC said that some members complained that the insistence on the separation of the sexes "caused complicated [*weitlauftigere*] establishments and costs."[45] The leadership considered this to be unbrotherly reasoning, but several examples from the records in the late 1780s and the 1790s illustrate the difficulties involved. In 1787, the UEC discussed the alarming situation in the Single Brothers House in Neusalz, in which "each room [had] its own milk and butter woman who [brought] her wares there to sell."[46] The central leadership sent Christian Gregor on a visitation, but it took until 1790 for the situation to improve.[47] Five years later, Jonathan Briant reported the same problem during a visitation to Gnadenberg. He noted that the Single Brothers House had "become a market house" where "brisk young stranger girls" came on the steps and in the halls to sell goods, and the Sisters "[were] as familiar in that house as in their own houses."[48]

Commercial traffic was not the only thing on which the leadership had to keep an eye. In late 1791, the Herrnhut *Aufseher Collegium* noted that some Single Brothers were prone to wander onto the walking area reserved for the Single Sisters. Admonitions regarding this apparently did little good because in 1793, the *Collegium* found it necessary "that once again the Single Brothers be reminded that those who in the future are found on the Sisters path against the ordinances regarding walks, . . . will be viewed as not fitting our ordinances and thus will shut themselves out of the *Gemeine*."[49] The Salem leadership was plagued with young people who insisted on traveling to the neighboring rural *Gemeinen* in mixed company and who mingled while helping with the harvest, not to mention bleaching their linen together "without any supervision."[50] The walls were clearly weakening despite attempts on the part of the leadership to shore them up.

In general, the minutes of the ruling bodies in Germany are more detailed regarding sexual offenses than are those of Salem and, thus, give a more full-bodied view of this particular issue. The UEC must have been painfully aware of the frustration caused by the marriage system in the *Gemeine*, especially the use of the lot, and by the separation of the sexes. Certainly, this awareness hit them squarely in the face in 1787, when young Count Heinrich Thirty-ninth Reuß, one of Zinzendorf's relations by marriage, abandoned the *Gemeine* to find a wife for himself. Quite clearly, despite his continued religious devotion, he preferred to marry someone, as he said, whose suitable character he could determine for himself.[51]

Since Reuß was from a noble family, the question arises of whether those of lower social and economic status shared his attitude. Other examples suggest that they did. In 1784, Andreas Riemer, a journeyman in Barby, told Spangenberg that he wanted to leave the *Gemeine*, even though he had no means to support himself, because he wanted to marry and already had a woman in mind. The Brethren did occasionally permit Brothers, but never Sisters, to suggest potential mates, so Riemer's desire to leave indicates either that he had made a connection outside the *Gemeine* or that his attachment to this woman was strong enough to make him unwilling to accept a negative decision from the Elders Conference or from the lot. He felt torn between his personal desire

and his devotion to the Savior. He told Spangenberg that "he [had] often be-
seeched God that he might take away *this* way of thinking; it remained however."[52] In this instance, his relatives succeeded where God had not and persuaded
him to give up his inclination. The fact that his biological family proved more
effective than did his spiritual connection underscores the shifting loyalties
among the second generation.

The Brethren were not always so easily dissuaded. In 1780, the Salem
Elders Conference needed to find a husband for the widow Baumgarten and
thought Jens Schmidt might be a good candidate.

> He, however, has a fantasy that Sister Eva Hein is the person deter-
> mined for him by the Savior. He even spoke with her about marriage
> but received the answer from her that she did not wish to act contrary
> to the *Gemeine* plan for she has yielded herself to the Savior. He nev-
> ertheless stirs up this thought within himself more and more. To the
> friendly counsel of Brother Reichel that he ought to desist from this
> inclination unfitting for a Single Brother, he said that he could not do
> so even if he were driven from the *Gemeine* as a tempter. We did not
> wish to do this. He then said he wanted to go and thus he took his
> leave.[53]

What is striking about this incident is Schmidt's use of the ideal of the Savior
as ruler to express his personal inclination. In essence, he asserted a personal
revelation in opposition to the Elders Conference, which held the sole right of
consulting the lot in order to determine the Savior's will. The German records
yield a similar case in which a Single Sister in Neusalz became engaged to a
preacher from Sebnitz. They met when visiting mutual friends in Neusalz (the
leadership did not worry about socializing for nothing), and he asked her whether
a person outside the *Gemeine* who wanted to marry an "honest and Christian-
minded [*Christliche gesinnte*] person" could have a Sister to wife. He then said
that he meant her. She saw this "as a direction from God," and she accepted his
proposal and her loss of *Gemeine* membership.[54]

A number of incidents from the late 1780s and the 1790s indicate that
in addition to simple inclination, active courtship also interfered with submission to the Savior. In 1788, the Gnadenfeld Elders Conference referred a local
problem to the UEC. A Single Sister there had received the Savior's approval
for marriage with a certain Brother Vogel but had turned it down. It came to
light that she had done so because of her inclination to a Brother Richter, with
whom she had a relationship [*Zusammenhang*]. When she became "uneasy"
and retracted her initial refusal of Vogel, Richter protested that she was "in no

way free of him," but he agreed to leave the decision up to the UEC.[55] Their solution was to transfer the Sister to Gnadenfrei. It is worth noting that the Sister and Richter, despite their obvious tie to one another, still felt the influence of the *Gemeine* ideal, although it is difficult to say whether their decision stemmed from genuine piety or from fear of the consequences of disobedience. In all likelihood, it partook of both.

When the leadership knew of such relationships beforehand, they usually refused to submit either party to the marriage lot. For instance, in 1792, the Herrnhut Elders Conference confronted Brother Beyer, who served in the local inn, with his prior "connection" with Sister Rohr, whom he had suggested as a possible wife. The Elders Conference said that this situation made the question of his marrying very doubtful. Beyer's response indicated a personal attraction and a practical view, or at least an attempt to seem practical. He said that he thought that she was suited to service in the inn, and he admitted that he "had an inclination to her because of her manner and behavior" but that nothing improper had occurred between them.[56] In the end, Beyer agreed to give up the idea of marrying Sister Rohr, but a similar case in Salem at the turn of the century illustrates why the leadership generally refused to consider putting such matches to the lot.

In 1801, Brother Ellridge told the Salem Elders Conference that he wanted to marry, and he suggested Sister Elisabeth Hauser. The conference hesitated to have dealings with this proposal "since it is known that these two have had an eye on each other" but agreed to ask the lot when Ellridge declared "that it was his mind to undertake nothing against the *Gemeine* ordinances and that he wished his marriage might take place in the manner customary in the *Gemeine*."[57] The lot then fell on the negative. A little over two months later, the minutes recorded that the connection between these two "has now gone so far that they have resolved to marry each other and to go away from here."[58] The Elders Conference had undoubtedly feared just such an outcome when they hesitated to ask the lot. The drawing of a negative answer thus put the young couple in the position of openly defying the Savior if they continued their connection. The fact that Ellridge insisted that the lot be consulted suggests that he either expected a positive answer or that he genuinely thought that he could abide by a negative one. It also indicates the hold that the *Gemeine* ideal continued to exercise on the minds of the Brethren, even if other forces ultimately overpowered it.

It is tempting to conclude on the basis of the aforementioned incidents that the American Brethren were more inclined than were the German Brethren to choose personal desire over devotion to the *Gemeine,* but three cases from Gnadenberg suggest otherwise. In 1785, the Elders Conference recorded what in their eyes was the troubling tale of a "child of the *Gemeine*" gone wrong. Under suspicion of pregnancy the young daughter of the widow König had "finally acknowledged . . . that [she] had sunk into serious carnal sins with a stranger journeyman blacksmith . . . and indeed in her mother's house."[59] The Elders Conference undoubtedly saw this as confirmation of the danger of parental foot-dragging because the elders remarked that they had told her mother earlier to get rid of her blacksmith and send her daughter to the Sisters House. It is possible that the mother had colluded in the relationship. As a widow, she may have viewed a young blacksmith as the best means of securing her daughter's future while easing her own economic burden. Recent research on family and property in early modern Germany has revealed that, in some cases, parents turned a blind eye to hanky-panky in the house if the match seemed a suitable one.[60] In this case, the journeyman was removed from Gnadenberg, and the young woman left for her uncle's house after telling the *Gemeine* leadership that she wished to marry the smith. The Elders Conference noted that it was "most highly disturbing to see a child of the *Gemeine* who so *willfully* falls into misfortune!" (emphasis mine).

In 1794, another Single Sister, excluded from Communion under suspicion of being pregnant, admitted "that she had sinned carnally with Josiah Wogwood from the Brothers House."[61] These two appear to have had no hesitation in marrying each other and accepting consequent expulsion from Gnadenberg. They were, in fact, taken into another village as protected subjects by the manorial lord of Gnadenberg, von Heithausen. Several months later, the Elders Conference noted "with pain" the "secret connection" of Gottlieb Weber and the widow Maria Elisabeth Verban, who had gone to Bunzlau to be wed after being officially expelled.[62]

The members of the Unity could be quite creative in developing ways to conduct these forbidden courtships. When the leadership in Niesky discovered the relationship between the schoolmaster and the schoolmistress, who had been "seen in the bush," the couple simply claimed to have been discussing school lessons. Significantly, the leadership was especially upset because several people in Niesky had known about this relationship for some time but had not reported it.[63] In an interesting violation of sacred space, Wilhelmine Reinekin and a shoemaker named Grunert shared a glass of wine in the darkened chamber of the *Gemeinsaal* before his departure for Neudietendorf, where he was sent on probation after the discovery of his "forbidden love connections" [*Liebes-Beziehungen*] with some Single Sisters, Reinekin in particular.[64] In another instance, a young man and woman used the pretext of close kinship, later discovered to be false, to establish "an inadmissible connection . . . which [went] so far that they [drank] coffee together here and there in the town" in the company of another Single Brother and Single Sister.[65] This led the UEC to remark on the need to keep a sharp eye on visits to relatives.

The Salem Elders Conference reacted similarly in 1785, when a group of young people used the opportunity offered by the construction of the Single Sisters House (after all, the women wanted to see how the work was going) to make each others' acquaintance, using siblings as go-betweens. The Elders Conference told the Single Brothers not to speak with their own sisters, let alone with the others, and threatened expulsion if they did not toe the line. A decade later, the Salem leadership uncovered another such web of forbidden relationships fostered by siblings.[66]

Several references in the German records reveal that the Brethren took advantage of their literacy to conduct their courtships through letters. This method, of course, also made them vulnerable to discovery. In 1791, the Herrnhut Elders Conference uncovered an exchange of letters between a stranger servant of Abraham von Gersdorf and Sister Johanna Roland, who served the von Ungern-Sternbergs. Their positions had allowed them to strike up an acquaintance, and the Elders Conference complained about the "very dangerous" practice of their noble Brethren keeping servants who were not members of the Unity.[67] During his 1792 visitation to Gnadenberg, Gregor reported that "a weed named Neuschüz," who had established an "entanglement" with a young woman and been expelled, had renewed his connection with her through letters.[68] That same year, the Neuwied Elders Conference thanked God that, through a lost letter, they had uncovered Sister Magdelena Kreymann's relationship with an assistant painter. In 1794, confiscated correspondence was responsible for the expulsion of Friedrich Schleiermacher from Niesky for conducting "a most highly forbidden acquaintance" with Frederica Müller, as well as for other offenses.[69] This latter relationship appears to have been encouraged by Müller's brother, a shoemaker who was a friend of Schleiermacher.

The involvement of Schleiermacher suggests a possible connection between such epistolary relationships and the influence of contemporary literature and thought. Unfortunately, not one of these "bad" letters has survived, so it is impossible to judge the impact of early romantic literature firsthand. Other evidence, however, reveals that the leadership in Germany did indeed perceive such a connection.[70] In 1792, the Herrnhut Elders Conference discovered the existence of an exchange of "bad letters" between young people in Herrnhut and Niesky that revealed a forbidden connection between two of them. The elders noted that the young woman involved had been given "all kinds of bad books, novels and plays" by her brother. The letters made it clear, the Conference maintained, that her "carnal inclinations" resulted from the reading of these "bad books."[71] The Kleinwelke Elders Conference made the same connection when it remarked that Maria Hollenz had not only had "forbidden relationships [*Umgang*] with men" but had also read "bad writings" and publicly sung "unfit" songs.[72]

Although neither entry specified the nature of the dangerous literature, their specific association with carnal thought and behavior suggests that the literature was probably representative of the Sturm und Drang movement, which upheld the primacy of passion in human nature. The emphasis on the interrelationship of sensual and spiritual passion found in such novels as *The Sorrows of Young Werther* was a disturbing mirror to the Brethren's emphasis on the need for a passionate attachment to Christ. This emphasis reached the height of its expression in the Sifting Period of the 1740s, when the devotional literature throbbed with tears and the tender exploration of Christ's wounds. Although by 1764, the official line of the Unity firmly discouraged excess of emotion, the devotional cycle still depended on emotional response for its efficacy. Under these circumstances, literature that celebrated intense emotion and that directed people's passions toward one another posed a double threat to the culture created by the Brethren.[73] As we will see, in the last quarter of the eighteenth century, the *Gemeine* ideal came under attack from the Enlightenment stress on reason, and from the early Romantic focus on passion.

The references to letters and long-term courtships found in the records suggest that for the younger Brethren, personal choice in marriage increasingly depended on "romantic" (sexual, emotional) attachments, not simply on practical considerations.[74] Yet their ties to the *Gemeine* and to its culture of holiness also remained strong. Thus, the records often reveal a true tug-of-war between love for an individual and love for the Savior and for the *Gemeine*. Although they had different outcomes, two examples, one from Salem and one from Herrnhut, illustrate the course of romantic entanglement very well. An entry from the Salem Single Sisters Choir diary of 1794 is particularly enlightening. In that year, Anna Elisabeth Steiner was allowed to assist her parents at the mill during her mother's illness. While there, she developed an attachment to a stranger day laborer who was working there. The head of the Choir told the following tale.

> After she returned to us we noticed an indifference in her toward the Savior and the *Gemeine* over which she was often spoken with, and sometimes without hope that the harm could be healed again. She herself testified how thankful she was that the Savior had helped her out of confusion, [and] went with us to Choir Communion at our festival. Soon thereafter she became gloomy again and appeared not to fit in with us anymore. Finally she went away. We had compassion

and fetched her back again. Now she improved and with many tears pled for forgiveness, which she received after she pledged her faith with hand and voice. It lasted only four weeks, however, then we noticed that despite counsel and warning her heart hung on the dissolute [*liederlichen*] man . . . to whom she ran on this day. The Savior's grace protect us from more of such deceit.[75]

Although the head of the Single Sisters viewed the errant Sister's actions as deceitful, the narrative suggests a genuine attempt to subordinate her desires to devotion to the Savior. The fact that she initially grew depressed after Communion may indicate a failure on the part of this central devotional celebration to make her satisfied with the Savior as the "bridegroom of her soul." She may well have felt alienated from her Sisters by her awareness of this. However, she apparently did not return to the fold voluntarily, and the pull of human passion proved the stronger one. What the diary entry does not say is that Elisabeth Reich, a friend of Sister Steiner's, was excluded from the *Gemeine* for aiding and abetting the courtship.[76] By the 1790s, this sort of cooperation was not uncommon.

The Herrnhut records give a view of courtship in which the Savior proved triumphant. In 1797, the Elders Conference reported that a tailor named Zöbel, already excluded for his connection and correspondence with a Single Sister, "has now, since he can no longer deny the matter, acknowledged that he has conducted an intimate friendship with the young Single Sister Anna Maria Rücker for half a year already, that they love each other sincerely, and that therefore he is minded to marry this Sister since he understands his profession well and intends to earn his bread with it."[77] The Elders Conference left the decision to Rücker's parents, who said that Anna Maria did not want to marry Zöbel. Things did not settle quite so easily, however. Zöbel enlisted the help of a girl in nearby Strahwalde in sending a letter to Rücker containing a pair of silver rings with their names inscribed. This letter, she said, reawakened her feelings toward him, but she became "completely tired of the matter" and said she wanted to give herself entirely over to the Savior. To this end she gave the rings to the head of her Choir, along with a written declaration that she was free of the persistent tailor.[78]

This incident tells much about the complications posed by romantic attractions. Zöbel's statement appealed to ties of "sincere" love, but it also linked marriage with the ability to support a family. It is difficult to tell just how "intimate" this friendship was, but the fact that the Elders Conference considered allowing marriage rather than a transfer to another *Gemeine*, although Rücker was ultimately transferred to Gnadenfrei, suggests that it may have been consummated. Given this possibility, it is noteworthy that, although

Rücker was drawn by the courtship element of letters and rings, in the end, security, piety, or both won out.

In both cases cited above, the couple received aid and comfort in their clandestine courtship. Other evidence reveals that these were not isolated incidents but were, rather, indications of a general shift in attitude toward marriage within the *Gemeine*. As previously noted, siblings helped each other over the wall that separated the sexes, and the Niesky Elders Conference lamented that several people had turned a blind eye to the relationship between the schoolmaster and mistress. The surgeon in Gnadau was discovered to have aided the secret courtship of a journeyman glover with his master's daughter by facilitating their exchange of letters. That the surgeon did not understand why his action earned him excommunication says much for changing attitudes.[79] In addition to these examples, in 1790, the Herrnhut Elders Conference noted that the Jäsckens had allowed Brother Friedrich Reichelt and Sister Palle Oberlin the opportunity to meet in their living room [*Stube*] and thus helped them to conduct a "forbidden connection." In 1794, the Elders Conference recorded a more direct hand in courtship when a Single Brother was excluded for helping his friend, a potter named Hille, to make the acquaintance of a Sister who he thought would make Hille a good wife. The aforementioned troubles in 1797 also were not confined to the Rücker incident. Two other couples had been seeing each other with the help of a Single Sister who carried messages for them.[80]

Evidence of various attempts to circumvent the separation of the sexes, along with the rise in secret courtships and the passive and active participation of other members in promoting "forbidden relationships," illustrates a growing unwillingness among the young people to subordinate personal desire to the will of the Savior. The fact that this unwillingness held true on both sides of the Atlantic suggests that the primary source of this conflict was generational.[81] There is, however, evidence of a cultural aspect: the records indicate that contemporary literature may have encouraged the romantic inclinations of the youth in the German *Gemeinen*. Whatever the source, by the late eighteenth century, romantic passion often overcame devotional passion among the members of the Unity.

The Culture of Holiness under Siege

In 1795, Jonathan Briant said the following after a formal speaking with the Gnadenberg Single Brothers Choir: "There are to be sure, people there, and no small number, who do not know what they want from the *Gemeine*, nor have any idea what purpose the Savior had in bringing them to the *Gemeine*; but [rather] live as freely unconstrained as other people." As discussed in the previous chapter, the Brethren created an alternative culture in opposition to "popular" and "elite" manifestations of worldly culture. At the heart of this culture of holiness was a devotional cycle designed to express and stimulate devotion to the Savior and to emphasize the union of individual member with the *Gemeine* and the Choir. Exclusion from the devotional cycle, not to mention exclusion from the *Gemeine,* cut the individual off from participation in the celebration of the larger community. If ritual serves as a process whereby a gathered church or community marks itself off from the world, the rejection of this ritual suggests a desire to reunite with the world.[83] Such a sentiment was at least attributed to the Single Brothers of Gnadenberg.

In ideal, the loss of fellowship was intended to spur the errant member to repentance. The problems with discipline and evidence of shifting loyalties point to an underlying weakness in the efficacy of the culture of holiness by the late eighteenth century. The second-generation Brethren were often distanced from the emotional religious experience of their elders who had formed the devotional cycle and the *Gemeine* regulations. The shared experience of exile and persecution that had bound many of the early members and, certainly, the leadership had also disappeared by this time. Although the basic pattern of devotion continued to affect the second generation, it became increasingly ritualized and less spontaneous. As church historian Werner Reichel observed, the use of "the power of the memory of the past" could become monotonous.[84] This monotony may have made Unity members vulnerable to the enticements of worldly culture.

The weakening of the culture of holiness allowed the incursion or re-emergence of elements of popular culture within the *Gemeine*. This occurred on both sides of the Atlantic, with the differences stemming from the different temptations provided by the environment. In the case of the *Gemeine* of Salem, the two primary sources of temptation came from participation in political life and from life in the backcountry. The Brethren always recognized the need to participate in public life in order to preserve their privileges. In Germany, they managed this through members of the leadership who doubled as lords of the estates on which the *Gemeinen* were built. In America, the political system required a broader base of participation, so many "ordinary" Brethren held voting rights and served as justices of the peace, as assemblymen, and as other local officials. The difficulty lay in the nature of public life in the eighteenth-century South. In his study of eighteenth-century Virginia, Rhys Isaac pointed out that elections and court days were notoriously unruly, comparable to the atmosphere at public executions in Europe.[85] Many of the Brethren appear to have been less than reluctant to do their civic duty by attending these riotous gatherings. In 1775, the leadership complained that too many Brothers sought every opportunity to go to court days and to the musters of the militia.[86] In 1783, a Brother was excluded from all devotional meetings for being very drunk at the elections, and, several years later, the leadership complained again that Brothers continued to frequent the courts.[87]

In addition to participation in a "rough and ready" public life, the Brethren's settlements in North Carolina were affected by the wilder life of their neighbors. In December 1777, for example, the elders canceled Communion in Bethania because the young people held a shooting match on which they gambled.[88] The minutes of the Elders Conference also contain several references to the hearty adoption of the practice of "corn huskings," in which both sexes gathered together in the evening to shuck corn and chat; the elders did *not* approve.[89] Corn huskings had their German equivalent in spinning bees, but the members of the German *Gemeinen* do not appear to have frequented these rural gatherings.[90] More "traditional" elements of popular culture, such as frequenting soothsayers for help with lost cattle and making accusations of witchcraft, also appeared, much to the distress of the elders who bemoaned the "demeaning character of such superstitious business in a *Gemeine.*"[91]

Like the Brethren in North Carolina, the German Brethren were influenced by the world that surrounded them. Although it, too, offered rowdy diversions, they unfolded in a different environment. Unlike the backcountry of North Carolina, the *Gemeinen* in Germany were surrounded not by individual family farms and scattered villages, but by towns, often sizeable, and by many villages, all within relatively easy reach. The members, therefore, had available a wider range of entertainment, of which many seem to have taken full advantage. We should also note that, although the *Ortsgemeinen* were artisanal, commercial communities, most of the villages that surrounded them were peasant communities.[92]

The lure of "superstition," for example, also surfaced in the European settlements. In 1793, several Single Sisters in Gnadenberg visited a "so-called wise woman in Bunzlau." For this visit, one Sister was expelled and the others were publicly excluded from Communion. Less than a year later, some Single Sisters in Herrnhut went to see a soothsayer in Bernstadt. The comment in the records indicates that these were not isolated occurrences.[93]

The major cultural temptation for the youth of the European *Gemeinen* seems to have been the popular theater. In the early modern period public theater tended to be rowdy and ribald. Thus, it was not considered an entertainment for "proper" people and certainly did not provide the orderly environment that had come to be treasured by the leadership of the Brethren. An overview of the records reveals at least six incidents of Brethren attending the performances of traveling comedy troupes, one of which performed *The Magic Flute,* in the years 1795 to 1798. All of these clandestine outings involved several young people and continued to occur despite severe warnings and disciplinary measures.[94] In one of the most significant examples of this form of "culture wars," ten Single Brothers from Herrnhut went to a comedy in Bohemia on the third day of the *Gemeine* Pentecost festival. One Brother even went so far as to try his hand at writing a comedy. He was expelled from Herrnhut for his efforts.[95]

The surrounding towns and villages offered other forms of theater that proved seductive. In 1790, the Neusalz Elders Conference appealed to the UEC to settle a dispute regarding the propriety of the practice that had arisen there of attending Midnight Mass and of the illumination of candles at the Catholic church. The central leadership promised to investigate the matter, and Friedrich Rudolph von Watteville said that, although attendance at Catholic services had been allowed, "no one imagined" going at night.[96] The UEC reported a more unpleasant diversion when they noted that "more Single Brothers" in Herrnhut had gone to an execution in Ostritz despite having been told beforehand that no one was allowed to go; two years later, the Elders Conference "presumed" that various young Brothers would try to attend the execution of a murderess in Ottenhein.[97] Interestingly, the primary concern of the Elders Conference was the potential "unpleasant impression" that the execution could make on the Brothers' emotions. As with the popular theater, the leadership feared the arousal of nonspiritual passions. This was certainly the case in 1799 when a group of "young and old" were "led astray" by one of the leaders of the Neusalz *Gemeine.* They saw him attending the performance of a tightrope walker and joined him. The text of the letter reporting this incident indicates the strongly sexual nature of the performance, at least in the eyes of Brother Geisler, in which, at one point, several men lay atop a reclining female.[98] This event probably took place at a fair, which also challenged the culture of holiness. One young man was excluded from Communion for going to a fair in Strahwalde during Communion. This case would, it seems, have indicated the inefficacy of excommunication as a disciplinary device.[99]

The younger European Brethren fell prey to the pull of other rowdy diversions, chief among which was joyriding in sleighs, occasionally in the middle of the night. The "joy" element of this becomes more apparent when we consider that most of these rides included some of the Sisters.[100] Aside from this, the records include references to Brothers attending a wedding feast, where they had the unfortunate boldness to dance; to gathering at a neighboring farmer's to sing folk songs instead of hymns; and to frequenting taverns during the *Gemeinestunde,* not to mention at other times.[101] The lure of tavern life was not confined to the Brothers who were artisans. In 1790, one of the supervisors in the seminary reported the expulsion of two students, one of whom had hosted a birthday party for himself in the pleasure garden of the seminary. The students had consumed seven flasks of wine among the twelve of them.[102] In this case, the students had reproduced the effects of a tavern on the grounds of the seminary and that was not the use for which the pleasure garden had been intended. Birthdays were incorporated as part of the devotional rhythm of the *Gemeine*, so the action of the errant Brethren probably held a particular sting.

One final example of an incident in Gnadenberg reveals how the language of popular culture competed with the language of devotion. During his visitation there in 1795, Jonathan Briant reported that, among other disturbances, Sister Frizel von Rohwedeln's dog, which often wandered into the Single Brothers House, had returned one day with a piece of sealed paper containing gunpowder inscribed "by express" tied around its neck. Sister von Rohwedeln's mother reportedly was "shocked to no small degree" and feared allowing her daughter to go out.[103] This little "joke" had multilayered meaning. Its message contained violence and sexual innuendo. It is noteworthy that, although the Single Brothers used the symbolic language usually associated with popular culture such as carnival, the nobility understood the message. It is possible that the direction of the message at a member of the nobility resulted from underlying social tensions as well as sexual ones. Whatever the case, its earthy roots emerge clearly, even if the motivation behind the message does not. Interestingly, this use of symbolic gesture does not seem to have a parallel in the Salem *Gemeine*. As we will see, the Salem Brethren generally expressed their frustrations more directly.

Tension between Brethren of different ranks was perhaps inevitable in a community that stressed the equality of Christian brotherhood and that downplayed rank while insisting that respect for rank be maintained. The mixing of Brethren of different social status also meant that the challenge to the culture of holiness did not come solely from "below." The alternative culture of the Brethren consisted not only of the devotional cycle, but also of an emphasis on simplicity in material culture and, particularly, in dress. The Brethren recognized the power of fashion to embody ideas or mind-sets. Early on, the women of the community adopted the cap of the local peasants as their own, and all the Brethren initially avoided the display characteristic of the eighteenth-century upper classes. It was difficult, however, not to allow some differentiation because the leadership never denied the distinctions of rank. This tension opened what the leadership came to see as a Pandora's box. The quandary of the Brethren was encapsulated in 1752 by Heinrich von Damnitz, who wrote the following regarding luxury in dress: "The first thought indeed is

that no one should dress other than how he can afford to, the second, that even
he who can afford it still should not wear what he is not entitled to by office,
rank, or birth, and the third, that, if for other reasons one would not give rise
to these distinctions of rank, better the nobility be completely brought to heel
[*ganz herunterrücke*], than the imitation by Brethren of lesser birth be toler-
ated."[104] It is difficult to be certain of what lay behind von Damnitz's opinion.
Concern for overspending played some role, as most likely did the ideal of
simplicity, but less savory attitudes also surfaced in this statement. Von Damnitz
seems to have been wary of letting those of lower social status get above themselves. Perhaps he felt that the estate system in Silesia and Upper Lusatia was
ingrained enough in other ways to withstand the abnegation of special dress on
the part of the nobility. Thus, for the nobility to dress down would be less
threatening than for the lower orders to dress up. In any case, the basic concerns he expressed continued to haunt the leadership. The Brethren do not
appear to have been easily brought to heel in this matter.

Although the Salem leadership fretted over fashion, this concern appeared
more prominently in the German *Gemeinen*. One of the first large-scale discussions of fancy fashion occurred in 1785. This detailed entry in the minutes
of the UEC is remarkable in its focus on "obscene" clothing, especially, of the
male variety.[105] In general, the leadership spread its condemnation fairly evenly
between the sexes, but this concern for sexuality in clothing focused on the
men. The overtones of the minutes indicate a concern for potential homo-
eroticism. The concern may be tied to ongoing problems with sexual misconduct in the seminary, but, because this entry is unique in its particular focus, a
firm conclusion is elusive. The conclusion that many of the Brethren blithely
ignored the fulminations on fashion is not so elusive. In 1792 the Neuwied
Elders Conference observed that the Choir leaders were not showing sufficient
vigor in combating "the increasing fashion mania and clothing folly among our
young people."[106] The next year the Herrnhut *Aufseher Collegium* complained
that all admonitions about the "striking clothing in which many young people
make themselves so conspicuous" were "fruitless," and only two months later
the Elders Conference made the issue more explicit when it discussed the need
for admonitions and possible disciplinary measures "regarding the high pointed
hats, extraordinarily tied neckruffles, and other equally striking clothing."[107]

Although, at one point, the central leadership identified Herrnhut as the
source of the problem, fanciful fashion was not confined to that *Ortsgemeine*.
On his visitation to Gnadenberg in 1795, Jonathan Briant included "clothing
folly" in his list of the common forms of behavior among those second-generation members who wanted to "live just as other people," and pointed to particular examples of this.[108] Franz Schlift, Briant said, although expelled, had

not left but, instead, had ridden around "in a jacket with yellow lining and a yellow vest." Briant also made an observation that poignantly drove home the opposition between the Brethren's culture and that of the "world." "In the sanctuary [*Saal*] increasingly few benches are occupied, and on the Brother's side one sees more powdered hair than I have seen anywhere in a *Gemeine.*"

These entries do not refer to the role of social rank in fashion, but this aspect did surface in a remark made by the UEC in connection with Gregor's visitation to Gnadenfrei. The UEC commented generally on the difficulties posed by the presence of "so many noble people" in the *Gemeine,* then pointed specifically to their tendency to dress in a more "worldly" manner than necessary.[109] A later observation by Johann Christian Geisler, himself of humble birth, during his visitation in 1799 to Gnadenfeld in Denmark reveals what the Brethren feared from this example. "Since in the colony even cobblers' wives are beginning to wear the so-called gowns," he wrote, "it is partly sad and partly laughable to me that the passion for fashion and clothing folly is also found among our poor folk, and the long women's dresses are worn by Sisters who should think about good body linen and other necessary pieces of clothing."[110] Geisler's lamentation indicates that the desire to indulge in the latest fashions did not necessarily require economic prosperity as the spur and suggests that many of the Brethren found the simple dress unsatisfactory and yearned to continue to "imitate" their social and economic superiors.[111]

It was not only in material matters that the Brethren felt the challenge of upper-class or, at least, literate culture. In 1782, Johannes von Watteville worried about the harm done to several Single Brothers in the seminary through their reading of "bad books."[112] In his study of Puritan culture, David Hall referred to the clergy's objection to "bad books" that provided fantasy or that provoked laughter instead of meditation on salvation. He pointed specifically to Puritan condemnation of romances, plays, and ballads that rivaled more "edifying" books such as spiritual autobiographies.[113] In part, the fear of bad books reflects a similar struggle for readership within the Unity. A memo from the Gnadenfrei Elders Conference lamented, "What sort of books are read? One hears indeed that novels exist in the libraries of our Brothers and are read secretly by their children, and what sort of free-thinking pamphlets do our [young men] bring here[?] . . . Should such shameful things be accepted, and read in our *Gemeinen?*"[114] "Worldly" books were a particular danger in the *Gemeine* because all children were taught to read and write. As we have seen, the leadership forbade the reading of harmful literature in the *Gemeine* ordinances and blamed plays and romances for the inclination to clandestine courtships. They also remarked the following of a young member who soon left for the university: "His soul is filled with nothing but pictures; he composes poems of such contents, and his mind [*Gemuthe*] is completely fixed on devoting himself to all pleasures."[115] This young Brother appears to have exchanged devotional pictures for those of his own imagination. In the judgment of the leadership, he had no room left for the Savior.

Romances and plays, although part of literate culture, were often closely tied to popular culture, especially as print and literacy spread over the social spectrum in the early modern period. As the reference to "free-thinking pamphlets" indicates, novels were not the only, or even the most threatening, "dangerous" books. In 1787, the UEC conducted a lengthy and intense discussion over whether to allow the seminary students to read the journal *Allgemeine Literatur Zeitung* which contained much that opposed orthodox religious teaching. In the course of the debate, the heads of the seminary remarked on the difficulty of enforcing the ban currently imposed by the UEC because the students had many ways of secretly obtaining "all kinds of writing."[116] The nature of these secretly obtained publications is made clear in an entry from 1794 in which the seminary director bemoaned "that many waste much time on unnecessary philosophical speculations" and, five months later, remarked that many young Brothers in the seminary had little contact with their Choir, seldom attended meetings, and were "too ardently addicted to the study of philosophy."[117] Given the language of these remarks, it is entirely likely that the "unnecessary books" referred to as having harmed young men in Neusalz and Niesky were also part of the rising interest in philosophy. This rising interest is indicative of the inroads made by Enlightenment culture into the *Gemeine*.[118] As we will see, this particular attack on the Brethren's ideal played an important role in the larger struggle over questions of authority and faith in the *Gemeine*.

In the first half of the eighteenth century, the Brethren had developed an alternative culture based on an emotionally compelling rhythm of devotion that, in ideal, served to stimulate piety and overcome dissension within the community. This culture of holiness provided much of the strength for the walls of discipline with which the Brethren surrounded their *Ortsgemeinen*. During the course of the late eighteenth century, however, the "world" began to make steady inroads into the *Gemeinen* in Germany and in America. These inroads are particularly visible in the areas of family life and relations between the sexes and in the interest in popular and "enlightened" culture. Ultimately, the lure of rival passions proved more compelling to many of the second generation than did the faith of their elders. Ironically, in responding to the challenge of a restless youth, which came to center on the use of the lot, the leadership let the Enlightenment in by the back door.

4

Gambling with God

REVELATION, REASON, AND THE USE OF THE LOT

Over the course of the late eighteenth century, no practice generated more discussion and debate among the Brethren than did the use of the lot. In many ways, these discussions encapsulated the challenges posed by the nature of the *Ortsgemeine* as a baptized town and the impact of cultural and intellectual developments. The extensive use of the lot in decision making marks the Moravian Brethren as peculiar in eighteenth-century Europe. Their belief that the lot represented the true will of Christ stands at odds with a century that had inherited a changing worldview in which a strong confidence in the power of human reason gradually replaced the assumption of God's providential power. Historian Andrew Fix has traced this intellectual shift as it affected the seventeenth-century Dutch Collegiants, who moved from a spiritualist to a rationalist approach to religious questions.[1] The Brethren resisted the triumph of reason over revelation into the late eighteenth century. Their resistance reflected the general hostility toward the emphasis on science and reason that was a hallmark of the Halle Pietists.[2] This similarity is not surprising given the ties between Halle and the Brethren during the formative years of the Unity.

Halle preceded the Brethren in a struggle over the role of reason in spiritual life. In the 1740s, the philosophy of Christian Wolff became popular among many at Halle, despite Wolff's having been removed from the faculty in 1722. Although the Halle Pietists did not reject science and reason out of hand, some among the faculty perceived a distinct threat to faith from Wolff's focus on reason as the divine source of human knowledge.[3] Wolff's ideas may have been prevented from entering the Unity in the 1740s because this decade saw the Brethren's piety reach a height of intensely emotional, even sensual expression. By the 1790s, however, it became clear that, at least among many of the lay members of the Unity, the Enlightenment stress on the primacy of reason was winning. Just as the Collegiants had come to view "free prophecy" as a function of human reason, several of the Brethren on both sides of the Atlantic came to see the lot as something open to human manipulation and objected to its use, arguing that decisions were best left simply to "brotherly reason."[4] A study of the Unity's use of the lot and its place within their spiritual life over the course of the century reveals this process. It also reveals something of the nature of authority within the Unity, for the change was driven by the laity while the leadership struggled, largely in vain, to maintain the old order.[5]

Although the Unity developed a relatively sophisticated administrative system, the will of the "true head" was determined in all major decisions through the use of the lot. Over the course of the century, the Brethren used a variety of methods to consult the lot, but the most common method consisted of writing down two statements expressing "the Savior's will" (i.e., "The Savior approves the proposal that Brother Heiz become *Gemeine Diener*" and "The Savior does not approve, and so forth"). A member of the Elders Conference then drew one of these out of a container. According to a brief history of its origin given by the Synod of 1769, the practice appeared almost simultaneously with the official founding of Herrnhut as a *Gemeine* in 1727.[6] At that time, Zinzendorf became strongly active in the affairs of the Brethren. Church historian Erich Beyreuther speculated that Zinzendorf may have become acquainted with the use of the lot in local civic government while serving within the administration of the central government of Saxony. Beyreuther further identified Zinzendorf's banishment from Saxony in 1732 as a significant turning point in the use of the lot. Zinzendorf's exile occasioned the formation of a new *Gemeine* that was not tied to any settlement. The formation of this "wandering" *Gemeine* increased an emphasis on pilgrimage, that, Beyreuther argued, encouraged a more radical attitude toward dependence on the Savior to provide for all needs and to guide all steps.[7] The designation of the Savior as chief elder in 1741 further intensified the use of the lot.

Precedents for Lot Use

To understand how the Brethren viewed the lot, it is helpful to explore the general historical background of the practice. Indeed, in many ways, the attitude of the Unity reflected much older attitudes. Ancient cultures often consulted the lot in the context of religious ritual. The Old Testament, for instance, contains at least thirteen references to it. These include specific references to the "Urim and Thumim," which appear to have been positive and negative dice seen by the Hebrews as God's occasional means of communicating his judgment through his priests.[8] The Brethren also used these terms in speaking of the lot. The Hebrew use of the lot presupposed an acceptance of its outcome as an indication of God's will and distinguished it from secular gambling. The language of the Old Testament, however, suggests a willingness to yield control over destiny similar to that involved in gambling. Proverbs 16:33 states, "The lot is cast into the lap but it is controlled by the Lord" (Revised Standard Version).

The practice of lot casting and its association with divine judgment did not die out with the ancient world. It was used in army discipline in the sixteenth and seventeenth centuries to determine life or death, but a more directly spiritual connection is evident in the proposal made by a London congregation in 1653 that Parliament be selected from congregational nominees "by lot after solemn prayer."[9] The Puritan minister Richard Baxter recommended this same procedure in his *A Holy Commonwealth or Political Aphorisms*, published in 1659, in which he laid out his views on the ideal Christian government. However, he cautioned that the lot should not be used indiscriminately but only "in cases of necessity, where judgment faileth."[10] In making this qualification, Baxter referred to the danger that use of the lot to choose one among a hundred candidates, for instance, rather than first electing a small number, would be a neglect of "their reason and God's gift," which qualified them to make the initial selection.[11] Nevertheless, he maintained that the lot was the best means of making the final determination because it was "a most rational, suitable course that he that stands next to God, should be chosen by God." Inherent in Baxter's ideas on the lot is an awareness of the tension between the use of God's gift of rational discernment and a desire to allow God to have a direct hand in the determination of earthly authority. In general, he seems to have erred on the side of caution in his attitude toward lot casting, which may reflect a more favorable Puritan view of reason that contrasts with the mystical bent of Zinzendorf.[12] A century later, the Unity members wrestled with the same tension in astonishingly similar terms. It is also worth noting that Baxter's view of reason was still thoroughly informed by a sense of God's immanent presence because he declared it "most rational" to allow God to choose his earthly deputies.[13]

In the context of the Brethren, perhaps the most significant ideas on the lot are those of Martin Luther, which are contained in his commentary on Jonah. Luther defended the validity of lot casting as a means of revelation in terms similar to those used later by the Brethren. In fact, Zinzendorf reprinted the whole of this section of the Jonah commentaries in his defense of the lot, issued in the 1740s. Luther's language also underlines the association between lot casting and gaming.

Luther declared lot casting to be "a real act of faith," although subject to abuse through human self-interest. He further emphasized that the lot represented God's decision and not that of any certain person.[14] In other words, when cast in a sincere desire to submit to God's command, the lot provided an acceptable means of ensuring that the decision was divinely guided. The willingness to accept the decision of the lot, however, rested on a "covenant" [*Bund*] among those concerned to regard the decision reached as one coming from God.[15] The concept that the validity of the lot rested on the foundation of an agreed voluntary submission also held a central place in the Brethren's theology of the lot, and they, too, used the term "covenant" in reference to lot casting. For Luther, as for the Brethren, the centrality of the covenant did not relativize the authority of the lot but served to define a true lot from an attempt to "tempt" God. Luther sought to define a true lot further by distinguishing it from what he identified as the "heathen" practice, which depended on fortune, but he used the language of gaming and play to make this point. He said that Christians must "not doubt that all that is given or taken through the lot or game is given or taken by God," and he referred to specific games of chance in emphasizing the need for voluntary submission to the outcome.[16] Despite the distinction between submission to blind fate and submission to God's command, the use of the lot involved the willingness to yield up human reason and action. Luther sought to offset any element of uncertainty by saying that "God is so beneficent and just that he will not allow the lot to err."[17] Nevertheless, people had no control over the outcome. Faith, in essence, was a gamble.

Zinzendorf and the Lot

Luther's ideas entered the Unity through the medium of Zinzendorf, who undoubtedly molded the Unity's theology of the lot. He and the first-generation Brethren were, in many ways, children more of the sixteenth and seventeenth centuries than of their own. This was particularly true in their view of the immediacy of divine intervention within human affairs. The seventeenth century had certainly seen a perceptible shift toward a greater faith in human reason and toward the "reasonableness" of religion. Thus, the Cambridge Platonists referred to reason as "the very voice of God."[18] For the Brethren, God spoke directly and for himself, although, as we will see, not without some aid of human reason. God's direct revelation of his will through the lot was necessary precisely because of the weakness of human judgment. Zinzendorf maintained, "I am not clever enough to seek out the Lord's will from my own ideas. An innocent little piece of paper is more certain for me than my own feelings."[19] Zinzendorf did not distinguish clearly here between reason and feeling. He implied, in fact, that human feeling/desires inevitably tainted the decision process and prevented a reliable understanding of God's desires. This same sense of the lot as a counter to human fallibility appears in the explanation of its use made by Christian David, one of the early leaders of the Unity: "The point of it [the lot] is this, that when we . . . cannot come to a decision in all kinds of important matters . . . and be certain of the will of God . . . we must then resort to the lot in order to avoid self-interest and self-will in all matters . . . and to allow everything to depend on the will of God."[20]The consequence of this view on the development of the theology of the lot was the opposite of what others have identified among Protestants in England and in the Netherlands. Barbara Shapiro, for example, argued that the roots of an increasing reliance on reason among seventeenth-century Anglicans lay in the conviction of human fallibility in the understanding of spiritual matters, and Andrew Fix made a similar connection in the intellectual transformation of the Dutch Collegiants.[21] In the case of Zinzendorf, the fallibility of human judgment in secular and in spiritual matters seemed to have required a faithful reliance on God's word, which could be clearly obtained through the lot. According to this view, the "enlightenment" of human reason paled to a glimmer in comparison with the light of God's revelation, most especially in matters of faith.[22]

Naturally this view presupposed a strong conviction of God's provident hand, a belief in the immediacy of his presence in the life of the Unity. Failing this, it would be difficult to trust that the lot was any more reliable than its human agents. In his writings on the lot, Zinzendorf insisted on the lot as Christ's means of acting as chief elder and stressed the need to accept its decisions with childlike simplicity. Christian David referred to "the basic reason" for the use of the lot by the Unity: "that we certainly know and are sure that the Lord is gracious to us and lives among us."[23] This sense of Christ's immediate presence emerges even more dramatically in a comment made by Zinzendorf in 1758: "The question in all great undertakings should always be, does the Savior want the circumstances, will he move heaven and earth? Or will he act gently?"[24] From childhood, Zinzendorf seems to have acted on the assumption of the ability to communicate directly with God through the written word. He is reported to have thrown little messages to Christ out of his window. This child's trust in a "direct line" to God permeated much of his later thinking on the lot.[25]

Like Luther, Zinzendorf also used the images of gaming and play in referring to the lot. In fact, his ideas on this were more thoroughly worked out than Luther's were, and they were tied to his general emphasis on simplicity in the Christian faith. Zinzendorf frequently referred to the lot as part of the "anointing" given by the Holy Spirit. As such, it took on the aspect of the Holy Spirit itself. Because, for Zinzendorf, the Holy Spirit acted as a mother teaching her children, so, too, did the lot. But it could also be a stern parent. While

Luther declared that God's just nature would not allow the lot to err, Zinzendorf spoke of a "punishing lot" that could reveal hidden unfaithfulness. The count, who was often not consistent, also said that human desire could spoil the lot.[27] Zinzendorf extended the image of the faithful believers as children in his use of a gaming reference: "The lot is a game of truth among us, in the sense of Proverbs 8:31; wisdom plays on their ground, and indeed a game that is truthful and reliable if we are children and allow it to play with us."[27]

This willingness to be playful children, referred to in his interpretation of Proverbs, fitted Zinzendorf's vision of the need for a simple faith, however complex his own theology. In his remarks comparing Paul's Epistles with the Gospels, Zinzendorf observed that Paul's greater learning often obscured his message and threatened to cloud the truth: "When Paul wrote down a truth, it likewise occurred to him how the truth might be spoiled . . . therefore he sought to protect one word through another. . . . The others had no need to do this, but wrote out their business as they understood it and left it up to the Lord how it would be understood in the future."[28] This speech could be viewed as prophetic of the later treatment of the lot if Zinzendorf is substituted for the apostles and the Unity Elders Conference for Paul.

As the use of the lot began to increase after Christ was made chief elder in 1739, the Brethren began to sound a note of caution regarding how it was used. In 1743, Zinzendorf proclaimed the lot to be "a special grace [Charisma] of the Gemeine" that "belongs among the miraculous powers in His Church. With this, however, it is as when one is near a fire, one can burn oneself."[29] The sense of this sentence approaches the tone of fearful reverence given to the Ark of the Covenant in the Old Testament.

Difficulties with the use of the lot sprang up even in Zinzendorf's lifetime. The most pressing area of concern within and without the Unity was that of obedience to the decisions made through the lot. During the 1740s and 1750s, the Unity came under fire from orthodox Lutherans for expecting absolute obedience from its members to lot decisions. In defending their use of the lot, Zinzendorf and the Unity Elders Conference continually maintained that questions were to be put to the lot or "asked [of] the Savior" only after careful deliberation and only when no clear decision could be reached. In practice, however, certain decisions, including proposals for marriage matches, confirmation for office, and readmission to the Gemeine after expulsion, were always put to the lot. The key to this apparent contradiction lies in the Brethren's skepticism about the powers of human discernment. The response of the Hernnhut Gemeine in 1739 to external criticism of the practice illustrates this. The Herrnhut Elders Conference stated, "The lot is never used other than when one knows no reliable counsel" (emphasis mine).[30]

Asking the Savior, however, could have uncomfortable consequences. In his observations on the lot, Luther spoke of the voluntary covenant to abide by the decision given. The Brethren also referred to the voluntary covenant as central to their use of the lot. The question then arose as to whether this meant that the individual must accept whatever a particular lot entailed, even when the individual had no hand in drawing up the question. As early as 1744, many members worried that they might suddenly find the lot sending them to Ethiopia and that they would have to obey. The synod meeting in that year emphasized the need for the prior "free will" of the Brethren in all issues decided by lot.[31] This rule allowed freedom only in the case of an affirmative lot, however. A negative lot closed the door to the proposal. Despite such thorny issues and much outside criticism of "blind obedience," in Zinzendorf's eyes experience confirmed the providential power of the lot as God's chosen instrument. For instance, as a result of the lot, Zinzendorf delayed the departure of a group of Brethren going to America only to have them arrive three months earlier than the ship that they had originally been scheduled to take.[32] Such events solidified confidence in lot casting, at least for some.

The Initial Controversy, 1760–1769

After Zinzendorf's death in 1760, the issue of the use of the lot became an increasingly hot one. In part, the ground for the debate was laid by the mechanics of the practice. Although a firm belief in the superiority of divine over human wisdom undergirded the theology of the lot, the Unity leadership also stressed the need for thorough debate of all issues submitted. Of course, the questions themselves were drawn up by human hands, a point clearly not lost on later members. The leadership sought to mitigate the human element through the inclusion of the blank lot. If a blank were drawn, the Brethren then had to determine its meaning. This was done by drawing up a possible meaning and then asking the Savior if it was the correct one. The process could get quite complicated, particularly if the Brethren kept drawing a negative, which did happen. In the view of the Brethren, however, this method allowed the Savior to correct an incorrectly worded question.[33] This too, though, contained a potential human pitfall. The practice of allowing some questions to be asked using only a positive or a negative and a blank increased the opportunity for human manipulation. As one Brother pointed out in 1769: "One runs the danger of making incorrect constructions; also the occasion can easily be taken to change the lot until it finally hits the way one wants it to."[34] By 1769, the Brethren had learned to be cautious.

Although the mixing of human and divine agency in the lot procedure provided yeast for difficulties, changes in attitude among the membership and problems with the practical consequences of its use caused gradual fermentation and finally produced severe limitations on lot casting. This process can be traced over the last half of the eighteenth century by looking at how the synods that met during this period dealt with the lot and by considering evidence of developments that fueled changes.

The Synod of 1764 met as the first official synod after Zinzendorf's death. The members' primary concern was the reordering of the central governing structure. They did, nevertheless, spend ample time on the lot. Their discussion reveals two particular issues that dictated much of the debate in this and future synods. One of these was the question of obedience to and respect for decisions made through the lot. The other concerned the potential tension between faith and practicality within a system where lot casting touched matters of everyday living such as house ownership and marriage.

The Brethren opened their discussion of the lot by lamenting developments in the handling of it. The use of gaming imagery is marked. They observed that earlier "the Brethren often wagered body and life on the lot. Afterwards, however, many explanations of the lot and issuances [Außtellungen] about it were made, thus the simplicity was disturbed, but we hope that this grace will be restored."[35] This statement contrasted the earlier willingness to hazard all at God's command with the increasing caution and definition of procedure that indicated a decline in simple piety. Such a lament seems quite ironic or, perhaps, poignant given the amount of paper dedicated in this and later synods to further explanation and declarations.

Many statements made during the discussion in 1764 continued to emphasize the special grace of the lot and its invaluable aid in decision making. One of the most revealing of these again contrasted limited human understanding with divine omniscience. The synod declared that the Savior's thoughts often differed from even the most carefully weighed thoughts of his *Arbeiter* and *Diener*, but He "sees in the future and all things are present to Him in their entire connection with dependent consequences. Our view, on the other hand, is indeed confined and imperfect."[36] According to this statement, limited vision prevented human reason from ever competing with divine understanding. It also assumed that the lot provided a reliable means for communicating this understanding.

Cracks in the foundation were showing, however. One Brother remarked that the very holiness of the lot raised the need to consider whether it was not used too often or incorrectly, thus allowing the opportunity for disobedience. He observed that one "must not perhaps think: dear Savior I would be happy if you thought as I! But he must . . . be so disposed that he can say wholeheartedly: dear Savior! I know nothing, I have no will, let me know thy will: I will gladly be obedient."[37] Obedience among the Brethren, or lack thereof, was apparently an increasing problem, as was the dreaded "self-will." As someone in the synod pointed out, such obedience depended on participation in the covenant with the Savior and a "heart-connection" with Him. Because this connection appeared to be failing among many members, the ground of the theology of lot casting threatened to give way. In the end, the members' unwillingness to submit to decisions made by the lot caused the discontinuation of its use in most areas of decision making in the Unity. Bishop August Gottlieb Spangenberg, who had replaced Zinzendorf as the dominant influence within the Unity, recognized the source of the trouble when he spoke of the conspicuous "reasoning" [Raisoniren] that resulted from the reluctance to obey a decision given by the Savior.[38] This statement identified the tip of an iceberg that damaged not only lot casting, but also the entire system of the Ortsgemeinen, which depended on the voluntary submission of individual desires to the good of the Savior and of the community. As the century progressed, the youth of the Unity were increasingly inclined to favor human reason over revelation, particularly in matters of everyday life.

The attempt of the Unity leadership to stem the tide of Raisoniren with regard to the lot involved them in lengthy debates over the process, which took them ever further from Zinzendorf's ideal of simplicity. One can sympathize with the tendency to "reason" over the lot when one considers some of the hoops the leadership jumped through in their attempt to keep the faith. Early in the discussion of 1764, one Brother reminded the synod of cases in which decisions made by the lot during Zinzendorf's absence were later overturned by him. The answer given to this is somewhat astonishing. The synod maintained that Zinzendorf's opposition contained "deep wisdom of God, since without this same opposition the intention of the Savior would not have been completely fulfilled."[39] It is difficult to see how God could have given one instruction when he actually intended another, but the leadership appears to have been untroubled by this paradox.

The existence of such a paradox reveals one of the basic difficulties with the use of the lot by the Unity. Lot casting could, and clearly did, throw a wrench into the administration of daily affairs. The very emphasis placed by the Synod of 1764 on the absolute need for careful deliberation before framing the question illustrates the leadership's awareness of the potential difficulties. One Brother spoke of the need for "patience and faith" in dealing with the "many tests" that resulted from lot decisions.[40] Although the synod did not discuss these "tests" in detail, later synods were forced to do so.

The tension between faith and the need to define the procedure of lot casting, given the practical problems, is poignantly clear in a speech made by Johannes von Watteville, who, like Spangenberg, had been a close companion of Zinzendorf's. He spoke of feeling the near presence of the Savior, who impressed upon him the importance of the lot for the Unity: "I had a pleasant impression, that the Savior had not taken it [the lot] away because He knows that it belongs to our way of grace [*Gnaden-Gang*] . . . He will act [and] teach us more justly in this according to his heart and always legitimate it as He has done 1000 times. Instead of now thinking much about it and how to wrap it up [*anzuwickeln*], it is better to worship and bow down [*hinzusinken*] and to feel ashamed of all mistakes."[41] In the next breath, however, he proposed keeping a record of all lots cast in order to better regulate the practice.[42]

The Controversy Deepens, 1769–1782

When the next synod met in 1769, the members took on the issue of the lot at great length. At this point, they discussed the possibility, even the desirability, of discontinuing its use. The debate indicated a deep difficulty within the system that continued to trouble the Unity for the remainder of the century. The Brethren's quest for the Savior's approval at all levels of administration and in some personal matters forced the leadership to consider the possible consequences of lot decisions under a variety of circumstances. They could not, however, allow their consideration to be entirely pragmatic because the ideal of the lot as the Savior's true voice remained very much alive. This set up a chronic tension between the everyday concern for problems with economic decisions and social welfare, and the ideal of faith in Christ's superior wisdom, which went beyond human understanding. The tension is also evident within the Pietist movement as a whole, which incorporated a "rational orientation toward social problems" and a strong emotional/mystical strain focused on the central experience of spiritual rebirth. Francke, for example, wanted new pastors and teachers to be well educated, but he also wanted to eliminate what he called "brain theology" and scholarly ambition.[43]

On the morning of July 14, 1769, the synod began to tackle the thorny question of the use of the lot by reading various memoranda written by the members. One Brother laid the cards on the table quite frankly by observing that the New Testament only mentioned the lot in the choosing of a replacement for Judas and that there was "not the least" reference to it elsewhere. This remark initiated a debate that was not brought to a settlement until four days later, after the synod had drawn up a series of points on the proper use of the lot. Their procedure at this juncture reveals how great a role the lot played within the Unity. Having agreed on various points regarding the lot, the synod asked the lot whether they should ask "about the lot," to which they received the affirmative. They then posed the question of whether the Savior had anything more to say about the lot, and, again, the answer was yes. After determining that the "more to be said" concerned the points that they had drawn up, the synod asked for and received the Savior's approval of these points.[44] No important decision, whatever the subject, was to be made without consulting the chief elder, even if it took four separate lot castings to settle the matter.

Despite the Savior's previous approval of lot policy, Spangenberg opened the matter again on the morning of August 10 when the the Brothers were reviewing the minutes. One Brother asked whether the approval of the points had not removed any reason to consider suspending the use of the lot. Spangenberg replied that this was not the case, that indeed they should examine whether it might not be better to discontinue use of the lot.[45] Spangenberg observed that the Brethren were not in as close agreement with the Savior as earlier. "Many indeed would gladly have the lot consulted in matters in which they had no desire of their own: however, if they would rather do this or not do that and feared that the lot might fall against their inclination, they would rather not have asked the lot."[46] The leadership as a whole feared that the lot was losing "legitimation" (legitimacy) in the eyes of the Brethren. The Synod of 1769 simply elaborated on what the Synod of 1764 had said about the need for trust in the lot as the expression of Christ's will: "The lot falls as the Savior wills it; and if we use the lot, we look to the Savior and, childlike, expect an answer from Him."[47] One of the synod members also used the image of the Brethren as children. He emphasized the benefits of submitting to the lot even when in difficult situations, because only a "wicked, self-willed or spiteful child" would try to manipulate one's father instead of trusting that the father's answer could never be "wrong or harmful."[48] This remark ignored Zinzendorf's concept of the punishing lot and, in so doing, diminished the sense of divine presence in favor of human action as the source of any difficulties with lot decisions. The denial that the lot could ever be harmful by God's will may also be tied to a perceived need to make the lot more appealing to a generation inclined to view it critically.

Many of the Brethren seem to have been bad children. In a letter sent to Johannes von Watteville just prior to the Synod of 1769, Cornelius van Laer observed, "I have now heard so many arguments [*Raisonnemens*], criticisms, and admonitions from everywhere, that I am astounded," and he expressed the "heartfelt" wish that the Savior would bring more respect for the questions put to the lot.[49] The problem, of course, lay in the fact that, as Spangenberg observed later, the questions put to the lot often dealt quite literally with where a person lived. The repercussions of a decision could thus be severe. During its discussions, the synod admitted that sometimes the Brethren had experienced many unforeseen difficulties as the result of particular lot decisions, although they insisted that the results had shown that "it had been [the Savior's] gracious will."[50]

The actual alterations in the use of the lot at this time were relatively minor but reveal a general trend toward restrictions on its use. For instance, they recommended that it not be used to determine the worthiness of Brethren to participate in Communion because a positive answer, allowing them to participate, might lead them to lose respect for the lot if their feeling of unworthiness was strong. Perhaps most significant in light of future developments, they emphasized that the lot was only to be used in economic matters with the prior permission of the *Gemeine* Council. The Synod of 1764 had enacted this regulation, but the *Gemeinen* had largely ignored it.[51]

Not all of the remarks about the practice of lot casting were as benign as the one that opened the debate in July 1769. The remarks brought by the representatives of the Herrnhut *Gemeine* included an expression of dismay that many members believed that the leadership "only wanted to lord it over people and do what they please," to which end they used the lot.[52] The leaders themselves were well aware of the dangers of human manipulation, which had led them to introduce the use of the blank lot earlier. The Synod of 1769 added the proviso that, in most cases, both a positive and a negative should be used with the blank; otherwise, the odds of drawing the blank were greater, and that could allow for the rewording and recasting of the lot "until finally it fell as one would have it fall."[53]

Despite all of the obvious concerns and headaches associated with lot casting, the Synod of 1769 did not opt to discontinue its use. Indeed, it seems likely that Spangenberg's main purpose in raising the question was to shock the Brethren into a serious attempt to revive reverence for it. The identity of the Unity was too closely intertwined with the lot to allow for its easy dismissal. As one synod member remarked, "We would have reason to mourn deeply [*zu Tod zuweinen*] if [the Savior] had to take this jewel from us, because that would be a sure sign that He acknowledged us as a people with whom He could not continue His former household."[54]

The synod member quoted above essentially feared that a discontinuation of the lot would confirm spiritual failure in the *Gemeine*. Historian David Hall has noted that, a century earlier, Puritan ministers in New England had reported problems with Sabbath-breaking, a decline in family devotions, and excessive "affection to the world." Hall linked this to a problem with restless youth who did not share their parents' religious experience. He cited the consequent difficulty with enforcing moral legislation in an environment in which the rhetoric of declension (the Puritan leaders' lamentation over the "decline" of piety in the current generation) did not seem to succeed in "awakening" the errant members.[55] As we have seen, during the years from 1769 to 1801, the Unity leaders wrung their hands over the same problem. Indeed, it is impossible to detach the debates about the lot from the environment in which they took place. In the period before each synod, we can see clear traces of growing discontent among the younger Brethren, particularly regarding the issue of marriage, and of an increasing emphasis on human reason. Each synod was, thus, pushed by "bad children" further away from the "good" childlike reliance so dear to Zinzendorf.

Developments leading up to the Synod of 1782 were less dramatic than those in later years, but they indicated important tendencies. A letter received by the Unity Elders Conference from Moritz von Dohna in 1773 illustrates the growing rift over the use of the lot, particularly in determining marriage proposals. Von Dohna was then serving as one of the local leaders of the Fulneck *Gemeine* in England. His concerns related to the issues of declension and authority. He observed that the use of the lot in marriage "no longer completely suits our time" because people "no longer give themselves simply to the will of the Savior as before."[56] Von Dohna's remaining comments clarify the source of the problem. He recommended that the leaders not tell the Brethren when they had asked the Savior about a particular match because that caused "too much argument [*Raissonemens*] and other sins."[57] This contrast of "argument" over the lot outcome with former "simple" acceptance indicates that many in the *Gemeine* viewed the lot with increasing pragmatism and that, in the eyes of the leadership, this altered view involved applying rational critique to a supernatural manifestation. The UEC, however, did not, at this time, see the need to change the regulations. Indeed, they denied that the behavior cited by von Dohna was in any way typical of the majority of the Brethren and maintained that "the parents in particular" exhibited respect for marriage proposals confirmed by the lot.[58]

The Unity Elders Conference's dismissal of von Dohna's impressions was in all likelihood misguided. During an official visitation to Herrnhut and Niesky in 1778, Friedrich Reichel, a member of the UEC, reported the frequent presence of "a spirit of opposition to the direction of the Savior."[59] Reichel did not specify which aspect of the "direction," which, for the Brethren, meant use of the lot, had raised objections; but, all was not well, particularly regarding the marriage regulations. Of the twelve expulsions (of sixteen total) from Herrnhut between 1773 and 1782 for which a reason can be determined, at least three, possibly four, were for sexual misconduct.[60] Protests against the "direction of the Savior" with regard to marriage appear to have increased along with sexual restlessness.

The Fruits of Declension, 1782–1789

When the Synod of 1782 met, the use of the lot once again became an issue. The Synod of 1775 had confirmed the points drawn up in 1769. The Synod of 1782, initially, did the same but was drawn into "a basic and very detailed" discussion of the points by one member's remark that allowing the Brethren to accept or reject decisions confirmed by lot seemed to him contradictory to a view of it as the "definite will of the Savior."[61] Once again, the Brethren were faced with the inherent tension between their view of the lot as the voice of their chief elder and the practical need for voluntary obedience and some freedom of choice. In their ideal world, everyone would accept the lot's decision, but this was increasingly not the case.

In all of the discussion in 1782, the synod members emphasized the primacy of heart over head and the need to understand Christ's supernatural working within the *Gemeine*. During this same synod, however, the question of specific practical issues surfaced. In particular, questions were raised regarding use of the lot in the cases concerning house ownership, permission to live in the *Gemeine*, and marriage. One member put the issue of house ownership in terms of the need for fair reward for service. He pointed out that it was often hurtful that a Brother who had spent a long time in the Savior's service and wanted to build or purchase a house did not receive permission to do so when the lot was consulted. He suggested that a distinction could perhaps be made between Brothers who were "old, proven and reliable" and those who were newcomers or of dubious history.[62] It is fascinating to note that this proposal appears to prefer human over divine wisdom and suggests that, in giving a negative answer, the Savior was being unfair to his faithful servants. This implication never seems to have occurred to the synod members, although some did remark that the Savior might give a negative answer because he intended to call the individual to service in another *Gemeine*, "not to mention other possible reasons."[63] The synod decided that it would not be advisable to change current practice and to make an exception for anyone. However, they managed to slip in two little exceptions to the requirement of lot approval for home ownership, both of which indicate slow adaption to practical needs: "new" *Gemeinen*, defined by the number of houses in them, which were still considered new when they "lacked accommodations"; and Brothers for whom being a renter threatened their livelihood.[64] There were limits on how willing the Unity leaders were to gamble with God.

The Synod of 1782 also faced the problem of continual criticism that marriages in the Unity were not free but were determined by the lot. The member who raised this issue at the synod remarked that the Brethren "were still in confusion" about how to answer this charge. Despite continued attempts to stress the voluntary nature of submission to the lot, many of the Brethren seemed to have had difficulty reconciling this freedom with the emphasis placed on the importance of submission to the lot. They probably also had difficulty with the fact that a negative answer eliminated all possibility of the match in question. The synod agreed that when the charge of forced marriages was made, the Brethren should simply point to the "covenant" made by the members to accept the guidance of "our dear Savior" in "a matter of *that* importance."[65]

The years from 1783 to the next synod meeting in 1789 saw the continuation of restlessness among the Brethren, in general and with the use of the lot in particular. The discipline patterns of the Herrnhut *Gemeine* and of the Salem *Gemeine* in North Carolina show a marked increase in expulsions during this period. Among the offenses cited for Herrnhut are thirteen cases of sexual misconduct, including one Brother who decided to marry without the lot. The Salem records show seven cases of clandestine courtship or elopement for the comparable period.[66] Anecdotal evidence indicates that the pattern was not unique to Herrnhut and Salem. The report for a visitation to Niesky in 1784 remarked that the *Gemeine* still evidenced an inclination to "independence," while a visitation to Gnadenfrei in 1788 gave rise to the comment that many members lacked trust and respect for their leaders and criticized the "rule of the Savior."[67]

A more dramatic and significant incident occurred in Barby, in 1787, when Count Heinrich Thirty-ninth Reuß, who had been serving in Barby as warden (administrator) for the Single Brethren, resigned his post and left the Unity to return to the Lutheran Church. The letter of resignation that he wrote to his immediate superiors is very circumspect, despite his avowed intention to give a "detailed" explanation. His primary concern was to assure the Brethren of his conviction that his resignation was Christ's will for him and not the result of the dreaded "irresponsibility" and all of its implications of self-interest. He confined his actual reason for leaving to a single phrase stating that life in the *Gemeine* was "no longer a way that, according to the understanding that I presently have of the Gospel, and especially of Protestant freedom, can remain my own any longer."[68]

Taken alone, no connection with the use of the lot is apparent. Fortunately, a letter written by his superiors to Johannes Loretz, a member of the UEC, reveals far more. Carl Baumeister reported that, in conversation, Reuß expressed frustration with the physical regulations of the *Gemeine* and, specifically, with the separation of the sexes. The meat of his dissatisfaction, however, was that "he wanted to marry and since he did not believe in the lot, and thus could not agree to give the direction of his future over to the lot, also did not want any wife proposed whose character and inclinations he had not first tested himself through sustained contact, he had decided to go to Berlin and take up residence in his house there, and expect a wife from God in whose company he could serve Him and love Him."[69]

This statement is significant for understanding the shift in attitude toward the lot and the complexities of the Brethren's faith. Young Reuß declared outright his rejection of the lot as the expression of the Savior's will. Furthermore, rather than viewing submission to it as part of a voluntary covenant, he saw it as inconsistent with "Protestant freedom." Beneath this, we can also see a desire to determine for himself the potential suitability of a prospective wife. This fact is particularly significant because the use of the lot for marriage grew out of Zinzendorf's belief that desire for a particular person or such things as concern for physical appearance had no place in the union of spiritual warriors.[70] Heinrich Thirty-ninth Reuß was definitely not a gambling man. The implication of his attitude was that the use of the lot was not a way to gain divine guidance in the area of marriage but, rather, that the sensible course was to establish oneself in good company and await the results. Of course, Reuß clearly did not reject God's intervention in his life, he "expected" that God would place the right woman in his path, but he expected this to occur through the natural social channels. He probably also wanted to allow for some individual desire in his choice of a bride.

Count Reuß's defection hit the Unity hard. Not only had he served in local Unity government, but his family had been closely involved with the Unity from its origins and was related by marriage to Zinzendorf. Baumeister's comments on the situation not only illustrate this general distress, but emphasize the continued importance of the lot within their piety and the perceived threat from renegade individualism. Baumeister posed several possible reasons for Reuß's action, including pressure over the succession to his inheritance, but also specified that he might have been "befogged by his own reason [Verstand] and his lust."[71] After admitting that the exact reason could no longer be determined, Baumeister declared it most likely "a darkness of his soul," the consequences of which he would deeply regret. In Baumeister's eyes, the rejection of the lot signaled a deep trouble in Reuß's soul, not a mere disagreement over the form of faith. Nevertheless, Reuß left the Unity to take up life in Berlin, still insisting that he was not motivated by fleshly lust but by his understanding of the Christian life in which God did not speak through pieces of paper.

The problems posed by the restlessness among the younger Brethren and an increasing desire for "independence" in personal decisions did not go away. At the next synod meeting, in 1789, the leadership was forced by this restlessness into another extensive discussion of the use of the lot. Some materials included as enclosures to the synod minutes bemoan the incursion of the cul-

ture of the Enlightenment into the protected ranks of the *Gemeine*. This undoubtedly played a role in the problems with the acceptance of lot casting, as
well as in the discipline problems of the youth cited earlier. The minutes of the
synodal committee on the Single Brothers expressed the frustration of the leadership. "How can we oppose the freedom in speech and frivolity from which so
much harm arises, since often mockery and free-thinking mix in under the
pretext of fun?"[72] The committee also pointed in specific to the "dangerous
spirit of satire and argument [*Raisonirens*]" that earlier synods had blamed for
resistance to the use of the lot. The Elders Conference of Gnadau had voiced a
similar concern in 1786 when it cited a "neological spirit" (an emphasis on
reason in theology) among the boys and blamed it for their "bad ways."[73] It
appears that many of those outside of the leadership were becoming increasingly vocal in their opposition to the traditional piety of the Unity and were
acting on Enlightenment ideas about the need for free discourse, which often
took the form of satire. This opposition included some of the students at the
seminary in Barby, which trained future leaders for the Unity. After much debate, the synod agreed to transfer the seminary to safer ground in an area of
Upper Lusatia where no universities existed. As far as satire and *Raisoniren*
were concerned, the synod could and did issue stern warnings against them,
but it could not stem the flow of change. Such a change in attitude toward the
relative place of piety and intellectual life also occurred within other Pietist
circles. When advised by his father to abandon "the latest, most learned" writ-
ers in favor of Luther, Arndt, Spener, and Bengel, one young man responded
that these might be acceptable "for a pious man" but were not sufficient for a
"scholar."[74]

Various memoranda sent to the synod by the *Gemeinen* indicated an
uncertainty regarding the use of the lot in decisions involving property or with
potential economic impact. Gnadenfrei expressed gratitude for the lot as the
Savior's means of guidance but suggested restrictions in the case of business
matters, particularly in the appointment of Brothers and Sisters to head businesses. Niesky worried whether it was "proper and advisable" to use the lot
when the Savior's will seemed clear from circumstances, such as when there
was only one suitable candidate to head a business. The Niesky memorandum
also questioned its use in cases of house ownership and commented that it had
hampered the "civil and economic course of the *Gemeine*," although it did not
specify how.[75] Interestingly, two non-German *Gemeinen* were bolder. Fairfield
in England and Zeist in Holland questioned how far the jurisdiction of the
Savior over "private property" extended. This remark hinted at the tie between
protests over the use of the lot and the restlessness with *Gemeine* control of
economic life. Although the records do not indicate that the American *Gemeinen*

raised the issue in these terms, their reference to "the American freedom" served much the same purpose.

Ultimately, the synod altered the use of the lot as a result of these concerns, but many members of the leadership denied that the bad consequences were the fault of the lot and continued to see advantages in gaining the Savior's stamp of approval on outward matters, particularly in the cases of positions of responsibility. As one Brother said, it would not be good to place business leaders without asking the Savior; such Brothers had great influence in the *Gemeine,* and a disputed appointment or a bad human decision could easily lead to faction within the *Gemeine.*[77] In the eyes of the majority of the leadership, decisions approved by the Savior were secure ones, despite the evidence of dissatisfaction over lot decisions within the *Gemeine.* Interestingly, this observation echoes Richard Baxter's comments, made more than a century earlier, on the advantages of lot casting. He maintained that decisions by lot prevented the manipulation of elections by factions and ill will on the part of the loser.[77]

The discussion did not end on that note, however. The synod members returned to the issue and reviewed past policy as recorded in the *Harmony of the Four Synods* (1764, 1769, 1775, and 1782). They discovered that it was not "positively prescribed" that the lot *always* be used in business appointments. At this juncture, the synod decided that in cases where only one really suitable candidate existed, that candidate could be appointed without the lot.[78] Although a small concession, it illustrates the synod's accommodation to practical necessity.

Having dispensed with the issue of the lot in business, the synod turned its attention to the second and somewhat related problem of lot casting in home ownership. As we have seen, this issue had been taken up by the previous synod, but the exceptions made then had failed to solve the problems. The summary made by the synod of the points raised by the German and the American *Gemeinen* make it clear that the old objections had only gotten stronger. The local Elders Conferences generally recommended a change in the regulations, provided, of course, that any such change was approved by the lot.[79] In each case, the objections all turned on practical problems that the "private" Brethren (the term used by the Unity to refer to members holding no official position) seemed increasingly unwilling to view through spiritual eyeglasses.

Faced with such clear negative consequences of the use of the lot in the matter of house ownership and an apparently solid desire for change, the synod proved more flexible than it was in earlier years. It pronounced the current regulations "uncertain and difficult" and observed that many *Gemeinen* did tend to make the exception the rule, thus voiding the regulations de facto. Given the general consensus, the synod moved to determine whether the Savior would approve any changes. The lot did indeed approve altering the current regulations and confirmed the decision to leave the matter of whether to consult the lot to the discretion of the local Elders Conferences.[80] The emphasis seems to have been on granting greater responsibility in decision making to the Elders Conferences. As the regulations stood after this discussion, it was possible for the local leadership to make all decisions on home ownership without supernatural intervention.

In the cases of businesses and home ownership, the debate centered on the suitability of using the lot in matters that seemed to have no clear spiritual element. One additional area of objection surfaced, however, that could not be classed as merely "outward." As might be expected given the problems with the marriage lot noted earlier, the Brethren also debated whether it was always necessary to ask the Savior before making a marriage proposal. From the tone of the discussion, it appears that the motivating force in raising this issue was an increasing desire for marriage on the part of the Brethren and the feeling that dependence on the lot hindered this by placing an additional barrier in the already delicate process of finding a suitable and willing mate.[81] According to Unity belief, marriage held an integral place in the work of the Gospel, so this issue held deeper implications than did the other two, and the synod formed a committee, all thirty-eight members of which were male, to discuss the matter. This committee, which included all of the members of the Unity Elders Conference, stood solidly behind retaining the requirement of the lot. In doing so, they cited the by now customary reasons, including the historical success of the use of the lot for marriage within the *Gemeine*, the origin of the practice in the covenant made by the Brethren, and the superiority of dependence on the Savior's judgment in such critical decisions. One Brother commented that the use of this method had been a great comfort to those who married.[82] One of the reasons cited, however, was new to the discussion and touched on the tie between the *Gemeine* system as a whole and the marriage lot. A committee member raised the question of whether the *Gemeinen* could continue to have "a well-ordered *Gemeine* constitution if each Brother chose a wife merely according to his conviction" and suggested that making exceptions might eventually eliminate "this covenant" to submit to lot decisions altogether.[83] This Brother linked the dependence on Christ's judgment even in, or especially in, this intimate matter with the entire order of the Unity. More prophetically, the Brother's observation suggests that once exceptions began to be made, the rationale that held Christ's approval to be necessary would be undermined. The concept of covenant seems crucial here because both parties to a covenant must keep their end of the agreement. If the Brethren now allowed individuals to avoid submission to the will of the Savior in marriage, the covenant, as a whole, would be severely weakened.

Despite the strong statements by committee members in favor of retaining the marriage lot, the evidence indicates the presence of strong dissent among many of the Brethren. In part, dissent was tied to the growth of a general suspicion that the *Gemeine* leadership used the lot to confirm their own predilections or to avoid the burden of "a tiresome investigation."[84] This appears to be the first overt suggestion of lot manipulation. That "private" Brethren would make such remarks implies increasing skepticism about the lot as the true voice of the Savior. It also illustrates the close tie between the use of the lot and the position of the *Gemeine* leadership.

From Revelation to Reason, 1789–1801

The years between the Synod of 1789 and the Synod of 1801 witnessed the continued unfolding of difficulties in the Unity, particularly among the youth. In Herrnhut, sixty-seven people were expelled from the *Gemeine*, although a few won readmission to other settlements. Of these expulsions, twenty were the result of sexual misconduct, which included marriage without the lot. The rise in the number of expulsions for sexual offenses outpaced the rise in the general number of expulsions; the earlier figures were forty-one expulsions, with eleven for sexual misconduct. This pattern later found expression in renewed objections to the marriage lot in 1801.

The records of the ruling bodies flesh out these figures. The Brother in charge of the Single Brothers in Herrnhut complained, in 1793, that "worldliness and the currently dominant spirit of licentiousness increasingly invades our Choir, especially among the young people."[85] As noted earlier, this "worldliness" was not confined to Herrnhut. On a visitation to Gnadenberg in 1795, Jonathan Briant, a member of the UEC, reported: "One heard of excesses, impudence, and licentiousness, pleasure outings to Bunzelau etc. sleigh trips of single and married Brethren, gossip clubs, wildness among the boys, gossip [*klatschereyen*] and argument [*Raisoniren*] in the houses etc."[86] The tendency toward rationalism also seems to have continued. In reporting on a speaking in 1796 with the Single Brothers in Herrnhut, Christian Gregor remarked that the conduct of some was "very dubious, especially such who through reading new writings think in an enlightened manner [*aufgeklärt dünken*]."[87]

The general restlessness with the *Gemeine* regulations also affected the attitude toward the use of the lot. In 1797, some Single Brothers in Gnadenfrei wrote a letter to the Unity Elders Conference in which they spoke in a "mocking manner" regarding the use of the lot in the remarriage of the master tanner very shortly after his wife's death.[88] The connection between objections to the lot and problems with the marriage regulations had surfaced earlier, if less directly. In 1796, the Unity Elders Conference first discussed the "very unseemly remarks over the use of the lot" being made by many inhabitants of the *Gemeinen* and from that discussion also noted the continued difficulties with the marriage regulations.[89] The members of the UEC found themselves having to cope with members' increasing willingness to sacrifice their positions in the *Gemeine* in favor of personal choice in a spouse. What they seemed most anxious to avoid was giving occasion for open rejection of Christ's leadership. Thus, when a Single Brother in Herrnhut was expelled for becoming engaged to his master's daughter after the lot had fallen out negatively, the UEC remarked that the Herrnhut Elders Conference should not have cast the lot over this couple because their "inclination toward each other had gone so far."[90] The Unity leadership recognized by this time that limitations on the use of the lot might be the only effective response to increasing willingness to defy it. In this instance, however, they were advocating neither a general policy change nor an exception allowing the couple in question to marry within the *Gemeine*.

Perhaps the most startling and strong rejection of the use of the lot came from the American *Gemeinen* on the eve of the Synod of 1801. In two letters written to separate members of the leadership, Gottlieb Schober, a prominent merchant in Salem, complained loudly of an injustice done him through the lot. He had become involved in a violent quarrel with a fellow member of the *Aufseher Collegium* in Salem and, as a consequence, both parties had been expelled from office and excluded from fellowship with the lot's seal of approval. In a heated letter to UEC member Johann Friedrich Reichel, Schober declared, "I said it, and I continue to say that no God can act in such a way and therefore it is a card game and the work of man."[91] By putting things in this manner, Schober identified the aspect of gaming inherent in the use of the lot from its ancient roots but also denied that such a gamble could ever be sanctioned by God. In effect, his remark implied that God was too "rational" to produce the decisions made by the lot. This concern over the apparent irrationality of lot decisions had been inherent in many of the criticisms over the effect of the lot on the running of the *Gemeinen*.

The next day, Schober wrote a calmer and more revealing letter to Bishop Johann Daniel Köhler, Salem's representative to the upcoming synod. In the course of laying out his general complaints about the structure of authority within the *Gemeine*, he took up the issue of the lot. He repeated his association of the lot with gambling, saying that its use could be "viewed as luck and bad luck" but explained that this was particularly the case when it was used in certain circumstances, such as "business between two people, or how this or that public house should be built," which matters could be decided "through brotherly reason [*Verstand*] if one wanted to take the time."[92] This remark echoed and amplified the objections to the lot raised in the Synod of 1789. Furthermore, it implied that the leadership had come to lean on the lot as an alternative to the proper exercise of their human reason, with which they were too impatient or too lazy to bother. Such an attitude, in conjunction with developments within the *Gemeinen,* sounded a clarion call to the synod that met in the summer of 1801.

The decisions made by this synod definitively altered the use of the lot in areas of practical concern such as business and, in general, continued down the path of restrictions on its use. Nevertheless, the ideal of adherence to the twenty points drawn up by the Synod of 1775 still stood. Thus the members of the 1801 synod "bound themselves anew faithfully to hold fast" to these principles.[93] Significantly, however, they also expressed concern that the Brethren, in general, and the youth, in particular, did not fully understand the lot regulations. They further admitted that many of them could never be won over to its use and would probably have to be expelled from the *Gemeine.*[94] Simply standing by the established practice threatened to bleed the Unity of much of its youth. Furthermore, the appearance of solid conservatism, which the Synod of 1801 tried to project, was essentially a fiction because many of the points had already been amended in previous years. The difficulty faced by the synod, of course, was the ever present dilemma posed by the fact that the lot was so closely identified with the will of the Savior. One of the memoranda sent to the synod offered a way around this dilemma while preserving the basic integrity of the lot. The memorandum repeated observations made in earlier synods that true care for the lot meant being sparing and cautious in its use, but it added something that seems quite significant in light of changing attitudes toward the supernatural aspect of the lot. It questioned whether the government of the Savior might not suffer "when one calls each and every use of the lot, even in insignificant matters, a question of the mouth of the lord, an instruction or order of the Savior, a declaration of His holy will etc."[95] The synod agreed with this statement and, in doing so, allowed for the possibility of viewing the use of the lot as a fully human action. The issue, of course, turned on the definition of "insignificant matters," which would undoubtedly vary. The action was still a far cry from dismissing the lot altogether, but it was also a considerable distance from Zinzendorf's ideal of simple faith.

Whatever the ideal position regarding the lot may have been, the synod had to grapple with the problems posed by its use. The reality was that the situation in the *Gemeinen* called for continued modification of its use. In the case of appointments to positions in the *Gemeine* businesses and election to the *Gemeine* Council, the Synod of 1801 dispensed with the requirement of lot confirmation. In both cases, it did so out of concern for the difficulties and "inconveniences" in the current system.[97] The comments made in the course of discussion over the election to the *Gemeine* Council shed more light on the shift in mind-set among the Brethren. One official from Herrnhut expressed concern that removal of lot confirmation would result in "bad people" on the council. This comment generated a brief exchange about the impact of majority vote. In the course of this exchange, one member pointed out that, in the past, the *Gemeine* members had complained that some of their choices had been negated by the lot and that some with only a few votes had received confirmation.[97] This exchange strongly suggests that the Brethren either felt more confidence in their own decisions than in those of the Savior or that they no longer believed the lot to be divinely guided. The synod made the decision to dispense with the lot in election confirmation, however, only after receiving affirmation from the lot that the Savior approved of this move. They could thus feel fully confident in their growing reliance on human decision.

With the removal of lot casting in business appointments and elections to the *Gemeine* Council, the Synod of 1801 moved further down the path of removing the immediate intervention of the supernatural in matters not directly spiritual in nature. One area that remained somewhat gray in this respect was the issue of marriage. While the Synod of 1801 did not restrict its use, the debate raised at this time set the stage for the showdown that brought about its removal at the next synod, held in 1818. Memoranda from the primary American *Gemeinen* and one memorandum from Herrnhut requested that the lot no longer be used to confirm marriage proposals. Although the minutes of the synod do not record any discussion of the memos from America, they do include a summary of the points raised by the memorandum from the "mother *Gemeine*" of Herrnhut. This memo makes it clear that some of the Brethren wanted marriage and courtship to follow a more "worldly" path than they had previously. It proposed that no proposal be made without prior parental consent and that proposals having such consent, where no doubt existed for either party, should go forward without the lot. Finally, and perhaps most significant, it urged that "the opportunity for people of both sexes to become acquainted with one another should not be so entirely cut off as hitherto."[98] Judging solely from the synod records, this memo might seem a voice crying in the wilderness, but when placed in the light of the disciplinary records and the memoranda from America, it becomes clear that it was a chorus. The Synod of 1801, however, refused to budge an inch on this issue, choosing instead to focus on the memorandums from the Elders Conferences of several German *Gemeinen* and one American *Gemeine* that supported the continued use of the lot in marriage.[99] The synod entirely ignored the suggestion that the wall separating the sexes be weakened and held fast to the view that the Savior provided the

surest source of wisdom in such an important decision. However, it emphasized that the lot could never be used in cases where the couple had already
fallen in love.[100] Such a comment had not been seen as necessary in previous
synodal discussions. Experience was eating away at the best attempts to hold
the line. By 1818, the American *Gemeinen* refused to allow for continued resistance to change in the marriage regulations and sent their deputies with an
ultimatum that led to the removal of the lot in marriage for all except officials
within the *Gemeine*. The road to this destination, however, was already cleared
by 1801. By century's end, the spirit may have been willing to gamble, but the
flesh was weak.

In many ways, the Unity's struggle over the use of the lot reflected changes
within the body as a whole. These changes, in turn, indicated subtle and occasionally not-so-subtle adaption of an attitude more clearly in line with the
eighteenth-century Enlightenment. In their journey from a strong emphasis
on a "childlike" acceptance of the lot as Christ's hand among them to an ever
more cautious view hedged by complex explanations and regulations, the leadership generally represented the voice of conservatism. They warned of the
danger of the loss of Christ's special relationship with the Unity, which was at
the heart of their system of "godly settlements." Their need to provide for the
inhabitants of these *Gemeinen*, however, forced them to deal with the lot in
increasingly practical terms in which human reason played a prominent role.
At the same time, this tendency was accelerated by a membership less willing
to accept the lot as direct supernatural guidance, particularly when it affected
their material welfare. Evidence suggests that this shift in attitude among the
"private Brethren" resulted from a growing reluctance to subordinate private to
public interest and from the influence of Enlightenment literature that they
seem to have used to back their defiance of *Gemeine* authority. These strains of
independence sounded in settlements on both sides of the Atlantic, although
more stridently in America.

Change in the regulations came very slowly and was driven more by
necessity than by desire, yet it did come. By looking at this process, we can see
the transformation of a communal mentality from one in tune with the sixteenth and seventeenth centuries to one primed for the modern world.

5

Testing Authority and Defining Freedom

A TALE OF TWO CONTINENTS

In 1818, the Pennsylvania delegates to the synod of that year made a speech in which they laid out all the various privileges and freedoms accorded to the American male citizen. "The effect of all this," they maintained, made it impossible to continue to impose the use of the marriage lot on the American Brethren.[1] This was a clear call from the local leadership for an official recognition of American distinction. As we have seen, the European and the American *Gemeinen* experienced severe challenges to the *Gemeine* ideal in the late eighteenth century, and earlier protests over the marriage lot came from both sides of the Atlantic. Indeed, one might well wonder how the leadership could have come to see anything peculiar about the American Brethren. Yet, clearly, they did, and evidence shows that the ground for this was laid by 1801.

The key to the distinction, as the speech of 1818 indicates, lies in the attitude toward authority and the ideas about freedom in the German and in the American *Gemeinen*. Challenges to authority within the German *Gemeinen* tended to be veiled in the language of symbol or in the concern for "proper" social roles. The Brethren in North Carolina expressed their objections more directly on the basis of "the American freedom." This "freedom" was associated closely with independence from economic regulation by the *Gemeine* in favor of individual initiative. To understand the implications of this development, we need to explore the ideas regarding authority and freedom within the ideals of the Unity and in the their respective environments.

The Ideal of Authority

In many ways, the structure of the *Gemeine* reflected a blend of secular models with religious vision. This was no less true for their views on authority and freedom. Because the Unity government exercised authority over practical and over spiritual matters, it is important to include some consideration of the secular traditions on which they drew. In his monumental study of the German concept of freedom, Leonard Krieger focused on the failure of the development of an intellectual justification for individual independence. Instead, "freedom" came to rest in obedience to paternalistic authority, firmly rooted in the feudal tradition that linked liberty with princely authority. However, as A.G. Roeber pointed out, an alternative tradition existed in southwest Germany that associated freedom with the absence of constraint and that was marked by a consequent suspicion of authority. This view was similar to the attitude that has been cited as typical of British America by the mid-eighteenth century, but it lacked the sanction of the English constitutional tradition.[3] Roeber also observed that the definition of freedom in early modern German dictionaries included a view of it as "self-will" contradictory to divine and social order.[4] The Brethren show evidence of both of these views of freedom, but their own view was also shaped by their concept of Christ as head of the *Gemeine* and by their stress on spiritual brotherhood.

From its beginnings, the *Ortsgemeine* rested in part on a manorial base. In 1727, Zinzendorf used the initial payment of homage on his Berthelsdorf estate to establish governmental and spiritual order in Herrnhut, and, in 1729, he wielded his position as lord of the manor to prevent separation from the Lutheran Church. An incident in 1733 illustrates the underlying paternalism and the spiritual overtones given it by the count. In that year, protest erupted over the monopoly on several staples that was granted to the tavern owned by Zinzendorf by Countess Zinzendorf. The monopoly on salt was a particular grievance. Several of the Brethren claimed that Zinzendorf sought his own profit at the cost of "harm to the Brethren," who could purchase better products at a cheaper rate elsewhere.[5] Zinzendorf responded with indignation. He reproached the Brethren for their ingratitude in light of the fact that he had freed them from their tenurial obligations. He then laid claim to the spiritual high ground, observing, "The disposition of Christ was: one should be silent and rather suffer himself to be wronged. The Brethren, however, sought their old Moravian advantages [*Vorteilen*] ." The remainder of the count's reply indicates that the Brethren had protested more than the monopoly. They appear to have rebelled against continuing in their particular tenurial status. Zinzendorf told them that if he granted them the bill of sale for their land, "it would not be good, they would fall into worldly justice. . . . They could have spared much expense which they would now have to give if they wanted to have the name of a people who would be independent from all authority."[6] This speech is quite revealing. Zinzendorf depicted his status as lord of the manor as a means of protection from secular society. Further, his tone with regard to "independence" was decidedly negative. Despite his high-handed tone, however, he lifted the prohibition on bringing in staples from the outside, although he did insist that the Brother who had instigated the protest be excommunicated.[7]

The connection between spiritual protection and freedom, and submission to authority is also evident in the Brethren's view of Christ as "patron, . . . protector and advocate" of the Unity.[8] As we have seen, Zinzendorf essentially made over his rights as lord of the manor to Christ, at least in ideal, who expressed His will through the lot. The human administration of the Unity was also presented as protective, in much the same terms that Zinzendorf had used about his own position. For instance, at the Synod of 1750, the count observed, "The plan of the *Gemeine* justice is such that would enable one to live in good order. Whoever lets himself be directed by the [presiding] Brethren will not have to lay out much money for court. He will not fall into the lawyers' hands."[9]

This paternalistic view of authority also applied to those Brethren who represented manorial and territorial authority. Such a view was important to the Unity because, unlike the Anabaptist groups, they viewed worldly authority as sanctioned by God for the maintenance of proper order in the world. Thus, we see not only a traditional assumption of power exercised as appropriate to each office, but also a stress on the benefits of this order. Because the Brethren rejected such traditional expressions of participation in worldly government as military service and oath taking, it was doubly important for them to stress their acceptance of secular authority. The Synod of 1789 noted that "it would be a misfortune for our *Gemeine Orte* if they did not have their [secular] authorities. These are not only there for the protection and representation of the *Gemeinen,* but also for the real exercise of their office in all projects."[10] The use of family imagery to describe governmental relations within the *Gemeine* undoubtedly reinforced a paternal view of authority.

In stressing the benefits of submission to a caring authority, Zinzendorf's ideas echoed the traditional stress on the protective aspect of the feudal structure. Human authority brought human problems, however. The *Gemeine* officials had charge of the use of the lot and held positions analogous to those secular authorities who stood between the locals and their prince. It appears as though they were subject to the same temptations. The members of the Synod of 1764 feared that the officials "forget they are *servants. . . .* They do not see so well how they can be useful to the Brethren and the *Gemeine* where they serve, but rather that they could enjoy honor and comfort themselves."[11] Although this lament occurred after a general sense of declension set in and may have been exaggerated, the synod reports of later years and the records of the ruling bodies indicate that resentment and mistrust of the *Gemeine* leadership was a recurrent problem in Germany and in America.

This tension between the necessity for human authority and the potential for its abuse in an "unbrotherly" manner lurked continuously beneath the leadership's discussions regarding *Gemeine* government. In 1771, for instance, a debate arose over the use of the word "counsel" [*Berathung*] with reference to the role granted to the Unity Elders Conference. Some of the UEC members feared that the use of this word would allow an opening for seeing their authority as merely advisory. The final word on the discussion illustrates the paternal view that they had of authority, the emphasis on the need for subordination, and the ever present importance of recognizing the boundaries established by their "true head," Christ. The records state, "All the Brethren were perfectly agreed that indeed the Elders Conference of the Unity does not have to insist for their own sake on the exercise of more power and authority; but it is nevertheless absolutely necessary for the sake of the Savior's business, that they have a real influence and due authority, whereby a course well-pleasing to Him can be established in His house, and harm avoided. In this we cannot and will not overstep the bounds of the regulations approved by the Savior."[12] In this statement, the UEC justified its authority as critical to the preservation of the *Gemeine* ideal, but the last sentence hedged this some. Human authority could never be absolute.

It is important to remember that all members were expected to submit freely to the government of the Savior and to subordinate their self-will to the good of the whole. An article in the section of the *Gemeine* ordinances that deals with relations between the "private" members and those Brethren holding authority refers to consent as the basis of the leadership's authority.[13] While there is no evidence that they thought of this in terms of constitutional theory, if members made a case that a leader was acting in violation of the ideal, and had thus lost "legitimacy," he or she was often removed from office. The leadership expressed continuous concern over the "legitimacy" of authority exercised in the Unity, and this word became a warning flag for strains between the leadership, local and central, and the private Brethren. In practice, this gave the private Brethren some measure of control over their leadership, but the final decision regarding the fate of any official rested with the UEC, subject to confirmation through the lot.

As far as human relations among God's people were concerned, Christian brotherhood may have downplayed distinctions of rank, but the leadership did not intend to level the social structure. The ordinances of the *Ortsgemeinen* emphasized the need for subordination in domestic service and in the handicrafts. More significant for the subject at hand, "free" behavior was usually condemned or, at least, viewed with discomfort. Here, too, something of a tension existed because the leadership encouraged free and open discussion in their governmental bodies and "open-hearted" speech in the pre-Communion speakings. The line seems to have been crossed when speech or behavior threatened to disrupt harmony in the community or to undermine the *Gemeine* system. An entry in the minutes of the Neuwied Elders Conference illustrates the boundaries: "It was observed that various [people] have drawn the conclusion from the free behavior which they perceived in some of the Sisters who have come here from Herrnhut, that it [Herrnhut] must not be so narrowly restricted as here. Brother Joseph [Spangenberg] remarked hereby; a little too much freedom is highly dangerous. We have a *rule* and peace is with those who act according to this rule" (emphasis theirs).[14] Here Spangenberg spoke of an individual, personal freedom that is in agreement with the German lexicographers' identification of it as potentially contradictory to good order. The association of liberty with the defiance of regulations proved influential in the Unity leadership's view of "American" freedom.

The Environmental Incubators

Ideas can never fully be separated from the environment that produces or fosters them. Historians have emphasized the physical and psychological impact of living on the periphery of what Europeans considered to be the civilized world. They have pointed out that conditions in the New World had, of necessity, an impact on all attempts to reproduce life as it was in the Old World.[15] As Henry James observed, young America had "no sovereign, no court, no personal loyalty, no aristocracy, no clergy, no army, no diplomatic service, no country gentlemen, no palaces, no castles nor manors."[16] If the absence of these marks of an entrenched hierarchical order in America is significant, conversely, we should not ignore the impact of their presence in Europe. James's litany of things absent indicates the various layers of authority, monarchical ties, and manorial ties that bound Europeans in an intricate web of vertical relations and obligations. This web became particularly complex in Germany by the eighteenth century as a result of the absolutist ambitions of the territorial rulers. Despite their sheltered community, the Brethren were by no means immune to the pressures that the layers of authority exerted. The Unity's German *Gemeinen* were concentrated in electoral Saxony, where the manorial system sat heavily, and in Silesia, whose new Prussian rulers were generally successful in centralizing authority.[17]

No discussion of the impact of environment can ignore the physical environment. The German *Gemeinen* were closer to other towns and villages than were their North Carolina counterparts, but there were other aspects of the landscape that reinforced a sense of order and hierarchy. Herrnhut, for example, conveyed precisely this sense of order and hierarchy, and the UEC was most often resident there. Its Choir houses were large and graceful buildings. A spacious baroque pleasure garden ran behind the Herrnhut manor house, which stood on the town square, and, across from the garden stood the imposing *Vogtshof*, which exceeded the manor house in size. Other sizeable houses provided living quarters for resident noble members. The Berthelsdorf manor house was a short walk down the road, as was Berthelsdorf itself, where the farming tenants lived who supplied Herrnhut with much of its agricultural needs. From the Hutberg, the site of Herrnhut's cemetery, one could see Berthelsdorf and the linden-lined road that led to the von Gersdorf estate, the hereditary holding of Zinzendorf's grandmother. Herrnhut was a sophisticated little town that played host to numerous dignitaries and rulers, including the elector of Saxony.

The records of the local and central ruling bodies of the Unity are shot through with evidence of the impact on the German *Gemeinen* of the web of obligations embodied in the landscape. Although the *Gemeinen* were freed from the most burdensome aspects of the manorial system, service dues and some monetary dues, the members were still surrounded by reminders of its power. Among these reminders was the ceremony of homage. All of the German *Ortsgemeinen* stood legally under the authority of the lord of the estate on which they were founded. This standing necessitated a formal pledging of obedience to the new lord whenever the estate changed hands. The connection between Herrnhut as *Gemeine* and Herrnhut as part of the Berthelsdorf estate emerges in an entry in the UEC minutes for 1789. They note that on the evening after the homage ceremony the *Gemeine* will hold "a solemn meeting in which the *Gemeine* will pledge proper esteem [*Hochachtung*] and love etc. to their new lord."[18] Because the women and men who held authority over the Unity estates were almost always members of the Unity, and frequently members of the UEC, the tension between the equality of status as a Christian Brother or Sister and the secular distinctions of rank affected the attitude toward the homage ceremony. Consequently, the discussion of homage often focused on downplaying the actual ceremony as much as possible.[19] It is also possible that this unease on the part of the Brethren reflected a growing resentment of the manorial system from both inside and outside the Unity ranks. Whatever the case, it suggests that many Brethren would have been quite content with the absence of this particular ceremony in America.

The homage ceremony was the most prevalent reminder of manorial ties, but not the only one. An incident in 1792 reveals another aspect of life on the manor. In that year, the Herrnhut Elders Conference discussed the potential admission of Anna Maria Hultsch to the *Gemeine*. At issue was whether she possessed a valid *Losbrief* releasing her from ties to her manorial lord. In the end, the Elders Conference tabled the question until they obtained more information on the legalities involved.[20] The consequences of this restriction could be widespread. In 1798, the UEC commented that the Gnadenfeld *Gemeine* was not growing "since in Schnellewalde, from which otherwise various people would move to Gnadenfeld, access is cut off through refusal of the *Losbrief* on the part of the manorial lord."[21] The centralizing tendencies of the German rulers could also restrict mobility. The Herrnhut records for 1789 remark that Prussian subjects should not be transferred to the *Ortsgemeinen* in Saxony "because as it is the Brethren stand under the suspicion of helping people leave the country."[22] It was not only spiritual standards and the lot that made joining one of the German *Gemeinen* difficult.

Manorial obligations formed only one strand of the ties that bound. A comparison of the German model of the 1770s *Gemeine* ordinances with the Salem version reveals the impact of territorial absolutism and bureaucracy on the former. The section on the relations with outside authority reveals this most strikingly. In the Salem ordinances, this section consists of three relatively short articles. The German model is twice as long. A closer look at one of the paragraphs clarifies the contrast. The Salem ordinances read, "We therefore recognize our obligation to love and honor our dear King George III and all his officials, especially those in this province, and to promote to the utmost the welfare of the land wherein the Lord has planted us."[23] This same paragraph in the German model contained the following additional phrase: "and in no manner to prefer our own or any other private convenience and interest to [that of] the sovereign."[24] It is noteworthy that the German version includes the specific denial of the pursuit of private interests in favor of those of the ruler. This statement would have sat very ill in eighteenth-century America. Indeed, it opposed the rationale for attracting colonists and the reality of the vast amount of land available, including the consequent economic opportunity.

The sentiment regarding the furthering of sovereign interests emerges in the minutes of the UEC in an entry that illustrates the dependence of the Unity on the territorial rulers for their various economic and religious privileges. The entry in question notes that the Durninger Company, which was Unity-owned, had, "through our dear territorial lord," been granted a merchandising right that they regarded as "a special mark of trust" on the part of the ruler.[25] This led them to express the wish that the *Gemeine* inhabitants would seek to promote the interests of the territorial lord as much as possible.

The growth of bureaucracy associated with territorial centralization also increased the Brethren's dependence on noble mediators and representatives at court. No one reading the records of the Brethren can fail to be struck by the heavy presence of the aristocracy in the German *Gemeinen,* or by their relative absence in Salem. It was no accident that the membership of the UEC from 1769 to 1801 counted a large number of nobles within its ranks. Of the twenty-nine men who held office during those years, ten came from the nobility. Other nobles served as local officials, such as *Helfer* or *Vorsteher,* or headed the district court. Occasionally, they served in a dual capacity as *Gemeine* officials and manorial officials. In contrast to the situation in Germany, only a handful of nobles resided in Salem during the period under study.

The noble element was a mixed blessing for the Unity. The need for a new manorial authority in Neudientendorf prompted a discussion of the frequent failure in noble members of a true dedication to the Savior's service and of the consequent strain in their relations with the members under their authority.[26] Apparently, they tended to become distracted by the administration of the estate and to keep largely to their manor houses. This made them appear to be outsiders, despite being members of the *Gemeine,* and alienated them from other members. Yet, the nobles were important to the running of the *Gemeine* system in Germany. A couple of remarks in the UEC records illustrate this. In 1780, the Neusalz Elders Conference asked that Ludwig von Marschall be allowed to stay longer because von Falkenhayn's health was bad and, except for von Marschall, there was "no one there who could look after the upcoming negotiations with the Council [*Cammer*] and government in Glogau."[27] A few years later, a member of the UEC made an even more revealing comment. He noted the Neusalz leadership's concern over their relations with the ministry in Breslau and remarked, "There is, however, at the time, no one here who can properly take on *that* business, and . . . apply with as much proper candidness as with required deference and foresight, for a better and more friendly disposition [from the ministry]."[28] Aristocratic training and connections were an invaluable asset to business at court.

Aristocratic members could be very helpful in maintaining control of *Gemeine* administration and in securing its privileges, but their presence could be intimidating to non-noble members. The Brethren in Gnadenfrei, for instance, complained of too many noble people in the *Aufseher Collegium,* "through which free discussion could easily be hindered."[29] Along similar lines, when her husband received an appointment as a *Gemeine* official in Gnadenfrei, Sister Scheuel said she felt shy about going, "especially in view of intermingling with so many noble Brethren."[30] Relations were strained in other ways by aristocratic presence, particularly in the uneasy 1790s. In 1796, the UEC records noted that some Brethren felt that the "deviations" of noble

Brethren were not taken so seriously as those of others.[31] As with the trappings of the manorial system, the nobility within the *Gemeine* served as a constant reminder of hierarchy.

Aside from the predominance of the aristocracy, the physical nearness of the central ruling body also distinguished the environment of the German *Gemeinen*. An initial study of the records of the Salem settlement impresses one with the extent of involvement of the European-based UEC in Salem's affairs, but an overview of the European records reveals the comparative lack of it. Of course, this only makes good sense given the distance, the relative slowness of the mail, and the expense of travel. Nevertheless, the impact of the presence or absence of the central authority, which did hold de jure the final word on all major administrative decisions, should be considered. A general pattern emerges from a study of the UEC records. Whenever relations within any of the German *Gemeinen* threatened to get out of control, the UEC could send a member to mediate or to serve as interim head. The Elders Conferences on both sides of the Atlantic frequently appealed to the UEC for support in keeping order and in protecting the ideal. The German *Gemeinen* were far more likely to get results. Conversely, the Salem records include complaints that the UEC was neglecting them. Visitations to America were costly and, consequently, approached with great caution; the distances between the German *Gemeinen* were relatively small, particularly because they tended to be clustered within their respective regions. Fires in Germany could be dampened more easily than those that sprang up across the ocean.

Interestingly, the leaders themselves seem to have believed that the German *Gemeinen* offered an environment peculiarly suited to keeping order. In a discussion of the potential difficulties with Francis Ockley, who apparently had a stronger mystical bent than suited the leadership, the Unity Elders Conference noted that he might be less harmful in a German *Gemeine* than in his current situation in England (he had previously been in Pennsylvania).[32] Taken by itself, this might not be particularly striking, but the UEC expressed similar sentiments regarding young Benjamin Heinrich LaTrobe, who had to be expelled from the *paedagogium* in Niesky for improper behavior. The UEC felt that sending him back to England would only put him in "still more danger" and that he should therefore be put in a German *Gemeinen* and tutored privately.[33]

Salem's landscape contrasted sharply with that of Herrnhut. The piedmont area of the Wachau was more rugged than were the gentle hills of the Berthelsdorf estate. The town consisted primarily of small half-timber or clapboard houses and had no manor house in sight. If Salem lacked the marks of manorialism, absolutism, and hierarchy, it possessed other defining environmental factors. These factors can basically be identified as participation in public life; the effect of the wilderness/frontier, in particular, the availability of land; and the distance from the central ruling body. Significantly, Jack Greene pointed to these three elements of the American environment as factors that influenced the development of the independent attitude of eighteenth-century British Americans.[34] They seem to have worked the same effect on the Unity members.

From its beginnings, the Unity recognized the need to participate in public life in order to preserve its privileges. In Germany, the Brethren accomplished this through those members who held administrative positions or who had "friends in high places." During the pre-Revolutionary period in the Wachau, participation in local government by "private" Brothers (i.e., those outside the Unity leadership) was also limited. The Brethren created false freeholds in order to obtain voting rights; but, before the Revolution, they sent only one or two Brothers to the polling place with proxy votes for the rest.[35] The Brethren did use their political contacts to gain the appointment of more members as justices of the peace than was usual for German immigrants,[36] but the leadership determined which Brothers received these appointments. Things began to change after the Revolution. The number of Brothers going to the polls expanded because proxy voting was no longer possible. Moreover, local participation in government became more important, and more Brothers were eligible to vote and hold office under the new regime. In an entry in the minutes of the Elders Conference for 1783, the leadership observed that "it is up to us to see that some Brothers are constantly acquainted with public affairs."[37] The minutes of the years following the Revolution also refer frequently to recommending various candidates for office to the Brethren. This responsibility contrasted dramatically with the layers of authority present in Germany, among which the private Brethren could only try to find the one most responsive to their desires.

In addition to opportunities for participation in government, life in Salem was marked by its location in the backcountry. The effect of this location consisted basically of two elements: the rough way of life and the availability of land. Between 1750 and 1770, the population of the state of North Carolina rose from 70,000 to 175,000, and then to 350,000 by 1783, with the greatest increase in the western area. It continued to rise in the following years, although at a slower pace, going from 350,000 in 1783 to 478,103 by 1800.[38] In their plans for the Wachau, the Brethren had anticipated a rise in population, but they got more than they bargained for. It became increasingly unlikely that, "buffer zone" notwithstanding, the Brethren could avoid close contact with their less savory neighbors. Although no definitive proof can be established, it seems unlikely to have been pure coincidence that the Brethren should record increasing problems with the three activities often cited as hallmarks of backcountry society, namely, drinking, shooting, and fighting. The frontier provided an atmosphere inimical to the ideal of the *Ortsgemeine* and to the order so crucial to the working out of the ideal.

Despite the leadership's efforts to keep Salem pure, they were undermined by the system established in the Wachau that linked Salem with the agricultural *Ortsgemeinen* and with the *Landgemeinen*. Because Salem contained the Choir houses, the great bulk of the trades, and the schools, it drew people from the outlying *Gemeinen*. Likewise, people from Salem frequently took temporary employment in the other *Gemeinen*. What happened in these *Gemeinen*, then, also affected Salem.

The significance of this for the discussion at hand lies in the fact that the agricultural *Gemeinen* and the *Landgemeinen* were more exposed to the influence of the outside than was Salem. Despite having their own local authorities, they were physically outside of the watchful eye of the Elders Conference except for occasional visitations by members, and, although the agricultural *Ortsgemeinen* were villages governed by village ordinances, their emphasis on farming drew their interests away from the center. In the *Landgemeinen* founded after 1770, the inhabitants lived on their individual farms, which were separated from the central village.[39]

The effect of this distance from the center surfaced in troublesome conduct. The Bethanians were the first to protest *Gemeine* control of house leases. They and inhabitants of the *Landgemeinen* took the lead in disruptive behavior such as shooting matches. The rough ways of the countryside also affected the Brethren in Salem. During the 1780s and early 1790s, a growing number of references to the young men who were going out hunting and shooting instead of working appear in the records. These references are also peppered with citations of rough speech and behavior. The fact that, when some Single Brothers walked off the job in 1778, most of them went out into the countryside says much for the pull of the "wilderness," as does the fact that, by 1787, the records report that many of the young people deserted Sunday meetings in favor of "roaming around in the countryside."[40] All of the references to the tendency of the Salem youth to frequent the countryside are laced with a sense of the disorder of the woods.

Availability of land also decisively shaped the life of the Brethren in the Wachau. As we have seen, that fact allowed the Unity to purchase a large block of land and establish the Brethren on family farms and agricultural villages. This opportunity also posed a danger, however, as Spangenberg recognized as early as 1760 when he warned of the potential for the Brethren in America to become "rich and content" through the availability of land and opportunity. This danger marked them off more clearly from their German Brethren than did their country ways. Some of the German Brethren were undoubtedly attracted by the possibilities offered in America. In 1771, Jacob Jorde wrote to the UEC that he wanted to go to the Wachau and "acquire some land," if he had money enough for this.[41] The ideal of the Brethren, however, had been expressly formulated for a mobile, artisan society. Zinzendorf had deliberately discouraged the Brethren from farming for fear that it was incompatible with the call to serve the Savior. This ideal of a "pilgrim folk" remained very much alive after the count's death, as a remark of the Salem Elders Conference shows: "We must inculcate the idea that we are a pilgrim folk at every opportunity, and seek to remove little by little everything opposed to this. The people whom we accept and receive must declare . . . their mind [*Sinn*] to be in all ways what the Savior wishes them to be, *to seek no ease, to attach themselves to no place,* but to be at home everywhere" (emphasis mine).[42] This statement stands in sharp contrast to the reality outlined in the minutes of the *Gemeine* Council for 1782: "The danger of forgetting this call of our *Gemeinen* is greater in America and especially here, than in *Gemeinen* where assignments to missionary and other posts happen more often and therefore the Brethren do not become so easily attached to outward things."[43]

Evidence reveals that these fears of "attachment" were not without foundation. In 1780, John Holland told the *Aufseher Collegium* that he was dissatisfied with his situation as assistant in the tavern and wanted to live "on his own piece of land where he can rest after the day's work has been done."[44] This desire necessitated living outside of Salem because the Brethren were not allowed to own land within the town. By 1790, the Elders Conference was moved to observe "that the inclination to establish farms at some distance from Salem, at the base of which impure intentions usually lie, increasingly takes the upper hand among our young people and so occupies their minds that through this many a one has been severely set back in his blessed *Gemeine* and Choir relations [*Gang*]."[45] Although the Elders Conference did not specify the precise nature of the "impure intentions," it seems highly probable that their desire to move to farms arose in part from an attempt to escape the restrictions placed on Salem inhabitants. In their attachment to the land, the North Carolina Brethren reflected the impact of an ideal in direct conflict with that of the pilgrim. One of the most popular cultural images in eighteenth-century British America was that of the independent farmer, sitting in front of his house, overlooking his fields, flocks, and dependents.[46] This was not what Zinzendorf or the other early leaders of the Unity had in mind, nor was it likely to be easily achieved in any of the German *Gemeinen,* except by those Brethren of noble birth. The Synod of 1764 encapsulated the degree to which the colonial American pastoral opposed the *Gemeine* ideal. The synod noted, "When you have eaten and are full [*satt*], and build beautiful houses, then your heart does not rise up."[47] A complacent, comfortable Christian would not be inclined to rise and go when called by the Savior.

This inclination to farming on the part of the younger members of the Brethren contrasts starkly with the lack of interest in agriculture among the early inhabitants of the Wachau and, indeed, among the early Brethren in general. According to Thorp, less than one in three of the adult males living in the Wachau in 1766 were farmers in any respect, and, in the early years in Bethlehem, Pennsylvania, the leadership noted the "total disinclination to farming" of most of the Brethren.[48] The role played by the increasing emphasis on the family in accelerating this new attachment to the land and the danger that such attachment posed emerges from the minutes of the *Aufseher Collegium* for 1794: "In general the desire for profit which lies at the base of these land transactions is unfitting for Brothers since it is more than likely that a piece of land which parents buy for their children brings harm to them and can give them occasion to abandon the *Gemeine*."[49] This entry indicates more explicitly the relationship between land possession and restlessness under the control of the *Ortsgemeine*. The plan for the Wachau was not compatible with the easy availability of land outside of the various *Ortsgemeinen,* nor had the Brethren fully anticipated the lure that this would present to the second generation.

The entry from 1794 also reveals another lure of the land, that of easy money. As the population of North Carolina grew, so did speculation in "the land behind the mountains." The first reference to speculation in land among the Brethren surfaced in the mid-1780s, when the Elders Conference admonished the Brethren in a public assembly on the unfitting nature of "land jobbing."[50] The problem may have subsided after this, but only temporarily. By 1793, the *Aufseher Collegium* commented on the fact that too many Brothers were indulging in land speculation. Although they were concerned that the poorer Brethren might ruin themselves financially, their strongest objection was that speculation was rooted in "greediness to become rich, which does not suit Brothers of this *Gemeine* at all."[51] References to land speculation crop up again in the records through the turn of the century. The temptation seems to have been a strong one. Recent research has revealed the extensive nature of land acquisition between 1770 and 1830 by residents of Salem and by the outlying settlements. In Salem, those most active in land purchase and sales were Brethren such as merchants, the tavern keeper, and the doctor, who had the most regular contact with people outside the *Gemeine*. Almost 10,000 acres went through merchant Traugott Bagge's hands between 1770 and his death in 1800.[52] Undoubtedly, they appreciated the possibilities of landownership. The fact that Gottlieb Schober, who became notorious for protesting the authority of the Salem leadership in business matters, was also an avid speculator suggests the role that property concerns played in shaping those protests.[53]

It is difficult to determine with any precision how unique this problem was to the *Gemeine* in the Wachau or even to the *Gemeinen* in America. Some land speculation did occur in Prussia toward the end of the century as land rents rose dramatically. This cannot really be compared to speculation in America, however, because the circumstances of these land transactions in Prussia were far more limiting. The Prussian land could only be leased, not purchased outright, and the lease of such estates required a large initial outlay of capital. In addition, those wishing to lease had to be approved by the *Domänenkammer*, which sought only "men of insight, activity, honesty, and ability"; the primary purpose of land lease was to increase the prosperity of the ruling dynasty and the nation, not of the individual. Speculation in Prussia remained confined largely to the nobility and, at any rate, could only have affected the three *Ortsgemeinen* located in that area. Frederick William II forbade further speculation in 1792.[54] In addition, no references to major problems with land speculation appear in the UEC records. It is unlikely, in any event, that speculation could have taken place on the same scale as it did in North Carolina. Spangenberg's premonition of 1760 had been all too accurate.

One final element distinguished the environment of the North Carolina Brethren, the institution of slavery. This institution stands in ironic counterpoint to the manorial system of eastern Germany. Both manorialism and slavery rested on the exploitation of human labor and embodied social hierarchy.[55] The existence of slaves, however, automatically raised the social status of white Americans. No matter how poor or insignificant, they remained free of physical bondage. Even indentured servants knew that eventually they would be free to make their own way in the world.[56]

The Brethren were active participants in the world of slavery, albeit reluctantly. Initially they shifted to slave labor as an alternative to the use of stranger day laborers, and, in Salem the first slaves were owned by the Unity, not by individuals.[57] The number of slaves in Salem rose over time, although it was always kept to minimum. The most significant growth in slaveholding came in the agricultural *Ortsgemeinen* and in the *Landgemeinen*. By 1790, the Unity and individual Brethren owned a total of forty slaves.[58] Despite the fact that the Brethren incorporated slaves into their spiritual life on a roughly equal parity as Brothers and Sisters, the slaves' position as legal chattel cannot have escaped them or their white Brethren. In a perverse way, the ability of anyone with the money to own another human being could be seen as another aspect of American opportunity or, even, of freedom.

Methods of Defiance

The leadership faced defiance of authority and the threat of disorderly freedom from the German and from the American *Gemeinen*. The different environments, however, seem to have produced different types of defiance. In the German *Gemeinen*, the incidents of defiance noticed by the UEC were usually indirect rather than open challenges to the system. In Salem and in its dependent *Gemeinen*, though, the Brethren were more ready to challenge the leadership directly. The German Brethren also appear to have been more inclined to oppose *Gemeine* leaders who also represented manorial or territorial authority (i.e., external authority), while the Salem Brethren opposed internal authority and occasionally used external authority as an ally. The different definitions of freedom that surfaced in Germany and in America reflect the differing attitudes toward authority shaped in part by the differing roles of authority in Germany and in America. They also hint at the impact of the respective emphases of the German and English Enlightenments.

An overview of the records of the ruling bodies reveals at least three forms of what can be called indirect defiance: pleading ignorance, anonymous satire, and avoidance of duty.[59] The first of these is well illustrated by an incident that occurred in Neudientendorf in 1782. In that year, a man escaped from prison in Erfurt and made his way to the Neudientendorf *Gemeine*. He went through the town, stopping at the blacksmith's and then the locksmith's to ask that his chains be removed, but his request for release proved futile, and he moved on to the neighboring village, where he was taken back into custody. His brief visit produced a considerable disturbance in the *Gemeine* that touched on issues of duty and relationship with authority.

Johann Christian von Damnitz, who served the Unity as local representative of the territorial ruler, was very upset at the failure of the Brethren to apprehend the fugitive. He reported that he specifically instructed some of the Single Brothers, who were standing outside their house, to seize the man, but that they "paid no attention to [his] cry," and, later, when he confronted them, said that it was not their responsibility and acted "really very injuriously" toward von Damnitz.[60] Von Damnitz was upset by the disrespect to his authority and by what he feared would be seen as defiance of the reciprocity agreement between Erfurt and Gotha regarding the apprehension of criminals. The failure to act, he said, could subject the negligent Single Brothers to severe punishment by the territorial government.

His was not the only voice to tell this story, however. Some of the Single Brothers wrote their own letter to the UEC. If we look at this carefully, some telling points emerge. The Single Brothers' letter specifically identifies the reason for the man's imprisonment as a struggle regarding his occupation

[*Profeßionsstreitigkeiten*]. This suggests two things: first, that he did more than simply request that his chains be removed; and second, that he shared the status of artisan with the Single Brothers. Thus, the Brothers may well have felt a kinship with him. Certainly, they did not seem to be eager to aid in his recapture; also, they did not refer to him as "prisoner," but simply as "man." They said that Connau Roemming went to alert the mayor, but that, in the meantime, the escapee crossed into the Altdietendorf jurisdiction. Most significant, the Single Brothers maintained that they "believed they had done their duty because it *had never been published* how one was supposed to behave in such a case" (emphasis mine). They contrasted the "brotherly" conduct of the Gotha magistrate, who was not a member of the *Gemeine*, with that of von Damnitz, who "used outside force against the *Gemeine* and did not behave as a Brother and member of the local Elders Conference." In addition, they asserted that Anton von Lüdecke, as former *mandatoriat* and a member of the UEC, would attest, they "had shown [themselves] at all times to be faithful and obedient subjects."[61]

Two salient points emerge from this remark. The Single Brothers claimed that they acted or failed to act out of ignorance of the law, not out of deliberate defiance, and they emphasized their reputations as obedient subjects. They also turned the heat on von Damnitz for having violated the *Gemeine* ideal. This accusation of "illegitimate" behavior possessed power because von Damnitz had apparently insisted that the Brothers swear an oath, something that the Gotha magistrate did not require of them.[62] However, the Brethren seem to have walked a fine line between ignorance and defiance: one of them (Noack) had responded to von Damnitz's order by saying that "he (Noack) was no bailiff."[63] Nevertheless, this statement, albeit gruff, was still a claim that it was not Noack's place to arrest people.

When the dust settled, von Damnitz was marked for transfer to another *Gemeine*, after being admonished that he should not have let the "fire" get out of hand.[64] This incident certainly provides the most thorough example of pleading ignorance, but it does not stand alone. A Sister in Gnadenfrei was excluded from Communion for taking in "the faithless Heinz woman" against the "express prohibition" of the manorial authority, Carl Christian Siegmund von Seidlitz, who was also a member of the UEC. She justified herself by saying that the mayor had not delivered the prohibition, so she had not taken her brother's warning regarding it seriously.[65] Apparently, the Unity leadership was aware of the tendency toward this particular form of indirect defiance. In 1794, the Herrnhut Elders Conference noted that although, out of concern for propriety, the new edict regarding illegitimate pregnancy could not be published in the *Gemeine*, if any single person appeared to be pregnant or in danger of being so, the edict must be made known to them privately "so they cannot *excuse themselves with lack of knowledge*" (emphasis mine).[66] Faced with the pressure of layers of authority and bureaucracy, claiming ignorance of the law probably seemed one of the most effective methods of defiance.

Anonymous satire also appears as a type of defiance in the German *Gemeinen*. Satire as defiance is often difficult to separate from general jesting, but some outbreaks that are directly connected with discontent in the *Gemeinen* surface in the records. The most clearly identifiable case of this occurred in Gnadenberg in 1795. The 1790s saw much unrest in the *Gemeinen*, but a visitation to Gnadenberg turned up a particularly sweet form of protest. Jonathan Briant reported one problem that stood out: "Offensive things and bad devices were written on the sugar hearts and sold by the baker, also lampoons [*Pasquille*] attached and found in the Brothers House."[67] Later, another lampoon was found that fit the first two, and an anonymous letter turned up in a family house. Unfortunately, the lampoons have disappeared, as, obviously, have the cookies, but Briant noted that in all of them, "much shrillness [*Gelle*] was spit out against Sister Kolesch," the wife of the *Gemeine Helfer*. In the course of his visitation, Briant commented that relations in the *Gemeine* were marked by "envy, suspicion, slander, and factions," with Sister Kolesch in the middle of much of it.[68] Attacking Sister Kolesch through anonymous mockery brought sharp attention to the perpetrators' dislike, without being easily traceable. Nor was this method confined to Gnadenberg. The Herrnhut *Gemeine* also reported difficulties with satirical verses "of punishable contents" found in public places, and had continual problems with lampoons and "bad" graffiti appearing on the observation tower that stood on the Hutberg.[69] It is worth noting that the 1790s witnessed the Brethren's increasing interest in attending comedies. They seem to have learned from the experience.

What the Unity leadership labeled "independence" could also be viewed as yet another form of indirect defiance, at least in its German incarnation. This form is most clearly demonstrated in the discussion of the strained relations between manorial and *Gemeine* government, this time in Gnadau. The UEC complained of a "perverse spirit" among the Brethren in the *Gemeine* who wanted to oppose manorial authority and to "be independent" of it. In connection with this opposition, the leadership noted their embarrassment over "the often noted inclination of many Brothers to use unpermitted and irregular means to promote their private interests and the improvement of their sustenance [*Nahrung*]."[70] The concern with promoting family welfare even at the expense of the *Gemeine* flew in the face of the Unity ideal and seems to have been on the increase. A later notation, however, indicates what in specific the leadership saw as "independence." In further discussion of the difficulties in Gnadau, the UEC noted the following, "Merely for the sake of the state of their sustenance, everything that belongs to good order and magisterial obligation in such cases seems to be a burden to them."[71] Earlier, the UEC had stressed the need for "the *punctual* following of the territorial laws and edicts" (emphasis mine), and Teutsch, the local excise collector, had asked to resign his office after being embroiled in a quarrel over proper legal procedures.[72] It appears that, confronted by the growing bureaucracy and demands of the state, many of the Brethren chose simply to do things their own way, or to ignore certain procedures. They did not, however, openly oppose the authorities or the *Gemeine* system. In fact, the UEC fretted over the Brethren's tendency to place greater trust in the *Gemeine* authorities than they did in manorial authorities.

The fact that the forms of defiance in the German *Gemeinen* were often indirect does not mitigate their role as modes of protest. Many historians of popular culture have noted the ways in which even apparently mundane words and actions can hold pointed meaning.[73] Any discussion of symbolic protest raises the question of the extent to which it acted to reinforce the established order by serving as a controlled safety valve. In the case of the Brethren, we can see evidence of effective opposition and continued stability. The leadership certainly did not view symbolic protest as controlled, and the protesters often achieved at least part of their goal. Nevertheless, veiled protests allowed the leadership to dampen the flames without any serious danger to the *Gemeine* system.

The Unity officials in Germany did face what they identified as the active desire for "freedom." This was usually depicted as a desire to obtain freedom by leaving the confines of the *Gemeine*. In addition, the "freedom" sought, at least what the UEC associated with that word, was intellectual freedom, freedom of conscience and the passions.

In 1774, "the young Lucius" expressed his unhappiness with the fact that his father would not say whether he would be allowed to go to the university. The UEC reported that Lucius feared he might be put to work in the missions department of the Unity "which [did] not harmonize with his avidity [*begierde*] to be free [*in Freyheit zu kommen*]."[74] The use of the word "avidity" is revealing; it implies a sensual, immoderate desire for the freedom offered by university life. This same association of university life, freedom, and passion occurs in a later notation in which three young men wanted to go to the university "to continue their ruinous [*verderbliche*] connection among themselves with more freedom."[75] University culture had a very real ability to invade even the most pious of institutions. August Hermann Francke battled in vain with student life at Halle that came to include drinking, pipe smoking, fighting, obscene songs, night carousing, and so forth.[76]

References to the desire for "freedom" increased in the 1790s. In 1792, the UEC noted "the spirit of freedom and unrestraint, especially among the youth" in Neuwied, and, in 1795, Jonathan Briant included the "thirst for freedom" in his description of the young people in Gnadenberg who wanted "to live thoughtlessly unencumbered."[77] Such a view of freedom was not confined to the leadership. In 1793, one boy commented to his companions that "now that he was excluded from the *Gemeine*, he enjoyed much more freedom than they did."[78] The Unity leadership identified this liberty with liberty to sin, which stood in direct opposition to the free joy found in adherence to the Savior's standards, as outlined in the *Gemeine* ordinances.

One entry in the records sheds a sharper light on how some of the youth of the *Gemeine* saw these "freedoms." During the same visitation that turned up the lampoons in Gnadenfrei and the problems with pleasure trips to Bunzlau and disorderly sleigh rides, Briant reported that many of the Single Brethren "maintain[ed] their alleged freedom and human rights, . . . and allow[ed] themselves all sorts of deviations."[79] The coupling of "freedom and human rights" as a defense of lampoons and the pursuit of pleasure in the face of the paternalistic attitude of the Unity leadership strongly suggests the influence of such ideas in the writings of many German thinkers of the period. The stress on the primacy of private conscience in matters of religion and morality seems to come particularly close to what the Single Brothers in Gnadenberg believed.[80]

Jürgen Schlumbohn observed that although by the last third of the eighteenth century, the use of the expression "liberty and property" rose, German intellectuals were particularly interested in freedom of the press and counted it as one of the central parts of general "freedom." They also linked this general freedom to freedom of thought and belief.[81] As we have seen, the reading of "bad books" was an increasing concern for the leadership; it seems with good reason. The culture of reading that developed in Europe during the eighteenth century gave them ample opportunity to indulge in forbidden books. Reading circles existed in Görlitz, near Herrnhut; in Bautzen, near Kleinwelke and Herrnhut; and in Gotha.[82] Evidence from the *Gemeine* records indicates that another of these reading societies existed near Neuwied and that it had been attended by some of the Single Brothers. Some of these Brothers continued to receive books from the society, even after they ceased to attend the meetings.[83]

There can be no doubt that the Unity leadership faced defiance of authority within the German *Gemeinen*, but the Salem leadership perceived the defiance they faced in the Wachau as distinctly American and passed this perception on to their UEC Brethren. An investigation of the attitude toward authority and freedom as exhibited by the Salem Brethren suggests that the methods of defiance suffered a sea change in the Atlantic crossing. This change was then nurtured in the atmosphere of the post-Revolutionary backcountry. In the environment of the New World, the Brethren became bolder in their opposition and redefined "freedom" in accordance with the American experience. This "American freedom" came to center, in particular, on property and economic life.

On the surface the actions of the Salem Brethren mirrored those of their German counterparts in many ways. Just as the leadership bemoaned the attempt of the Brethren in Germany to skirt regulations and ignore admonitions, the Salem leadership complained of Brethren who went their own way. As early as 1776, the potter Georg Aust's refusal of three different orders regarding his apprentices prompted the *Aufseher Collegium* to remark peevishly, "What good then is a collegium at all if the people in the *Gemeine* do anything they want to."[84] Their lament seems to have gone unanswered. In 1778, for instance, the Elders Conference perceived the need to announce in the *Gemeine* Council "that no Brother should engage in an agreement or binding obligation with another without the knowledge and approval of his *Arbeiter* or respective superior."[85] In another case, Charles Holder wanted to resign as road supervisor and so had the local court appoint Heinrich Walther as his successor: "This all happened without notifying any authority here. . . . It will be announced in the *Gemeine* Council that no Brother is allowed to use the secular court to get rid of his office in such a way."[86] In this case, Holder's relationship with external authority was the reverse of that found in the German *Gemeinen*. Rather than attempting to use the *Gemeine* leadership as a buffer against external authority, he turned to external authority to achieve his goal. In the American environment, outside authority offered the Brethren support for independence, rather than putting restrictions on it in alliance with the *Gemeine* leaders.

The 1780s and 1790s saw a rising number of references to the attempts of various inhabitants of Salem to skirt the authority of the leadership. In 1781, for instance, the Elders Conference observed with regard to domestic help that "the Brethren must not turn to private individuals regarding work, but to the *Vorsteherin*," and, in 1787, they complained, "It is indeed rather late to seek to obtain the consent of the Conference after everything has already been arranged and the trip definitely scheduled."[87] When Gottlieb Fockel was excluded from the *Gemeine* in 1791 for leaving his profession to work at the paper mill, the *Collegium* observed, "We cannot tolerate our people to go from one profession to another or from one master to another just as they please."[88] The problem persisted, however. In 1793, Gottfried Schulz took steps to relinquish his management of the Single Brothers farm and prompted the Elders Conference to observe, "Generally it appears to the Conference to be altogether contrary to the character of the Brethren when, as has happened in other matters, Brothers act only for themselves."[89] This activity indicates a general restlessness with the leadership's control of individual decisions in economic matters and an increasing reliance on individual ties.

An entry in the minutes of the *Gemeine* Council indicates that the leadership saw a trend not only toward independent action, but also toward disobedience or indifference to the decisions made by the ruling bodies: "When this or that is resolved in the Conferences for the best of our *Ort* and its inhabitants, it is to be expected according to our government and the entire purpose of our being together, that each one will act accordingly. . . . For some time, however, it has often happened that when the *Gemeine* Council, *Helfer Conference,* or *Aufseher Collegium* gave reminders, these were not universally obeyed."[90] All was not well in paradise.

These sorts of attempts to circumvent the authority of the leadership occurred in Germany and in America, but, in the Wachau, the leadership specifically associated them with the desire for freedom, and some of the Brethren openly protested the *Gemeine* system, at least in its business restrictions. In this context, it is worth noting that while four of the expulsions from Salem resulted from disobedience to the *Aufseher Collegium,* the Herrnhut records show no comparable expulsions.

In 1780, the Elders Conference struggled with what they saw as a very dangerous attempt to upset the economic system of the Wachau. The store assistant was being encouraged by some Brethren in Salem and in Bethabara to open a store in Bethabara independent of the Salem store. This was a direct challenge to Salem's position as the commercial center and to the *Gemeine* profit because the Salem store belonged to the *Gemeine.* The Elders Conference referred to the supreme authority of the Savior, the lot, and insisted that if any store were opened in Bethabara it would have to be a branch of the central store. From the further observations of the Elders Conference, it seems that the troubles went deeper and touched on the "hot button" issue of marriage practices. The elders noted the following: "People think tediously over these sorts of notions . . . and spoil their destination. It does not stop just with the notion to set up a business or trade, but the Brethren bring such people to seek out for themselves people to marry, which . . . is not only improper for us but also a harmful thing for the soul."[91] This statement indicates a close tie between economic restlessness in the Wachau *Gemeinen* and growing resistance to the marriage lot. Opening a business usually necessitated marriage, so restrictions on one interfered with the other. The American Brethren were not happy with restrictions on either.

In 1782, the Salem Elders Conference noted the inclination of the young people to want to leave their assigned trade to earn higher wages outside "with-

out being bound."[92] The Brethren were unique in colonial America in insisting
on a full seven-year apprenticeship; their tendency to seek work outside the
confines of the *Ortsgemeine* appears to have been a reaction to the example of
greater freedom among their neighbors.[93] The Brethren utilized "freedom" in
other instances. In 1789, the *Aufseher Collegium* complained that the inhabitants of Bethania used promises of "more freedom and other advantages" in
their bid to draw artisans from Salem.[94] Gottlieb Schober openly challenged
Gemeine control of his business interests in 1790 when he objected to several
points in his lease of the land for his paper mill. The objectionable clauses
included the requirement that he sell the mill only to a member of the *Gemeine*
and that he not sell or lease any part of his land without the permission of the
leadership.[95] In all of these cases, individuals sought to determine their own
economic destinies in an environment that offered various options.

The records of the ruling bodies also reveal a notable lack of deference to
authority, particularly among the second-generation American-born members.
These members did not cloak their feelings in anonymity. One of the earliest
and perhaps most revealing examples of this lack of deference emerges from
the minutes of the *Aufseher Collegium* for 1774. Some of the younger Brothers
complained that Johannes Heinzmann, the Single Brothers *Diener,* took over
the Single Brothers' farm and businesses "as if they were his own," at which the
smith, Georg Schmidt, commented "that it would be time to chain him or to
make one for him."[96] The Brothers clearly resented the control that Heinzmann
exercised over their outer affairs and were willing to voice it. A similar impatience with the local leadership can be seen in at least two other instances.
When the heads of the Single Brothers Choir called Johannes Flex to answer
for stirring Christoph Reich's father to oppose a decision of the Elders Conference. Flex "answered scornfully [that] they could wait," and when the *Aufseher
Collegium* instructed the shoemaker, Kuschke, to stop his "unauthorized" tan-
ning business, he refused to give up his hides or tools and said he would stop
when he had finished with his current supply of hides.[97]

A walkout of artisans in the Single Brothers House provides a dramatic
indication of the increasingly direct defiance faced by authorities in Salem. In
March 1778, the Elders Conference recorded "much debate" [*Raissonemens*]
among the Single Brothers over "the inequality of wages between those who
worked for the Choir account and those who worked for themselves." A letter
from one of the Single Brothers pointed out that all the Single Brothers were
required to bear the same expenses regardless of wage.[98] The Elders Conference
and the *Aufseher Collegium* discussed the problem and agreed to a raise for all
the Single Brothers, except the day laborers, whose wage they declared to be
high enough; but, they also increased the cost of lunch by four pence. When

this was announced to the Brothers, "all were quiet" initially; but, soon, the younger Single Brothers became very angry and agitated. The next day, a number of them left their work and walked out into the countryside.[99] They returned to work the following day, but their action sent shock waves through the leadership, for it was an overt challenge and a show of solidarity from youth raised in the *Gemeine.* The challenge so took the leadership aback that they attributed it to the work of Satan. The UEC records mention no comparable occurrence in the German *Gemeinen.* It is indicative of the mind-set of the younger Brothers that, even in his letter of apology written after the walkout, Ludwig Moeller managed to make his point about the basic unfairness of the wages assigned to the journeymen and day laborers, "on which they could not exist."[100]

The more confrontational nature of the Salem Brethren also surfaces in a comment in the records regarding the potter Rudolph Christ. In 1776, the *Aufseher Collegium* noted:

> In regard to the pottery journeyman Rudolph Christ, who goes his own way, feels superior to everyone, and would ask no one anything, but already for some time defies us to fire him if things do not go according to his conceited mind, because he believes that the pottery cannot function without him, this recommendation was put forward: If Ludwig Moeller really and entirely changes his behavior so that we can establish him, we could perhaps put Christ on probation, reproach him with this conduct in the shop, his neglect of work, going quickly out to hunt with his rifle, another time trapping birds and the like, and see afterwards how it turns out with him.[101]

Rudolph Christ obviously sensed the power that his skill as a potter afforded him and felt free to take full advantage of it. Two years later, he was among those who participated in the walkout. The description of his outside activities also gives further evidence of the effect of the backcountry on the behavior of the Salem youth.

As in the German *Gemeinen,* evidence exists that this defiant behavior may have been fueled by the introduction of new ideas that shook the underpinnings of the *Gemeine* ideal. Although the ideal survived, the incursion of the Enlightenment stress on reason and self-reliance may have played a role in the impatience of the second generation in Salem with restrictions in material matters. Certainly, the leadership suspected such a connection. Unlike the German records, the Salem records contain only a few references that indicate the penetration of the Enlightenment into Salem, but they are significant within a system whose ideal was directly opposed to dependence on reason and self. During a visitation in 1780, Johann Friedrich Reichel of the UEC remarked with concern on the situation among the Single Brothers whereby some were reluctant to express devotion to the Savior because of "reasoning and ridicule at sincere expressions about the Savior and His grace to poor sinners." A few years later, one of the Single Brothers was taken to task for introducing "frivolity" into the singing of devotional songs.[102] Although it is impossible to pin down the exact nature of this spirit of "ridicule" among the Brothers or to pinpoint its source, in 1794, the *Aufseher Collegium* and the Elders Conference expressed deep concern over the "bad books" being read by the youth of Salem.[103] According to the *Gemeine* ordinances, the Brethren defined "bad books" primarily as those "wherein scoffing [*Spotterei*] over Religion and its servants, even indeed over the Holy Scripture itself, is given occasion to mislead."[104] What they inspired in the Wachau, however, was, not a call for freedom of conscience or even for "human rights," but a defiance of *Gemeine* authority over matters involving economic life and property. This particular focus seems peculiarly English because the English concept of natural rights was rooted in property.[105]

The focus on individual economic rights suggests that these new ideas may have had a distinctly native flavor. In 1781, the Elders Conference expressed concern over Martin Lick's frequent visits to Johannes Reuz because they feared the influence of "principles of freedom" on Lick.[106] Given the connection between Reuz and these principles, it is worth noting that he had served as a justice of the peace and as a member of the local committee for war affairs. He was, thus, in a good position to have absorbed revolutionary rhetoric about individual liberty. At least one other piece of evidence indicates that the Brethren were becoming political. In 1775, the Elders Coherence somehow obtained a letter written by Mattheus Weiss to a former member of the Salem *Gemeine* who had been expelled and gone to Pennsylvania. According to the Elders Conference minutes, this letter indicated young Weiss's strong sympathies with the revolutionary cause and prompted the Elders Conference to discuss "the useless and indeed harmful correspondence between the young people here and in Bethlehem."[107]

A Different Kind of Freedom

The records for 1785 reveal that after the Revolution, the inhabitants of Salem found a justification for their objections, not to the moral and spiritual ideal of the *Ortsgemeine*, but to the outward workings of its system. The following entry appears in the minutes of the Elders Conference for that year in conjunction with a discussion of Gottlob Krause's desire to leave his masonry business and start a pottery in Bethabara, a plan to which the leadership had expressly objected: "We noted thereby that *a spirit that would establish the American freedom* is evident among some in the *Gemeine* and [we] held it to be good to have a discussion and prudent inquiry in the *Gemeine* Council in order to arrive at the reason for this and to abolish such a dangerous thing from among us" (emphasis theirs).[108] The leadership clearly had no sympathy for such ideas. The minutes of the *Gemeine* Council, which was held over this issue, reveal more about what underlay this desire for "the American freedom" and why the *Gemeine* authorities found it so objectionable: "It was noted that for some time it has become common with some to call on American freedom in contradiction to human order. This expression reveals at the least a great lack of understanding since the proper subordination, without which no human society can exist, is held even in the so called free countries just as in others. Thus, for example, a journeyman must surely do what the master of his trade orders. If however, someone would use the mentioned freedom against the town ordinances, of which we have already seen signs, he demonstrates through it that he would be better residing elsewhere."[109] The response of the leadership indicates their continued stress on hierarchy, and their use of the reference to a journeyman's subordination to his master suggests that economic regulations were at the heart of the matter. Indeed, the leadership's refusal to allow Gottlob Krause to set up a pottery in Bethabara probably stirred up this particular hornet's nest.

It is possible that the Brethren's new fear of "American freedom" is an example of redefining deviant behavior to combat the perceived threat to their social structure.[110] In many ways, the behavior exhibited by the disruptive Brethren does not appear to have been anything "new." As has been noted, however, the American Brethren were far more willing to take their concern for their livelihood to the streets or, at least, to the woods. In the eyes of the leadership, this represented a new challenge to the established order and one based on a misconception of the very "freedom" by which the deviants justified their defiance. Both elements within Salem society sought to come to terms with their new status as part of "America." One group did this by challenging the system in the name of the new nation, and the other, by denying that their new situation (i.e., as Americans) justified any significant change in their ideal.

In their response to the threat of "free" ideas, the Salem leadership did not view themselves as being antiliberty. An observation regarding the internal dynamics of many German towns is useful in illuminating the mind-set of the leadership: "Hometown equality and hometown democracy meant the subjugation of everybody in the community to everybody, to limits set by the whole community."[111] Despite the fact that the protesting Brethren undoubtedly did not believe that the "whole community" was agreed on the limits, in the eyes of the governing bodies, their particular form of "freedom" threatened the equilibrium of the whole *Ortsgemeine*. The American concept of individual liberty did not sit well with a leadership whose ideal had been formed within an earlier German context. The leadership made it plain that "American freedom" had no legitimate claim in their eyes to disrupt the system of the *Ortsgemeine*. What the quotation from the *Gemeine* Council minutes indicates, however, is that some of the Brethren viewed American ideas on liberty as a means of justifying their objections to restrictions on their daily lives.

The leadership denied that "American freedom" justified objections to the *Ortsgemeine* system. They maintained that this system did not, in fact, contain anything contrary to American ideals when these ideals were correctly viewed. Whether it did or did not, the significant fact is that enough of the Brethren thought that it did or were, at least, willing to argue that it did in order to disturb the administration. An entry from the minutes of the *Gemeine* Council for 1794 shows that this identification of freedom in practical matters with American ideas continued. In that year, the Elders Conference expelled Johann Georg Ebert for continuing to build in violation of the fire ordinances after he was ordered to stop. In making the announcement of his expulsion to the *Gemeine,* the Elders Conference noted that the fire regulations were "a matter which is strictly held not only by us but in all well-constituted cities outside of us, *even in America*" (emphasis mine).[112]

Despite evidence of the beginnings of a spirit of skepticism among the youth, the objections raised over the extent of *Gemeine* control do not necessarily indicate that the Brethren in Salem rejected the concept of the *Ortsgemeine* as a gathering of "God's people." Indications do exist, however, that they were beginning to reject or, even, to fail to understand the fusion of the practical and the spiritual that served as the backbone of the *Ortsgemeine* as developed in Germany in the 1740s and 1750s. The failure to understand is hinted at in the dismay expressed by Mattheus Oesterlein on being excluded from the *Gemeine* for establishing his own forge without permission and for making it a meeting place for gossiping. When confronted with his fate, Oesterlein said that he "had not thought these things could have such heavy consequences."[113] By the mid-1780s, many of the Salem Brethren apparently felt that actions in outward matters indeed should not have such consequences.

The identification of a specifically "American" freedom within the North Carolina *Gemeinen* is intertwined with the development of a distinctly American identity on the part of the *Gemeine* members, and the perception of this on the part of the leadership. An early articulation of this different identity suggests that it may have developed in Pennsylvania before it entered the Wachau. In 1773, Marschall received a letter from Andreas Schober of Bethlehem (father of Gottlieb) that strongly challenged the ideals of the Unity. "My dear Marschall," he wrote, "I cannot help but ask how it comes that you have bound my son [as an apprentice] without asking me or reporting it to me. I believe that it is well known to you that we are not in Germany and thus no one has the power to bind my children. As long as I live that [right] belongs to me alone. I cannot lie, I have wondered very much that someone can conceive so to do in an English land and [to make] a provision which, perhaps, is against his temperament. What are you thinking?"[114]

Aside from the fact that Brother Schober obviously lacked an attitude of submission to a Unity leader, not to mention, an aristocrat, this letter hints strongly at the "liberties" that some of the Brethren in America thought to be theirs even before the Revolution and gives evidence of the role of the impact of the English tradition on attitudes of the American Brethren toward authority. Schober clearly believed that what was acceptable action for the Unity in Germany was not so in America. The Elders Conference thought decidedly otherwise. They pointed out to Schober that he and the other parents had given up their rights when they allowed their sons to be sent to Salem and recommended to the Elders Conference "that they care for them as parents and assist [them] to learn a useful profession."[115] In the eyes of the leadership, the dedication to the *Gemeine* should not be any different for the American than for the European Brethren. Over the years, however, the Elders Conference continued to feel threatened by an air of freedom that they labeled as peculiar to America.

The majority of references to the "free" environment appeared in the letters from America to Europe but not in the reverse correspondence. The first such reference occurred in 1775 and illuminates the perceptions that colored the thinking of the Elders Conference. In this year, Marschall wrote to thank the UEC for appointing Brother Wallis as *Gemeine Diener*. Marschall specified that he was particularly grateful "because," he said, "I can now hope that the outward regulations of Salem will not run wild in my absence, as it is similar in spirit to the Indian country and likewise has a great effect on the inner course of a *Gemeine*."[116] Marschall here expressed his fear that the disorderly country in which Salem was situated would taint the spiritual life of its inhabitants. As we have seen, his fears were not groundless. This emphasis on the "backwoods" nature of the Wachau did not go unnoticed by the UEC. Both they and Marschall may have been predisposed to see America as an unregulated land because earlier German immigrants held similar views, but, what concerned Marschall was the potential impact on the Unity.[117] It was in this same letter that Marschall emphasized the different nature of the American circumstances with regard to the use of the lot.

Before the Revolution, the "freedom" of the New World was not specified as "American." By the time the war itself drew to a close, however, this situation had changed. In his visitation report from 1781, Reichel noted that Bethania, particularly the obstreperous upper village, had "really declared themselves for Americans too loudly."[118] Marschall was all too aware of the confusion brought about by the Revolution and its effect on behavior. In 1782, he observed to von Lüdecke, "If, however, one yields to such times, then the confusion of the earth can affect [one] within, an example of which we have in America."[119] In the next year, Marschall reported, "The inclination to independence, which indeed is to be perceived in all our *Gemeinen,* is entirely extraordinary here in this country" and that the concern of the Elders Conference over this had led them to renew their prayer fellowship.[120] This latter action excited the UEC members more than did the situation that produced it, although, as usual, they expressed their sympathy with the troubles of the local leadership.[121]

By 1785, the association of disorderly behavior with American behavior appears to have been firmly established in the minds of the Wachau leadership. One of Marschall's letters to Europe indicated that he feared that the "free" reputation of the American *Gemeinen* had crossed the Atlantic. When he offered to help with the expenses of any Brothers coming from Europe he added that this could only be done "if they do not bring with them false suppositions as if here is an independence from the *Gemeine* ordinances."[122] He wrote even more explicitly in a letter of 1786 that dealt with the need for new artisans. Marschall warned that he wanted no one to come whose inducement was the hope of gaining property, "since experience [had] taught that some people who came to America [were] more harmful than useful to themselves and others."[123] Later in the letter, he clarified what he meant by this. He argued that "as little as the desire to make one's fortune can be the reason for wanting to come to an *Ortsgemeine* in Europe, so little can that be the case in America," and he expressed his deep concern regarding those who had the idea "that a freedom exists here that is not restricted by laws or that one is allowed to be less bound by the *Gemeine* ordinances."[124] Here Marschall juxtaposed the assumption that American freedom equaled freedom from law with a desire to be free of certain *Gemeine* restrictions. He also tied this lawless freedom to the desire for economic prosperity and the acquisition of property. Neither of these was acceptable, no matter which side of the ocean members were on, but, clearly, Marschall felt that some looked to America as the land of freedom to prosper. It is probably no coincidence that these letters were written close to the time of the meetings about "American freedom." The leadership's experience of Brethren who agitated for greater economic leeway had made them wary.

An incident that occurred in Herrnhut in 1796 throws some light on one possible ground for this association of America with greater economic opportunity and freedom on the part of the German Brethren. Early in the development of the *Ortsgemeinen*, the leadership decided to eliminate the guild system within the economic life of the *Gemeine*. After a special visitation to the Single Brothers because of several months of "disorderly" behavior, Christian Gregor reported that many of them had said that they would "gladly" leave the *Gemeine* if they had learned their professions in the guild system.[125] The lack of guild training and membership severely restricted the options of the youth within the German settlements.[126] The Herrnhut leadership was aware of this problem and the attendant tendency of "unsuitable" Brethren to stay in the *Gemeine* for economic protection. Since 1790, in particular, they had made an effort to alleviate the difficulty by allowing some of the Brethren to join guilds. The expense and the invasion of rival loyalties (the various guilds each had their own special culture) made them hesitant to grant this permission, however, so, in practice, the situation remained largely unchanged.[127] In America, the guild system had declined in favor of more open competition, thus enabling artisans trained under the Unity greater freedom to leave without endangering their livelihood. This fact suggests that the Brethren's ideas about "American freedom" may have sprung from practical as well as from conceptual grounds.

The Wachau Brethren themselves came to view their particular freedom as differentiating them from their European Brethren. In a meeting of the Salem *Gemeine* Council in 1789, the Brethren discussed the increasing tendency of many of their members to ignore or circumvent the ordinances, particularly in practical matters. In specific, recent developments included Jacob Bonn's outright rejection of the leadership's proposal that he turn his house over in trust to the *Aufseher Collegium*, which would find a buyer for it, and Christoph Loesh's engagement to buy a house in Bethania in spite of the prohibition of this by the Bethania and the Salem leaderships.[128] The Brethren had discussed this type of defiance previously in terms of the desire for "American freedom," but, in this instance, the minutes indicate that the rebellious Brethren drew a distinct line between their situation and that of their European Brethren: "Many *Gemeine* members lack the willingness to submit to the rule of the Savior and on the other hand [demonstrate] an inclination to direct their course and circumstances themselves. Furthermore, [they] lack the willingness to accommodate themselves to the *Gemeine* ordinances and institutions. . . . Thereby the idea appears in many as though here, as in a free land, one did not have to act according to the *Gemeine* ordinances, as, for example, in the European *Gemeinen*, if one just complied with the law of the land."[129] This statement linked a desire for greater autonomy in material matters with what the Brethren viewed as the freer atmosphere of America. The American Brethren not only argued for more freedom on account of their American status, but also indicated that the European *Gemeinen* might well be held to a different set of standards. In doing this, they also implied that the ideal of the *Ortsgemeine* was derived from cultural circumstances.

By the late eighteenth century, many of the Brethren in the American and in the German *Gemeinen* became increasingly inclined to prefer their private interests over the interests of the community and of the Savior. The methods by which they sought to accomplish this, however, differed. The German Brethren tended to cloak their opposition to *Gemeine* and manorial authority. This opposition could take the form of claims of ignorance of the law, anonymous lampoons aimed at objectionable leaders, accusations of "illegitimate" behavior on the part of the leaders, or avoidance of duty. In a world marked by layers of authority and increasing bureaucracy, these indirect methods of defiance may have seemed the most natural ones and the most likely to have the desired results. In the less hierarchical atmosphere of the North Carolina backcountry, the Brethren developed a bolder manner, at least in the eyes of the leadership. They protested openly and, often, loudly against the extent of *Gemeine* control of business affairs.

The issue of authority also involved varying definitions of freedom. The Unity leadership seems to have identified a "good" freedom and a "bad" freedom, both within the context of German tradition. Within this context, "good" freedom consisted of free submission to the paternal authority of the Savior and to His agents, who were designated through the lot. "Bad" freedom was associated with the desire to indulge in unregulated and disorderly behavior. Some of the younger German Brethren protested this idea and implied that true freedom allowed them to determine their own behavioral boundaries. In general, however, they seem to have sought this freedom outside of the *Gemeine*. In America, the leadership faced a different vision of freedom, one influenced by the English Enlightenment's association of freedom and property, in particular, the individual's rights to dispose freely of property and to determine his own economic destiny. This concept of freedom provided the Brethren in the Wachau with a justification for their objections to the leadership's authority in matters affecting their livelihood. After the Revolution, "American freedom" became a weapon with which the Salem Brethren began to fight a war of independence of their own.

6

Hands across the Water

THE CHALLENGES OF A TRANSATLANTIC RELATIONSHIP

By the end of the eighteenth century, some inhabitants of Salem viewed the American *Gemeinen* as significantly distinct from their European counterparts. In effect, the protests of the American Brethren that peaked in 1818 over the issue of the marriage lot called for a type of independence from the standards imposed by the central ruling body in Germany. It appears that by the late eighteenth century, the "private" members of the Salem *Gemeine* were pulling away from their German roots, while the leadership on both sides of the Atlantic sought to shore up the spiritual and cultural bridge that connected the Unity's two continents. The situation, however, was not so simple. The fact that the American *Gemeinen* were governed by and economically tied to a body located in Germany makes their experience closer to that of the Anglo-Americans than to most other German immigrants, whose ties to their motherland were largely private in nature.[2] Some similarities do exist between the Brethren and the German Lutherans, whose ministers were basically appointed by Halle. One of these ministers, Henry Melchior Muhlenberg, labeled the movement among immigrant Lutherans for congregational control of pastoral appointments as an outgrowth of American freedom. However, the Lutherans' network of ties to Germany disappeared during the Revolution, and, afterward, any sense of unity with Germany also disappeared.[3] The situation of the Brethren made such a break impossible.

The attitude of the American Brethren toward their transatlantic ties was complex. Evidence indicates that they felt a continued attachment to their place within the Unity, but they also began to express a sense of alienation. In this, they resembled the Anglo-Americans who, while they developed a "modernized mentality" that celebrated freedom from traditional restraints, still depended on the mother country for social and cultural models, trade ties, and protection.[3] In the case of the Unity, the second-generation American-born

Brethren expressed a sense of alienation the most vociferously, but the distance from their roots also affected those members raised in Germany. This mentality is perhaps best measured by looking at the leadership, for they were most closely tied to the Unity.

The Salem leadership could not and did not watch over their *Gemeinen* in isolation. Their actions must be viewed in the context of the Wachau's position as one unit of a larger whole. Just as each individual Brother or Sister existed as a member of a particular *Gemeine*, so, too, each *Ortsgemeine* existed as a member of the Unity. The relationship between the individual *Ortsgemeinen* and the Unity reflected the same need for cooperation and subordination that marked the relationship between the individual member and the *Gemeine*. The Brethren embodied this need in their administrative structure. They also used devotional texts to instill in the members a sense of dedication, not just to the *Gemeinen*, but also to the Unity, as the link between all of "God's people." Salem, however, was in what the Brethren referred to as a "*wüster Ort*," or "desert place." Zinzendorf viewed its relative isolation as advantageous in maintaining the *Ortsgemeine* in its purity. As we have seen, the wilderness proved a dubious blessing and the isolation less than complete. While Salem did not remain isolated from its rougher neighbors, the sheer distance from its parent *Gemeine* in Germany threatened to isolate it from the source of its ideal. This situation gave added importance to the devotional texts and letters as a means of maintaining the link between the Unity and the area to which the Brethren referred as "one of the most distant settlements" of their body.[4]

The Ties that Bound

To understand the particular dynamics of the relationship between the European leadership and the leadership in the Wachau, it is necessary to explore the ideal and the ground rules under which they functioned. To maintain the Unity as a viable structure, the needs of the various *Gemeinen* had to be balanced with the status of the entire collective body, which, by 1785, numbered twenty-eight *Ortsgemeinen* and twenty-six *Land* and *Stadt Gemeinen*. This was a formidable task because, at least in the case of the *Ortsgemeinen*, it included the care for the economic and the spiritual welfare of each settlement. This meant that, while the local leadership had to be consulted in matters concerning them, only the UEC could be expected to understand the whole picture. The structure that the leadership built to accommodate this dynamic emerges most clearly in the various synod reports. Each synod reviewed the governmental and devotional structure of the Unity and revised it where deemed necessary, always, of course, subject to the approval of the lot. An overview of these reports from

1764 through 1801 reveals a subtle tendency to increase the emphasis on the authority of the UEC.

The first synod held after Zinzendorf's death allowed the local Elders Conferences a good measure of authority, if not of autonomy. This synod, in 1764, declared that "the special guidance and service of each *Gemeine* and its Choirs depends on the Elders Conference of the same, and the Directorate [the central government] decides nothing in the *Ortsgemeine* and their Choirs except through the Elders Conferences."[5] The Synod of 1769 drew up a more detailed plan of the "orderly" relationship between the Directorate, now termed the UEC, and the individual Elders Conferences. The essential sense of 1764 remained intact. On the side of the UEC, they were forbidden to change any specific circumstance in a *Gemeine* until the individual Elders Conference had been consulted, and decisions about the fate of a *Gemeine* member, such as a transfer to another *Gemeine,* necessitated the consent of the Elders Conference.[6]

The limitations on the UEC were balanced by the obligations of the individual *Gemeinen* toward the UEC. They were to ask counsel and instruction from the Unity in "all matters which affect the whole and the *Gemeine* plan," especially in the case of any undertaking "which with time could effect [*anschlagen*] the whole adversely."[7] The UEC came closest to control of the local *Gemeinen* in its provisions regarding the governing officials. The Unity required the individual *Gemeinen* to await the nomination of the heads of the *Gemeine* and of the Choirs from the UEC with the provision that they, in turn, consult with the local Elders Conference before the final decision to see "whether they [had] something considerable in objection to this person."[8] The final point given in the report exhorted the individual *Gemeinen* to contribute what they could to the prosperity of the whole. This undoubtedly covered physical as well as spiritual aid.

At the Synod of 1775, the UEC used the difficulties in correspondence to claim a privilege in its relationship to the *Gemeinen,* particularly those "far away." The UEC still pledged to wait for the proposals of the Elders Conferences regarding the appointment of officials but now added that it could not *always* wait, "much less be bound thereon," because its first duty lay in the fast replacement of officials "with the proper people."[9] It is worth noting that already, in 1775, the UEC felt it necessary to spend so much time dealing with the appointment of local officials. The problem of a shortage of competent and devout leaders mentioned by the synod grew sharper over the decades.

The Synod of 1789 sharply emphasized the need to submit to the decisions of the UEC in the transfer of *Gemeine* officials and specified that if an official recalled from a post by the UEC did not relinquish the office and return to Herrnhut the errant individual would be cut off from the Unity for this disobedience.[10] This same synod, however, reiterated an earlier provision that concessions had to be made for those *Gemeinen* in more distant regions. Such concessions were never general ones but applied only to certain circumstances.

The resolutions of the various synods provided the basic framework within which the individual *Gemeinen* interacted with the UEC. The minutes of the UEC and its correspondence with the Salem Elders Conference yield a more intimate and detailed picture of the dynamics. It remains a somewhat limited view because, with a very few exceptions, the only voices heard are those of the leadership. It was, however, the leadership that was entrusted with the task of preserving the ideals of the Unity in their spiritual and their physical manifestations. In addition, the *Gemeine* elders were often strongly tied to the central leadership by shared experience and family ties, yet they held direct responsibility for the survival of their particular *Gemeine*. These things all combined to make them barometers of the pressures brought on by distance and time.

As stated previously, the relationship between the individual *Gemeinen* and the central body as a whole was one of mutual dependency. This dependency can be divided into two basic categories: the practical and the spiritual. Of these two, the spiritual ties weathered the ocean voyage most successfully. As might be expected, however, the strain brought on by physical dependency also affected the sense of spiritual unity. The Salem *Gemeine*, in particular, was caught between its role as an opportunity for a fresh start for the Brethren, and the reality of its existence in a "wild place." Nevertheless, the correspondence between the UEC and the Elders Conference reveals the surprising strength of the concept of a unified body despite an increasing sense of otherness on the parts of the Elders Conference and the UEC.

Before we can discuss the strain on the Unity, therefore, we have to understand the nature of the dependency between Salem, or, more accurately, the Wachau, and the UEC and to consider its positive aspects. In the practical sphere, dependency boiled down to three primary areas in which Salem was tied to the UEC: the placement of local officials, finances, and the immigration of new members from Europe. These areas all touched the very heart of the *Gemeine*. The UEC also had a strong vested interest in them. In each of these spheres, local need had to be considered in tandem with the current status of the Unity. With regard to local officials, the Unity had to provide for all the *Gemeinen* from an increasingly small pool of candidates but needed to choose those most trusted to uphold Unity ideals. In the realm of finances, the UEC supported its *Gemeinen* with loans or grants when necessary but expected contributions to the common funds in return. Last, the need for artisans could pose difficulties in maintaining the *Ortsgemeine* ideal. This situation gave the UEC's oversight of immigration to the *Gemeinen* great importance. Thus, neither party could afford to ignore the other. To further complicate matters, we must always bear in mind that the separation into practical and spiritual spheres, when dealing with the Brethren, can never be viewed as clean. The Savior was always the court of last resort, regardless of whether the matter was "practical" or "spiritual." Dependency also surfaced in the intangible area of emotional and spiritual ties. In terms of the maintenance of the ideal of the Unity, these ties played an important role and cannot be ignored, however eager we might be to concentrate on conflict and change.

The Ties of Person

In the matter of the appointment of local officials, the practical dependency of the Salem Elders Conference on the UEC was outlined in the synod decrees. The interrelationship contained far more subtle elements, however. The majority of the Salem leadership shared the experience of the years in which the Unity ideal and the *Ortsgemeine* took shape. In several cases, they also had ties of friendship with Zinzendorf and other influential leaders, including members of the UEC such as Johannes von Watteville. The original government of Salem thus worked within a unified set of experiences and ideals that were closely tied to their home base in Germany. The backgrounds of those officials sent later from Europe indicate an attempt on the part of the UEC to maintain this general profile. By century's end, however, those sent had no personal experience of the early years of the Unity.

Aside from their experiential ties to the European leadership, the Marschalls shared the bond of kinship. Sister von Marschall was a von Schweinitz by birth. This family was quite large, and exact relationships are difficult to determine, but she was a cousin of Hans Christian von Schweinitz, whose eldest son, Moritz, married a cousin of Zinzendorf's. Ties to this branch were strengthened when the Marschalls' daughter married Moritz's younger brother, Hans Christian Alexander, who headed the Bethlehem *Gemeine* until his call to membership in the UEC in 1801. Hans Christian Alexander's second wife was the granddaughter of Zinzendorf and the daughter of Johannes von Watteville, who presided over the UEC until his death in 1788. The Marschalls were thus linked by marriage to some of the Unity's leading families.[11] The widows of the Brethren often returned to Europe, and, in a few cases, officials serving in the American *Gemeinen* sent their children to Europe to be educated.

The correspondence exchanged between the UEC and the members of the Elders Conference confirms the strength of these ties of family and friendship as well as the mutual spiritual interest that bridged the ocean. The majority of the extant correspondence is addressed to Marschall, but examples of those to and from other officials share the same characteristics. Despite the synod's admonition to keep correspondence to the point at hand, many if not most of the letters contain news of various marriages, births, deaths, and even, occasionally, gossip.[12] This information almost always pertained to members of the UEC or leaders in other *Gemeinen* and their families. A letter from Brother Johannes von Watteville to Brother Graff spoke movingly not only of friendship, but also of the sense of its ability to bridge the ocean. Referring to his forty-year friendship with Graff, Johannes said, "We are now really old and perhaps near the end of our pilgrimage. I thereby stretch out my heart and hands once more to you across the great water."[13]

Expressions of personal friendship from both sides of the Atlantic became particularly poignant toward the end of the century as the old leadership began to die out. Marschall wrote to Christian Gregor, "I wish you could come here after the synod and travel to the Wachau once again. Whether you will see me again, however, I know I cannot judge."[14] Gregor told Marschall, in turn, that he thought of their walks together every time he walked on the Heinrichsberg. He also wrote to Johannes Stotz, who was Salem's *Gemeine Diener* at the time, "What you most dear Brother write of yourself and your state of health can I answer thus, humility and thanks, praise and apologies, pass every day between the Saviour and me."[15]

Ties of Devotion

Aside from evidence of strong personal ties, the correspondence contains multiple expressions of the spiritual and emotional ties that bound the American and the European *Gemeinen*. Just as devotional practices such as the reading of the *Gemeinnachrichten* bound the individual member to others within the particular *Gemeine*, these expressions also functioned to remind members of their place in the greater body of the Unity. In the case of some devotional texts, such as the *Memorabilia*, the Unity leadership drew up a special version in which they reported events of significance to the Unity as a whole. The UEC also held responsibility for the *Losungen*, biblical texts that the members of the UEC drew out in lottery form for each day of the year and compiled. By such means, the members in the Wachau were kept aware of their ties to the European Brethren. The synod reports and diaries also served as a link across the ocean. The diary of the synod, for instance, allowed those who did not attend the synod to participate in it by imagination; it recorded the daily events rather than simply reporting the decisions. The correspondence and the minutes of the ruling bodies indicate that these devotional aids succeeded in maintaining a sense of spiritual unity between the European and the American *Gemeinen*.

The correspondence also reveals a strong emotional bond between the European and the American leaderships that continued throughout the eighteenth century, even under stress.

Expressions of mutual interest became especially strong during the years of the American Revolution. This seems ironic given the role the Revolution played in straining the ties between Europe and America. Much correspondence was lost during this time, but those letters that did reach America displayed an anxious care on the part of the UEC for the fate of the American Brethren. This concern surfaced even before the actual outbreak of hostilities. In early 1772, Brother Wollin wrote, "Many sighs are sent to our Saviour that He would take our dear Brethren in the Wachau in His gracious protection in the unrest of these times, of which we read descriptions in the papers here."[16] A letter from January 1777 opens with the sentences, "Oh how often have we thought on you dear Brothers in this difficult wartime and are often very anxious to know how you fare. Many prayers and sighs have been sent to our dear Lord on account of this in order to protect you from everything which could harm you in body and soul."[17]

Bishop Spangenberg wrote two open letters to all the American Brethren in 1778. The general purpose of these letters was to encourage them in a time of crisis and to assure them of Christ's protection. The rhetoric used by Spangenberg, however, particularly in the second letter, stressed the familial nature of the Unity: "As it is with a mother who in her chamber knows that one or more of her children are in a fearful storm at sea, she frets more than her sons who experience the storm themselves, so it is with us."[18] Family imagery constituted an integral part of the ideal of the Unity as it stood in 1769. Its use here served a double purpose: it conveyed an urgent and loving concern for the welfare of the American *Gemeinen* while, at the same time, reinforcing the paternalistic or, in this case, "maternalistic" authority of the UEC. Spangenberg then turned to the theme of unity in experience saying that "in all the *Gemeinen* we see a heartfelt sympathy with you. How true are the words that all members suffer when *one* member suffers."

The European Brethren also expressed their concern in a more tangible way. In 1783, the Salem Elders Conference reported that the Brethren in Europe had collected money for the poor Brethren in North America "out of sympathy for what they suffered during the war."[19] These assurances of Europe's interest in the American *Gemeinen* did not cease after the Revolution. As late as 1797, Brother Gregor wrote to Brother Marschall, "I only wish that I could show you fully how the heart of the collective UEC is situated toward you."[20]

References to the emotional and spiritual ties between the UEC and Salem most often occurred in the context of a discussion of the impact of the

Salem *Gemeinnachrichten* and diaries. As stated earlier, these newsletters and diaries formed another means of knitting the Unity together. From the evidence contained in the correspondence, they appear to have been successful in maintaining a sense of shared experience, at least among the leadership.

Johann Friedrich Reichel made a direct connection between the letters and diaries received from the Wachau and the continued interest on the part of the UEC in the affairs of that settlement. "I cannot express to you," he wrote, "what sort of feelings, thoughts, joy, also sorrow and tender sympathy your letters and diaries have excited in our hearts."[21] This letter was written while Reichel was in America on a visitation, and his letters written in the years thereafter contain occasional references to his fond memories, which bound him in a special way to the Wachau. For instance, in 1783, he wrote, "I still indulge in the joy of walking around in Salem, Bethabara, and Bethania, in spirit from time to time. . . . All the names which I find in the diary interest me and I have as yet found little that is unfamiliar."[22]

Unfortunately, very little correspondence from America to Europe is extant. What does remain demonstrates that the relationship was not one-sided on the part of the UEC. Just as Gregor sighed over his advancing age and regretted that he could no longer travel to the Wachau, so, too, did Marschall with regard to Germany: "We still often think on all the dear Brethren in Herrnhut whom we enjoyed there but now will scarcely see until we meet with the Saviour." Marschall's unexpectedly lengthy stay in Germany in the late 1770s appears to have reinforced his ties to the "mother *Gemeine*." In this same letter, he said wistfully, "If I could only be present at the synod in Berthelsdorf for a few days and see the new building in Herrnhut it would please me very much, especially since I have also not seen the *Gemeine* lodging and wings for the *Arbeiteren*." His following sentence, however, shows the strength of his sense of duty and his conviction that his true place lay in Salem: "Yet I can assure you that despite all the difficulties which have occurred here I am still thankful that the Saviour has brought me here."[23]Feelings of close ties with Europe were not confined to a purely personal level. During the period from 1771 to 1801, only three official visitations from the UEC to the Wachau occurred: one in 1771, one in 1780, and the last in 1786. The letters from the time immediately following each visitation shed some light on the impact that they had. The visitation of 1780 seems to have made a particularly strong impression. This may well have resulted from the fact that the Wachau was effectively isolated from any steady contact with Europe and was deprived of their chief leader from 1775 until this visitation. The Brethren did not view a visitation as primarily disciplinary, but rather as a cooperative effort to smooth the administration of a *Gemeine* and encourage its members. Thus, in their announcement of the impending visitation of 1780, the UEC asked that the hearts of the Elders Conference be with Brother Reichel and that the elders support him with prayers, assist him in his work, "and serve him faithfully with the insight that you have of the circumstances of the country, of the *Gemeine,* of the Choirs, and of each soul."[24] This excerpt demonstrates the dependency on the part of the UEC on the special knowledge of local circumstances possessed by the Salem Elders Conference.

Little evidence of any negative reaction to Reichel's visitation exists in the extant records. In his report to Europe regarding this event, Marschall spoke glowingly of its effect on the *Gemeine* and, especially, on the spiritual lives of the members. During Reichel's stay, the area had been disturbed by a rising of Tories that, in turn, brought in the Continental Army, which quartered in Salem. Marschall reported, "During all these circumstances in the *Gemeine* we enjoyed the peace of the Saviour in this place, and it manifested itself in particular in the activities of Brother Reichel in so exceptional a way that throughout all this commotion from outside no one was disturbed."[25] Later in the letter, Marschall returned to the response to Reichel and assured the UEC that "Salem indeed enjoyed the Reichels' residence excellently."

Something of the same reaction appeared in a letter from Christian Ludwig Benzien, then *Helfer* of the Single Brethren, to Gregor written during the visitation of Brother Johannes von Watteville in 1786. Benzien apologized for not sending in his report on the Single Brethren the previous year but said that he was expecting to communicate with Brother Johanne (the name by which von Watteville was known) "over all our circumstances" during the visitation. He then reported that his hopes for this had not been in vain and that the Lord had granted them in Watteville "a man who entered into our matters with much love and concern, in whom we could have perfect trust."[26] Benzien further observed that the Single Brethren were particularly blessed by the meetings that Watteville held. The Elders Conference noted, "It should be mentioned especially that the Single Brothers Choir found a new closeness and quickening through our dear Brother Johannes' Speaking and his reconciling [*bandmäßig*] conversation with the members in their Choir meetings."[27] In the case of the special meetings of communicants for the purpose of renewing the *Chorbund,* the visitation revived the desire for these after they had been discontinued because of poor attendance.

Ties of Duty

While the Salem settlement looked to the UEC for spiritual renewal and guidance, the UEC felt quite strongly its obligation to provide for their spiritual and their practical needs. As mentioned previously, the individual *Gemeinen* depended on the UEC for the official appointment of their *Gemeine Diener* and *Helfer* and of their Choir officials, although the local Elders Conference could appoint someone to such a position temporarily. The *Gemeine* were also closely linked to the UEC financially. In the early years of Unity activity, the *Ortsgemeinen* had received substantial assistance from the common funds in establishing and maintaining their communities. The massive debt that plagued the Unity in the 1750s made the leadership increasingly cautious, and, in 1769, they vested greater financial responsibility in the individual *Gemeinen*. Nevertheless, they retained considerable control over local finances. All officials in charge of money matters had to submit an annual report to the UEC. The UEC could then require that the wealthier *Gemeinen* assist the poorer ones and that surplus funds be turned over to the Unity for the use of the whole. The UEC, thus, played an important part in shaping the fate of the Wachau and had a keen awareness of this responsibility.

The UEC's sense of obligation to care for its settlement in North Carolina was especially evident in the early years of Salem's founding, which entailed the dismantling of the general *Oeconomie* that had been in place up to that time.[28] In 1771, two members of the UEC, Loretz and Gregor, made a trip to the Wachau for the express purpose of helping Salem's economy and administration to its feet.

While the UEC owed support to its fledgling *Ortsgemeine,* Salem, in turn, owed a very real debt to the Unity as a whole. Writing in 1772, J.F.D. Smyth observed that the Brethren "by their unremitting industry and labor have brought a large extent of wild and rugged country into a high state of population and improvement."[29] Smyth was only one among many visitors to the Wachau to wax eloquent regarding the accomplishments of the Brethren. What such expressions do not reveal, however, is the fact that, at least for approximately the first twenty years, Salem and its environs stood on a solid mountain of debt. The initial land purchase consisted of one hundred thousand acres, seventy thousand of which the Unity used, in 1753, to set up a land company for the purpose of financing its ambitious venture into the wilderness. The company was to consist of thirty-five shareholders who would bear an equal portion of the expense for the purchase and surveying of the total holding and for the cost of settling it during the first five years. The men who drew up the plan anticipated settling 424 people during this period and looked to have revenue of seven thousand pounds (Carolina currency) with which to do so. Not surprisingly, things did not turn out quite as expected. Delays in obtaining subscribers and in transporting available money to America left the colonists without money from the land company until 1755, by which time the first two groups had been settled at the expense of the Bethlehem *Diacony*. Almost as quickly, subscribers, of which there were, at best, only twenty-six, began to default and return shares to the company. At the end of the five-year period, the Wachau had fewer than seventy-five inhabitants, the site for Salem remained unchosen, and only £3,622 had been received. Thus, by 1771 the Carolina project, far from having turned any profit, had a three thousand-pound deficit, underwritten by Bethlehem, the Unity, and individual members and friends.[30]

The existence of this deficit provided an added incentive for the UEC to keep in close touch with the Salem Elders Conference, which had charge over the entire Wachau region. As in the case of the more ethereal bonds of unity, the correspondence from the UEC emphasized the interdependence of all *Gemeinen* while assuring the Elders Conference of the UEC's particular interest in the welfare of the Wachau. As of 1797, however, Salem had more than doubled its surplus and was thus able to offset Bethabara's then rather substantial deficit. The most significant impact of the status of Salem's finances is evident in the fact that, in 1799, the total amount paid by Salem and Bethabara into the Unity sustenance fund made up one fourth of the total paid by all of the *Gemeinen*; and neither Salem nor Bethabara required help from the fund, the only American *Gemeinen* to accomplish this. Of the remaining six *Gemeinen* in this category, only Christiansfeld in Denmark paid in a larger amount.[31] While this confirmed the hopes of fruitfulness with which the UEC had begun the Wachau settlement, it also laid the ground for the imminent severing of one of the ties that bound the settlement to its European parents.

Straining the Ties

Despite the very real ties to Europe and, to some degree, because of them, relations between the Wachau settlement and the UEC were often strained. An overview of relations in the first thirty years of Salem's existence reveals an increasing identification of the local leadership with the American situation, while the UEC came to view the Wachau as a mission field. This development is particularly significant in light of the fact that the North Carolina and German leaderships faced common difficulties in the late eighteenth century. Ultimately, practical stresses, enhanced by the process of accommodation to a "new world," ate away at the bonds of unity.

As in the case of the ideal structure of the *Ortsgemeine*, the ambition of the Unity in seeking to weld the American and the European *Gemeinen* into a unified body made their system vulnerable to change. The *Gemeinen* on the frontier of North Carolina during a period of revolution could not possibly function in the same manner as did the *Gemeinen* in Germany. Aside from legal and social differences, the *Gemeinen* in the Wachau suffered from their distance from Europe, which made dependence on the UEC for the appointment of local officials a real hardship. Although the ocean's width also separated the Pennsylvania settlements from their European counterparts, they received mail far more quickly than did Salem because all mail for the American *Gemeinen* was sent first to Pennsylvania. But, the UEC faced the consequences of its expansion during the 1740s and 1750s: it was left with the responsibility for a large number of *Ortsgemeinen* and *Landgemeinen* in the midst of a shrinking number of adult converts and a troublesome younger generation.

The outbreak of the American Revolution and the subsequent development of a new nation combined with declension within the Wachau to enhance the stress already present. By the beginning of the nineteenth century, the Brethren in the Wachau viewed themselves, with some justification, as the stepchildren of the Unity; they came to express a sense of themselves as distinct from their Brethren across the water.

Correspondence between the UEC and the Salem Elders Conference from 1771 through 1801 reveals four major areas of concern: the desire for a steady flow of information between Europe and America, including devotional material such as the *Nachrichten;* a desire for unity of practice in devotional and governmental matters; the need for *Arbeiter* in the Wachau; and the need for artisans in the Single Brothers House. Each of these areas bears evidence of the effects of cost, distance, an aging leadership, and "American exceptionalism." In addition, the attitudes of the UEC and of the Wachau leadership toward these various issues illustrates the difficulties caused by the different responsibilities borne by each body. The UEC had to look to the needs and preservation of the Unity as a whole, while the vision of the Salem Elders Conference was, of necessity, primarily focused on local concerns.

A Sense of Loss

Difficulties in correspondence undoubtedly produced the greatest impact on the relations between the UEC and the Wachau. Laments over missed and suspended contacts run consistently throughout those letters that have survived. These difficulties reveal the tensions created by war and distance, and they forced the UEC to allow the Wachau certain exceptions to Unity regulations. The delay in the reception of the *Nachrichten, Losungen,* and synod reports also drove a subtle wedge between the North Carolina Brethren and their European counterparts.

The extant correspondence for the 1770s through the 1790s contains several specific references to letters gone astray en route from Europe to America and vice versa. Three letters were apparently lost in 1773. An unspecified number, including the yearly accounts from the Wachau for 1783, were lost in 1782 and 1783. All the initial information regarding the calling of the Synod of 1789 was also lost.[32] Delayed letters also posed a problem. In early 1775, Marschall told the UEC that the letter containing information on some Brothers being sent from Europe had gone astray and had arrived some days after the arrival of the party from Europe.[33] Again, in 1783, Marschall reported that he received a letter from the UEC, about which he had been told "something" by one of the officials in Pennsylvania, very late.[34] In the same letter, Marschall spoke of the eagerness with which the Wachau Brethren awaited a letter from the UEC containing the news of which Brothers were coming to settle in the Wachau, because this news affected "all kinds of projects." He added that when one considered "how many dangers and transfers [*Abwechselungen*] letters go through before they reach our hands it is a real wonder that we could have so much connection with one another in these times."

Although only a few specific references to lost and delayed letters occurred, the correspondence between Europe and the Wachau rang with lamentations over the difficulties that beset the exchange of news. In 1777, the UEC remarked that it had been a long time since they had received any report from the Wachau, "and it will perhaps have been much longer that you received nothing from us."[35] The letters contain strong references to obstacles that stood in the way of communication. Assuredly, the most poignant lament came from Brother Gregor in 1790: "I am sorry that the world between you and us and between us and you seems as if it were boarded up with planks. . . . We waited very long this time for the joy [of hearing from you] and we must wait patiently to see something from your dear hand again."[36]

The American Brethren were fully aware of the problems caused by uncertainty on the sea. In 1780, when the Elders Conference was anticipating a visitation from Europe, Marschall wrote of the frustration of trying to plan for their arrival without having any details regarding it. He then expressed their joy when they finally received the information: "It can scarcely be conceived in places where one is accustomed to steady information and regulated post, how pleasant this joyous news was after such long uncertainty and complete seclusion."[37] In addition to the uncertainty over correspondence, this letter expressed a very real sense of being in the wilderness and strongly implied that the European Brethren could not possibly identify with this from the vantage point of their more "civilized" situation. Two years later, Marschall told Anton von Lüdecke, "You are finally the only correspondent that I have in Europe. The others have all given up hope of their letters reaching me."[38] He pointed out that, as a consequence, the Wachau Brethren remained ignorant of who had filled Brother Pfohl's position on the UEC. Clearly, the Brethren in North Carolina felt isolated from the mainstream of the Unity.

The circumstances of the American Revolution heightened the anxiety of the Brethren in America and in Germany, but particularly in the latter. In 1778, the lot approved a visitation but, as a result of cost and of the continued threat of war, the UEC remained apprehensive at the prospect. They wrote the Salem Elders Conference that they had resolved on a visitation not knowing whether Brother Reichel could reach America from England: "Our love, prayers, and blessings, accompany him and [we] hope to God that He will open a path for him."[39] As in the letter from Gregor sent in 1790, this letter expresses the sense of a barrier between America and Germany. The Wachau received the worst wounds of the war toward its end, a fact of which the UEC proved well aware. In 1783, the UEC wrote, "We are always happy when we hear something from your area. . . . We can well imagine that you might still be in such a position as to be not yet free from all trouble."[40] The coming of peace and relative stability in America might have restored communication to its normal, if slow, pace; but, by the 1790s, war threatened it once again, this time from the other side of the Atlantic.

In their correspondence from the 1790s, the Brethren struck the same note of worry as they had earlier. Indeed, they seem to have become almost resigned to the precarious nature of their communication. Many of the letters from Germany at this time were almost despondent in tone: "One can, however, never be certain of the arrival of letters, neither to you nor from you, which is right troubling"; "We are very sorry that . . . in the present course of events many of the *Nachrichten* from us are perhaps lost"; "Were we not so far from you and one did not have to fear anew that in this present wartime the letters could be lost, then I would certainly write to you more often"; "This [the present "uncertainty on the sea"] makes one, however, entirely reluctant to write because one has to fear that it will perhaps be in vain."[41] As in the 1770s, the distance of the Wachau isolated them from news to a greater degree than it did other settlements. When the settlements in Zeist and Neuwied were threatened by invasion and turmoil, Christian Gregor maintained that the Brethren in the Wachau must have been especially worried because of the length of time for which they had to await the report of events.[42]

The most significant development that resulted from problems with the correspondence was the gradual loosening of the UEC's hold on the appointment of local officials. In a letter written in 1774, the UEC took the Elders Conference to task for authorizing the ordination of some Brothers without first consulting the UEC. Marschall's reply to this was an odd mixture of submission and defiance: "I assume that . . . nothing has occurred among us that did not originate from a perfect sense of subordination, and from hearts yielded happily [to the Savior], but since we do not receive an answer from Europe in less than a year [the best time was actually five months] I assume it is acknowledged that many things must be decided locally."[43] He then pointed out that, in 1761, the Unity leadership had decided that marriages of nonofficials and decisions regarding building could be determined locally "and, I beg to say, the same for ordination." Thus, Marschall not only argued that the UEC's insistence on controlling ordination would harm the spiritual life of the local members, but also implied that the right of tradition lay, in this case, on the side of the Wachau officials. His view prevailed, and, three years later, the UEC granted local officials the authority to decide on ordination.[44]

The Synod of 1789 allowed the American *Gemeinen* to replace officials in the *Landgemeinen* without prior consultation; the *Ortsgemeinen*, however, were held to more inclusive standards of obedience and piety. The synod members were inclined, though, to make an exception for the offices of *Gemeine* and Choir *Diener*, which dealt with issues of daily administration. A letter from Gregor illustrates the reasoning behind this decision: "We indeed suppose, and see increasingly from your dear letters, that many things occur with you where the distance and uncertain manner of communication with the UEC often holds up matters very long, [even] a year long. . . . Since the correspondence between the Wachau and us is so very precarious, *I* think no one can think badly of you if . . . for the sake of necessity you seek to procure more freedom in these matters [the appointment of local officials] than in Pennsylvania where the correspondence is still easy." [45] In this instance, Gregor hinted at his sympathy with any attempt the local leaders might make to extend their autonomy even further. Throughout the eighteenth century, the UEC continued to insist on control over the distribution of leaders in those offices of primarily spiritual responsibility. Marschall, however, understood that even these offices required more than spiritual strength. In 1801, he "strongly requested" that the determination of the *Ort* in which the new *Landarbeiter* (pastors in the *Landgemeinen*) would serve not be made in Europe but, rather, in the Wachau *Helfer Conferenz für Ganze*, "which best knows the requirements of the place."[46] However great the pull of the traditional structure of authority, local interests could not be understood by a group of men an ocean's distance away.

The correspondence that did reach America from Europe was not always unedited. Sometimes the UEC suppressed information, especially when it sensed that it might upset their American Brethren. The Unity leadership made a more significant omission in the copy of the minutes of the revisions committee of the Synod of 1789 that they sent to the Wachau.[47] One item dealt with by the committee was the marriage of Marschall's assistant, Ludwig Christian Benzien. The Wachau copy says that the elders first proposed Marschall's daughter, Anna Johanna, but the lot was negative. The original of the minutes tells a different story. Anna Johanna and her sister, Agnes Justina, were, indeed, among those Sisters considered as possible for marriage with Benzien. Many Brothers thought Anna Johanna would suit Benzien "right well . . . nevertheless there were still doubts expressed regarding the *inequality in rank*" (emphasis mine).[48] Hereditary nobility meant little in post-Revolutionary America, but, in Germany, it was another matter. The UEC did consult the lot about Sister von Marschall but only so far as to ask the preliminary question of whether they should include her in those Sisters considered for Benzien. The negative answer relieved them of any possible embarrassment. Despite the fact that the UEC supposedly sent a complete copy of those sections of the minutes pertinent to the Wachau, that copy gave no hint of the doubts expressed regarding the match.

In conjunction with the frustration over the difficulty with regular correspondence, the Brethren expressed considerable frustration over the delay and loss of their devotional writings and synod reports. As we have seen, these documents helped bind the Unity together in spirit. In addition, the *Nachrichten* helped give members in one *Gemeine* news of relations in other *Gemeinen*. The extant correspondence contains many references to lost *Losungen* and *Nachrichten*.[49] When the correspondence did arrive, it was almost invariably late. As a result, the Salem Elders Conference was often forced to draw *Losungen* for the Wachau from among those of previous years. The Brethren in Salem were as little pleased with this as with the constant delays in correspondence. In a letter regarding finances, Marschall voiced their frustration: "You can imagine, however, how it must concern us when we receive the Unity *Memorabilia* [the year-end newsletter] two years late, by which time we have already seen elsewhere that almost everything has changed."[50] The UEC was sympathetic to their troubles but claimed such delays could not be helped and cited their own burden of work.

Visitation provided another means of maintaining cohesion in the Unity. Because of the distance from the German base of the leadership, visitations were especially important for the American *Gemeinen*. The UEC and the American leadership recognized this fact. In the committee for America at the Synod of 1775, the Pennsylvania representatives requested that a member of the UEC occasionally stay for a while in America and that one of the Brothers who had served in America for some time be brought back to Europe as an advisor. The UEC, however, dismissed the latter request as not possible at that time. The

UEC members did favor the former, which, they pointed out, had also been Zinzendorf's plan, but the cost of the journey troubled them. Here, again, the expense of transatlantic travel interfered with the ties between the American *Gemeinen* and their European leadership. The matter was settled for the time being when the plan, despite having the blessing of the "blessed disciple," did not obtain the same from the Savior.[51]

The ordination of a new Bishop for America would have alleviated some of the need for a visitation, but, again, circumstances in America made the UEC hesitate: "A doubt was expressed, whether, because of the distance and uncertainty of correspondence, now was the time . . . to place a chief official [*Hauptarbeiter*] in America."[52] The issue of a bishop for America remained unresolved for years. Another visitation was approved in 1783, although it did not arrive in North Carolina until late in 1785.[53] The visitation of 1783 was to be the last approved for nearly twenty years. The UEC minutes for the 1790s record several fruitless attempts to gain the Savior's approval for a visitation, which circumstances made increasingly urgent especially among the Pennsylvania Brethren.[54]

Unity versus Local Need

The increasing need for a visitation was viewed from different angles from the different sides of the Atlantic. In 1788, Marschall observed, "we have . . . wished in various cases that a synod might be held once in America, where our local circumstances would be seen from close up since we could then hope to see the mind of the Savior more closely in many things."[55] Marschall appears to imply that the Savior's will regarding His American *Gemeinen* could be more accurately determined *in loco*. This implication illustrates the tension between the practical and the spiritual quite well. What Marschall undoubtedly had in mind was the idea that the synod could more accurately know what questions to put before the Savior if it were actually in America. In 1796, he expressly requested a visitation from the UEC prior to any synod that might be called. His reason for this spoke movingly of the ambiguous position in which the American Brethren felt themselves to be: "The number of Brothers in the UEC who are acquainted with America is decreasing and yet we are a part of the Unity."[56] The American Brethren clearly thought that in order to serve the best interests of the American *Gemeinen* the UEC needed to become reacquainted with its distant Brethren.

The UEC had a slightly different reason for concern. By 1801, the elders were troubled by the "embarrassment" in all of the American *Gemeinen* "in which the right trust of the Brethren toward their *Arbeiter* appear[ed] to be very much lacking," and, thus, the UEC regretted very much that for many years they had not had a visitation from the UEC.[57] Both Marschall and the UEC were concerned for continued unity, but, while Marschall stressed the need for an understanding of American circumstances, the UEC stressed the need for a restoration of proper order.

These differing emphases also shaped the disagreements between the UEC and the Elders Conference over general practices and the adherence to Unity regulations. This was most particularly the case with regard to the status of the *Landgemeinen* in the Wachau. The *Landgemeinen* did not share the mixture of secular order and spiritual ideal to the same degree that the *Ortsgemeinen* did; neither did they have Choir houses. For precisely these reasons, the UEC viewed them with a strong measure of suspicion. Thus, the Synod of 1769 urged that the reception of people into the *Stadt* and *Land Gemeinen* occur with even more "care and caution" than it did in the *Ortsgemeinen* "because with these the danger of degenerating into a dead religious constitution is great."[58] The Unity feared that because members of these *Gemeinen* could partake of particular privileges, such as exemption from military duty, without being subject to the stricter structure of the *Ortsgemeinen,* people would seek to join the *Landgemeinen* without the true call to be one of "God's people."

In the 1780s, a dispute arose over the use of the lot to determine marriage proposals in the *Landgemeinen*. To a degree, the matter appears to have been something of a tempest in a teapot, but the dynamics are very revealing. In 1783, the UEC members discussed the fate of the marriage lot in view of their desire to promote more marriages among the Brethren. They rejected the lifting of this requirement as a means to this end, but noted in their discussion that the Synod of 1775 had allowed for exceptions "when, for example, the [possible] proposals [for marriage partners] in a *Landgemeine* were too few."[59] In other words, when the pool was limited to begin with, the UEC allowed the local Elders Conference to dispense with the lot to avoid its being left with no approved partner. Apparently, this flexibility on the part of the UEC was far from clear to the Salem Elders Conference. In August 1787, the elders wrote a long letter to the UEC in which they asked "permission to lay before the dear Brothers of the Elders Conference of the Unity some points over which they request[ed] their advice and instruction."[60] Then they proceeded to explain in detail the difficulties incurred in the Wachau by their attempt to adhere to the marriage lot. These involved not only a restriction on the number of marriages, but also the necessity of expelling those members who chose either to marry without the lot or in defiance of it. In their explanation, the Elders Conference pointed out that the generally unregulated nature of the *Landgemeinen* created an atmosphere inimical to submission to the lot, as did the pastoral locale

itself: "They are under no protection from a Choirhouse, have few formal principles, [and] the spirit of the country and the entire institution is such that
people can not easily remain single." As indicated earlier, the agricultural nature of Bethania, Bethabara, and the *Landgemeinen* led to an increasing emphasis on the family and a greater susceptibility to the temptations of the
backcountry.

The Elders Conference seems to have anticipated a renewal of the admonition of the Synod of 1769 to restrict admission to the *Landgemeinen,* and
they went straight to the difference between religious circumstances in America
and those in Europe.

> Where there is a religious domain in which people can baptize their
> children, go to holy Communion, and adhere closely to our society,
> the *Gemeine* circle can be kept narrow, without people who are not
> suited to a narrow rule. . . . Here in [this] country, however, where
> each sect has the same privilege and prerogative, indeed even in the
> same no Christian ordinances and institutions exist, it would, accord-
> ing to our thought, be of no help for the business of our Savior if one
> required the people to keep to the denomination from which they or
> their parents came and which have here no Church constitution . . . if
> they could not obtain holy Communion. We think the Savior des-
> tined our *Landgemeinen* to help with this lack.[61]

The lack of ordained clergy in the North Carolina backcountry, coupled with
the variety of "religions" needing clergy because there was no single recognized
church, meant that people of various denominations were often unable to obtain ministry from within their "religion." The Wachau Brethren thus found
themselves to be the only spiritual resource for many people. In this letter they
presented the possibility that God had given their *Landgemeinen* a special calling, which would be spoiled if admission to them had to be severely restricted
or became so de facto by the need to expel those who rebelled against the
marriage lot.

The UEC's response to this detailed letter was curt. The elders pointed
out that this matter had already been discussed in Pennsylvania during Reichel's
visitation, "and we have already acknowledged in the synod that it is difficult
and almost impossible to treat the Brethren in the *Landgemeinen,* especially in
North America, entirely the same with regard to marriage [as is] our practice in
the *Ortsgemeine*." They added that "it appear[ed] necessary" to clarify this matter
in the next synod and that Marschall should take comfort in this.[62] Marschall,
however, repeated his observation regarding the problems with the lot as an

example of the need for a synod to be held in America. It is difficult to determine why Marschall continued to complain about the situation regarding marriage in the *Landgemeinen* when the synod report and the UEC acknowledged the possibility of an exception for the American settlements. The answer may lie in the confusion over the nature of the third *Ortsgemeine*. Bethania was a thorn in the side of the Wachau authorities from its foundation, and its upper village, which had originally been made up of nonmembers, proved particularly obstreperous. In his letter regarding the marriage lot, Marschall wrote that Bethania's upper village was not distinguishable from the *Landgemeinen* in its manner of thinking. Nevertheless, it was an *Ortsgemeine*, not a *Landgemeine*, and so could be viewed as falling under the stricter standards of the *Ortsgemeine*. By 1790, the leadership in the Wachau had taken the matter of Bethania into their own hands. They accepted the synod's decision to omit the lot in marriages in the *Landgemeinen* and added "wherein we can count Bethania after a certain fashion."[63] With this declaration, they also freed Bethania from the marriage lot without consulting the UEC on this particular action. Local independence was growing.

Although the problems in the *Landgemeinen* caused the biggest disputes over unity in practice, issues of a similar nature arose in other matters. In 1773, Marschall wrote to the UEC to protest the arrangements made for the administration of the Wachau after Salem's foundation. The UEC noted, "Brother von Marschall has complained in a letter to Brother Johannes that our Brothers deputized to America have disarranged the effort to further the improvement of the Wachau . . . because the free disposition of the local funds and possessions is too much confined, and through this, also the means of defraying certain general expenses."[64] Marschall believed that he needed immediate authority over local finances to see to it that matters were taken care of promptly. The UEC responded that because they held the ultimate responsibility for the finances of the entire Unity and had granted the Wachau settlement quite generous terms, Marschall was seeking too great a freedom, which appeared to be neither in line with synodal principles nor necessary, in their opinion.[65] Authority over economic matters remained a sore point the next year and prompted the UEC's decision to call Marschall to the synod, "where we believe that he will learn to accommodate himself to the manner of thinking assigned to us by the Savior."[66] In this instance, it was the UEC who wished to have the American officials meet them on their territory. More important, they clearly felt the Savior to be on their side. Local need must not be allowed to threaten the divinely ordained regulations of the Unity.[67]

The Need for Leaders

One constant theme of the correspondence between Europe and America was the need for Brothers to fill leadership positions in the Wachau. As mentioned earlier, the immediacy of the need to replace officials led to increasing independence on the part of the Salem Elders Conference in this particular area. The search for new officials illustrates very well the difficulties involved in reconciling the needs of the individual *Gemeine* with the needs of the whole, and in balancing practical and spiritual requirements. In addition, two general trends compounded the problem in the years 1771–1801: first, the increasing lack of Brethren considered proper for leadership positions, particularly in America; and second, the frequent failure of those leaders sent from Europe to serve in the Wachau. The lot, of course, served as an ever present "wild card" in the entire process.

From the point of view of the Wachau leadership, there was too much work for too few hands. In late October 1771, Ulrich Muschbach, the *Diener* of the Single Brothers, whose primary duty was to administer and supervise their trades, asked to resign after a dispute with the storekeeper over the establishment of a standard monthly payment to the store account. Despite his manifest unhappiness and acrimonious letters to Marschall, his resignation could not be officially accepted until his place was filled. To this end, the Elders Conference wrote to the UEC. Although Muschbach remained in office, his effectiveness was severely hampered by the fact that he refused to attend the meetings of the *Aufseher Collegium*, and, in August 1772, he left for Pennsylvania despite the fact that the Elders Conference had yet to receive a response from Europe.

Marschall's departure for the synod brought the shortage of help into high relief. Before leaving for Europe, he urged the UEC to appoint another Brother to help Johann Michael Graff with the spiritual care of the *Gemeine*. In doing so, he referred to potential internal stress if the need for help remained unanswered. The care of Salem alone, he pointed out, would be more than enough for Graff to handle, and "it could not but result in the disadvantage and neglect of the other *Gemeinen* and *Orte* if this Brother is bound to Salem alone."[68] After the UEC rejected one Brother who was suggested for this office and another proposal failed to win the approval of the lot, the matter was set aside until after the synod, and Graff had to bear the burden alone for the next five years. The UEC itself recognized that the situation was stressful. In a letter informing Graff of the continued delay in the Marschalls' return, Brother Andersen wrote, "When we come to think that our dear old faithful Brother Graff was left almost entirely alone . . . our heart is very moved."[69] Such expressions of sympathy were probably small comfort to Graff, who was having a difficult time at home.

The Marschalls were not the only Wachau officials to be detained in Europe. The UEC appointed Johann Daniel Köhler as Paulus Tiersch's replacement in March 1776 but then appointed him interim to a series of posts in the German *Gemeinen* while they waited for him to be able to make the trip to America. Finally, in March 1780, when the lot negated Köhler's traveling to America that year, the UEC admitted that this position could not remain vacant and authorized Brother Reichel to appoint someone within the Wachau as interim *Gemeine Helfer*. This Brother, was not, however, intended to replace Köhler permanently. The UEC thus found it necessary to note that "one does not doubt that such a Brother, when Brother Köhler arrives . . . could be used very well in another way."[70] This observation indicates the intense need for officials but also hints at potential conflict over authority.

Köhler's arrival continued to be delayed, and Marschall continued to feel the burden of his office. In a letter to the UEC in July 1783, his hope and frustration surfaced quite clearly. Marschall reported that the Elders Conference had accepted the postponement of the meeting of the American Committee as a good thing "since at that time you still lacked the news of the various deaths and thus the deliberations over the appointments would have been very imperfect. Here in the Wachau our Provincial Helper Conference is diminished, our bishop has died, despite which we still lack a preacher for which Brother Köhler was destined, and various Brothers have become widowers [and so] they can only half administer their *Gemeine*."[71] He went on to say that this created personal difficulties for him and that they certainly needed someone to help with the business of administration "if a great loss were not to be risked." As it happened, Köhler's departure for America had been approved in late January 1783, although news of this did not reach the Wachau until much later. The UEC did not settle on a coadministrator to assist Marschall, however, until April 1787.

The UEC faced a number of obstacles that impeded its ability to satisfy the Wachau's continual pleas for leaders. These included their responsibility to the other fifty *Gemeinen*, not to mention their areas of Diaspora work; the loss of many potential leaders, particularly among the young nobility; the cost of transportation; and the reluctance of many Brothers to go to America. Finally, and, perhaps, most significant, the decision of the lot often destroyed the best-laid plans. Regardless of the validity of the reasons for their delays, the result was to increase the sense of otherness on Salem's part. The varying agenda of the UEC and the Salem Elders Conference were not easily reconciled. The Unity as a whole suffered from a lack of willing and capable leaders, and the

UEC was constantly short of officials to fill the large number of posts that existed by the 1780s. In the letter sent to Marschall in 1783 announcing the departure of Johann Daniel Köhler and Gotthold Reichel for America (the latter to Pennsylvania), Johann Friedrich Reichel exclaimed: "Oh my most dear Brother Marschall! How poor in *Arbeiter* are we! It will be right difficult to replace Gotthold Reichel and Köhler. Christiansfeld also lacks a preacher."[72]

The hesitation of Brothers to leave the relative security of Europe for the wilds of America presented another obstacle. The transatlantic voyage continued to be viewed with trepidation into the late eighteenth century.[73] As early as 1764, Marschall anticipated particular difficulties in persuading people to leave Germany for the Wachau. In a letter to the UEC, he observed, "In my opinion it would cost more to transport people from Europe than it would bring in and because the climate there is much hotter than in Pennsylvania it would not draw many."[74] Although this hesitation surfaced more often among "ordinary" members (i.e., nonofficials), those elected for leadership positions did not always accept gladly. When Johann Caspar Heinzmann was informed of his possible call to the Wachau as Single Brothers *Diener*, he replied that he "himself would indeed not have chosen such a plan, however he entirely surrendered to the will of the Saviour and was willing to go and serve therein."[75] Occasionally, the UEC met more than resistance. When Moritz von Schweinitz, who was suggested by Marschall for the position of preacher in Salem, was rejected by the lot, the UEC considered Brother Cranz but had to eliminate his candidacy because he had "expressly forbidden" any call to America.[76] In 1783, during a search for new wives for several widower-pastors in the Wachau, Reichel observed, "I do not believe that Single Sisters from here will go to America."[77] Given the difficulty that the UEC had in finding ordinary Brothers willing to go to America, it is a credit to the strength of the Brethren's devotion to their Savior and to their *Gemeine* that those called to positions of leadership were as willing to go as they were.

The Need for Workers

References to the need for ordinary Brothers to work in the Single Brothers House and in other trades appeared more frequently in the correspondence of the Brethren and in the records of the UEC than did references to the need for officials. The lack of capable workers increased Salem's vulnerability to declension because the Brethren were often reluctant to expel artisans whose trade they considered essential to the welfare of the *Ortsgemeine*. The Brethren were also forced to allow a growing number of "stranger" workers into Salem, whose presence frequently proved disruptive. In fact, the number of references to the need for artisans rose steadily from the 1770s through the 1790s in tandem with declension within Salem. Unfortunately, tension between the UEC and the Elders Conference over this matter rose almost proportionally, which is not surprising, because the records of the ruling bodies in the German *Gemeinen* suggest that the Germans did not have many artisans to spare. The majority of the American references consisted of pleas for Brothers from Europe while, on their part, the UEC members lamented the increasing difficulty in finding suitable Brothers and paying for their transport. In this instance, as in others, the responsibility of the Unity leadership for the whole body severely limited their ability to meet the needs of the Wachau. The proximity of the European *Gemeinen* to each other and to the seat of Unity government made it easier and cheaper for the leadership to tend to their wants than to those of their "most distant" *Gemeinen*. For the most part, the extant evidence reveals no lack of will on the part of the UEC leadership, but they did have a number of practical difficulties. The same obstacles that hampered their efforts to provide the Wachau with officials also affected the extent to which they could send artisans. They needed to find Brothers who were suitable both in training and in spirit, who were available, and who were willing to make the voyage. They then, of course, had to receive the approval of the lot. It was by no means an easy task.

By the 1790s, German Brothers exhibited an increasing unwillingness to go to America despite the lure of the land. When told of the possibility that he would be sent to the Wachau, Andreas Vierling said that although he would prefer a post in Europe, "he was still willing to go to America if it be the Saviour's will."[78] Clearly, it was not Vierling's will. Occasionally, a Brother needed much persuading. The clock maker, Eberhard, told the UEC that he was "now more willing" to go to the Wachau since the proposal (the lot) for this had fallen on him for the third time and "at that moment he believed that this could be the will of the Saviour for him."[79] One young man did not even have the chance to decide, for his father "forbade that his son be proposed for [service in] the *Anstalt* in the Wachau."[80]

In letters written in 1795, Gregor attributed the reluctance to go to America to an unwillingness to exchange the known for the unknown, particularly given the present full employment in the German *Gemeinen*. In his letter to the officials in the Single Brothers Choir, he said, "One should indeed think that in these troubled times in Germany, there would be enough Brothers who would gladly go to America where there is quiet and peace. If, however, they do not have a prospect of improving themselves there [i.e., becoming head of a trade], then they easily think: If I should be a journeyman cobbler, or tailor, or weaver there just as here, then I had rather remain where I am. The former mindset to be anywhere one is requested is not so commonly found as in former times."[81] Even those who did go to America did not always live up to their promise. Brother Becker originally proclaimed his willingness to work for the Single Brothers *Diacony,* but, soon after his arrival, he insisted on setting up his own shop.[82] This may well reflect the impact of an American emphasis on economic independence. The Elders Conference learned from this incident, and, a few years later, Marschall warned that if Brother Katchler came as saddler, he must not expect that his own shop and a wife would be soon granted to him.[83] These examples indicate that economic self-interest was an increasing problem in the European and in the American *Gemeinen.* However, emigration to the American *Gemeinen* appears to have been specifically linked with economic opportunity.

Aside from being willing, artisans had to be available. The need for masters of specific trades was often very difficult to meet.[84] This situation proved especially hard on the American *Gemeinen,* for the European *Gemeinen* had a larger pool of Brothers from which to draw. As the number of "suitable" Brothers decreased, the European *Gemeinen* became increasingly reluctant to give up their artisans. One Brother requested to go to America and was approved by lot only to have his Elders Conference refuse to let him leave.[85] In 1795, Gregor wrote to Marschall that "even those who might possibly have the desire to go to the American *Gemeinen,* the *Gemeinen* [in Germany] do not gladly give up," and, a month later, he reported that although the UEC had sent out many requests for Brothers, the *Gemeinen* had answered that they needed the same thing "for themselves."[86] While attempting in 1800 to find a master tailor for the Salem Single Brothers House, the UEC noted that the need in Upper Lusatia "[was] itself very great."[87]

Of course, even when Brothers were willing and able, they still had to be approved by the lot. To try to follow the often torturous path of all Brothers suggested for service in America would be frustrating and tedious. The year 1785, however, witnessed an intensive search on the part of the UEC and can serve as a good example of the vagaries of selection. A surprisingly large number of Brothers reported their desire to serve in America in response to the memo sent out by the UEC in that year. Out of the sixty-three who reported, fifteen received final approval, of whom ten were farmers, not artisans.[88] These fifteen were then divided between Pennsylvania and the Wachau. It is not surprising that the American *Gemeinen* felt that they had little support from Europe.

To some extent, all of the *Gemeinen* faced problems with willingness, availability, and the lot. As with so many other matters, however, the American *Gemeinen* faced the added factors of distance from Europe and the cost of the trip. The sending of Brothers for professions, therefore, often took a backseat to providing the Wachau with officials. During the discussion of Salem's need for a doctor, the UEC maintained that "since the trip is so costly, we did not consider it necessary to send someone to the Wachau for any purpose except for the position of a preacher in Salem."[89] Unfortunately, the need of the American *Gemeinen* for adult artisans increased just as the threat of war began to hang over Europe again. Thus, in 1787, the UEC expressed its sympathy for Marschall's request for Single Brothers but said travel at the time was very dangerous, rare, and costly by any route.[90]

The European and the American *Gemeinen* shared in the difficulties caused by the shortage of workers in the late eighteenth century. The cost of sending Brothers to America, however, and their frequent reluctance to go, made it easier for the UEC to meet the demands of the European *Gemeinen* than those of the American *Gemeinen*. The Wachau Brethren, on their part, felt a greater need for Brothers; their smaller size left them with fewer candidates from which to draw. This shared experience, then, increased the sense of distance between the Brethren in Europe and those in the Wachau.

Toward a New Identity

In tracing the strains that developed in the relations between the UEC and the Wachau, one of the most revealing elements is how the two parties came to view the American *Gemeinen* as distinct from the European *Gemeinen*. Granted, they were aware of certain distinctions from the beginning, such as distance and a different legal system. As time passed, however, the Elders Conference and the UEC each began to refer to the free spirit evident in the American *Gemeinen*. This free spirit extended beyond the political sense traced in the last chapter to include a difference in character. The UEC also put increasing emphasis on missions in America. At the same time, circumstances forced the Wachau Brethren to become involved in local government. After the Revolutionary War years, evidence surfaced of a new awareness of themselves as American. They began to contrast their identity as Americans with the European identity of the *Gemeinen* across the Atlantic. Ties with Europe remained intact, but the nature of the relationship had changed by the early nineteenth century.

Language provides a basic measure of shifting identity. Although the Salem Brethren kept their official records in German until the mid-nineteenth century, the records are shot through with English words and expressions. For the most part, they follow the general pattern for eighteenth-century German American usage in being confined to legal and economic, rather than to domestic or spiritual, terms.[91] There are some exceptions to this pattern, however, such as "situation," "intention," "inclination," "constitution" (meaning health), "distance," "confusion."[92] By the 1790s, the Brethren preached an English sermon on a regular basis, and, by 1799, the *Aufseher Collegium* decided that tomb inscriptions should be in English.[93]

The European perception of "free" American manners as distinct comes through in a remark made by a newly arrived Brother. When Christian Thomas Pfohl made his first report as head of the Salem *Anstalt* in 1793, he noted that "in the beginning it was very noticeable to me . . . that a particularly free manner [*Wesen*] was evident among them, which seemed like impudence to me in the beginning but which now, since I am somewhat better acquainted with the manner of the Americans, I have learned to excuse more and more."[94] He went on to specify that his charges were generally sincere and friendly. It is well worth noting that the manner of the American children seemed alien to this Brother newly arrived from Germany. It is also notable that he identified his charges as "American." Cracks in the Unity were showing.

The Elders Conference's expressions of concern over the free spirit of America, discussed in the previous chapter, gradually affected the attitude of the UEC. In 1795, the UEC rejected one Brother proposed for America because his "character and heart's inclination [*Herzensgang*]" were too uncertain for him to be placed in an American *Gemeine*.[95] Another example reveals something of the ambiguity with which the UEC viewed the Wachau. In their discussion in 1796 over whether to send Brother Wried to North Carolina, the UEC members admitted that he lacked the "proper legitimation and sense of humility" that was expected of a servant of Jesus. "We believed, however," they continued, "that he would find much schooling from the Saviour for him in America."[96] This allusion to America and, by implication, to the Wachau, as the Savior's school carried positive and negative tones. The UEC foresaw a closer relationship with the Savior for Wried if he went to America. Their statement strongly implied, however, that they expected this closer relationship to result from Wried's increased need to depend on Him under difficult circumstances. Given the evidence of Muschbach, Wallis, Schröter, and Köhler, it seems that the tones were probably more dark than light.

In another case, the UEC eliminated a Brother from consideration because of the "increasing number of examples of Brothers in the Wachau who had become unhappy through the misuse of strong drink," which made them reluctant to send one "who had already shown himself weak in this regard."[97] Their aforementioned hesitation to send their youth "far away," literally, "into the distance," may also stem in part from fear of the "wilds" of America. It certainly indicated some sense of America as an alien shore.

As the local leadership came to blame disorder in the *Gemeine*, in part, on the nature of its American location, the UEC placed increasing emphasis on the Wachau as a mission field. The plan to use the American *Ortsgemeinen* as a base for missions work went back to the first group of Brethren sent from Europe to Pennsylvania in the 1730s. The Wachau, however, was not originally intended as such an outpost, at least not by Zinzendorf. By the time of Salem's foundation, the Unity had shifted its position on this matter. In 1772, when Mattheus Stach told the UEC that he wanted to preach the Gospel to the Cherokee, they commented that it was regrettable that this had not yet been done in the nineteen years during which the Brethren had lived in North Carolina, and in the following year they urged Marschall to foster a missions program.[98] Toward the end of the century, the UEC increasingly conflated the desire to serve among the heathen with a call to America. In 1788, for instance, Brother Michael Harnap expressed a willingness to serve among the heathen, so the UEC proposed that he go to the Wachau as an artisan, while, in 1791, a Brother offered to go to America, using the phrase "service among the heathen."[99] In a heroic attempt to kill two birds with one stone, the UEC considered filling the need for Single Brothers in America with those Brothers who reported for service among the heathen, for an increasing number were willing to serve in this capacity.[100]

As with the issue of freedom, the Wachau Brethren themselves may have contributed to the increasing emphasis on missions in the Wachau. In a letter written in 1795, Brother Köhler made the following observation: "Here in this land is freedom to believe in the crucified Savior and to confess Him, but there is also freedom to live as a heathen who knows nothing of God nor wants to know. The number of such here is greatest, as one can see."[101] Köhler's words lay bare the relationship between American freedom and disbelief in the eyes of the Wachau leadership. The UEC's interest in missions may have arisen partially in response to the crisis perceived by their American counterparts. The result was to point up the "differentness" of the American *Gemeinen*.

Ironically, the concern of the Unity for the preservation of their privileges drew them into public life and, in the case of the *Gemeinen* in America, contributed to an awareness of themselves as citizens of America. This development can be traced chronologically. Interestingly enough, the UEC encouraged the Brethren in their relationship with the government, although the Wachau officials generally took the lead. What the UEC failed to realize was the truly revolutionary impact of this relationship on the self-perception of the American Brethren.

Before the Revolution, the UEC urged the officials in the Wachau to establish contact with those in power. "It would be good," they advised, "if it could happen more often that one or another Brother would sometimes visit

. . . a meeting of the Counsel and Assembly of these lords, as well as the Governor." [102] The Brethren also secured positions as justices of the peace in order to ensure a measure of control over local litigation and to remove outside influence. Nevertheless, the Brothers who held this office moved into the public sphere. Undoubtedly it was no coincidence that the first member of the Unity to be elected to the North Carolina House of Commons after the Revolution also held the office of justice of the peace before the Revolution.

The Brethren walked a very thin line during the early Revolutionary period. Caution was clearly their watchword, but, by 1778, they had drawn up an affirmation of loyalty to the Revolutionary government that they proposed to take in lieu of the standard oath required by the rebels. They firmly maintained that this affirmation could not be equated with an outright renunciation of the king, for it was carefully worded to avoid this. So, the fact that they drew it up at all indicates a willingness to accept the validity of the new government. [103] Undoubtedly, their faith in the Savior's providence played a large role in their adaptability.

As we have seen, by the early 1780s, the Brethren were increasingly active in local politics. In 1781, the records contain the first reference to the Brethren's being encouraged to vote for those candidates endorsed by the Elders Conference, and, in 1782, Brother Bagge was elected a member of the North Carolina House of Commons after friends had advised the Elders Conference to put forth their own candidate in order to have a voice in protecting their interests. [104] In this same year, the synod gave spiritual sanction to the new government when it noted that, because the president of the Pennsylvania congress treated the Brethren as "a people of God," this provided grounds to pray for the congress by name. [105] In 1790, the UEC gave its final seal of approval to the new country when it proclaimed the adoption of the federal Constitution by the North Carolina assembly to be "right good." [106] They did not seem to object to "American freedom" as long as it did not affect the government of the *Gemeine*. Of course, adoption of the Constitution also provided hope for an orderly civil government.

The significance of the changes in attitude brought about by the Revolution can be seen in the issues of landholding and citizenship. As early as 1778, Marschall had warned the UEC that his nephew could no longer be designated as his heir to the Unity lands in America, which Marschall held in trust, because the nephew had not "subscribed to the Act of Independence." [107] By 1787, Marschall lobbied for the Unity's name to be removed from any mention in the deeds; instead, the lands should be held solely by "inhabitants of America" because the American authorities might object to "foreigners" taking money out of America. [108] Five years later, he requested the North Carolina assembly to be allowed to possess the lands "as a citizen of the United States."[109] Benzien used the phrase "as an American" when he advised the UEC that he could not hold lands in the West Indies, which were under British rule.[110] The distinction that developed between American Brethren and immigrant Brethren is indicated by the fact that when Eberhard arrived from Germany in 1800 he could not hold property in his own name because he was an alien. Instead, his house was deeded in the name of one of his creditors who was an American member of the Unity.[111] Thus, by the turn of the century, the Wachau Brethren were citizens of a country in which, in the eyes of the UEC, much was "entirely different from Europe."[112]

Perhaps nothing epitomizes the tension between the ideal of unity and the growing sense of otherness on the part of the American *Gemeinen* than an incident in 1791. In that year, the UEC declared that the Brethren would celebrate the fiftieth anniversary of the festival of November 13, the date on which the Savior's election as chief elder was announced to the Brethren. Brother Ettwein, an official in the Pennsylvania *Gemeine,* questioned whether the American Brethren should celebrate with the European Brethren or should wait until 1798, "since that will be the first fifty years since the example of September 16, 1741 [when the Saviour was elected] was made known in the North American *Gemeinen.*"[113] For reasons that are unclear, the Savior's eldership was not extended to the American *Gemeinen* until 1748. The UEC responded quite firmly, "We held it to be most proper that *all Gemeinen* might celebrate this Jubilee at the same time and indeed this year." The UEC also stressed unity when they informed the Wachau of this celebration: "Since it is fifty years that this festival has existed for the collective *Brüdergemeine,* it follows that you in the Wachau also have a Jubilee to celebrate."[114] This sense of unity seems to have been less clear to the American Brethren. The growing sense of distinction appears even to have affected the ties of devotion that were designed to hold the Unity together.

In contrast with other German settlements in America, the settlements of the Brethren functioned as one unit of a larger whole that was based in Germany. This situation meant that the settlements benefited from an official contact network to maintain ties with their mother country, but the interdependence of the relationship with their German leadership proved problematic. The Unity founded the settlement in the Wachau to be a refuge in the wilderness and a source of economic strength to the whole, with Salem as its crown jewel. The Wachau soon became an additional source of strain on Unity resources. The years of interrupted communication and the simple fact of distance itself led the leadership in the Wachau to act more frequently as an independent unit. They continued to feel a strong bond with the UEC, however, in their role as preservers of "right order" in the face of disorder among the younger members. These first decades of Salem's existence also saw the Brethren in America come to view themselves as different from their Brothers in Europe and, eventually, quite explicitly, as "American." By century's end, in the eyes of those Brothers charged with guiding and preserving the Unity, the wilderness had invaded the refuge.

Epilogue

THE SHATTERING OF THE IDEAL

Although the Synod of 1801 changed little in the ideal to which the Brethren were held, the Synod of 1818 allowed for some significant alterations. In effect, this synod officially recognized the drive toward greater individual autonomy evident among the North Carolina Brethren in the 1780s and 1790s. In doing so, the synod brought to the surface similar dissatisfactions among the German Brethren. The American Brethren, however, took the lead in promoting change.

In preparation for this synod, the American Brethren in Pennsylvania and in North Carolina drew up a list of their primary concerns. This list dramatically illustrates the change in mind-set that had taken place since the Brethren first settled in the new world.[1] Not surprisingly, their most urgent request was that the lot no longer be used for marriage and that its use in government appointments be limited. Although this desire undoubtedly stemmed from the practical difficulties arising from the use of the lot in these areas, the fact that this request had the endorsement of the local leadership argues loudly for the strength of the American Brethren's concept of themselves as now distinct from their roots.

By looking at the presentation of the petition to the synod, we can confirm the role played by the Americans' sense of distinction in their requests. When the European synod members asked the Pennsylvania deputies to explain their stance, the Americans placed their objections to the lot firmly in the context of their status as American citizens. After a lengthy description of the constitutional privileges granted to "Brothers in such a free republic," the deputies concluded, "The influence of such a national constitution [*Landesverfaßung*] on the mindset and actions of our *Gemeine* members is completely unmistakeable and equally completely unavoidable; so too the relationship between them and the other inhabitants of the country is entirely different than in the case of the members of the other *Brüdergemeinen*." The deputies also claimed that the American Brethren felt themselves to be considered "an unimportant part of the Unity" because the impact of their peculiar circumstances was being ignored by the European Brethren. They did not, they said, want to demand any privilege but simply to be given release from the marriage lot "out of a true sense of necessity." The deputies ended by saying that it would be "certainly futile" to attempt to force the American *Gemeinen* to adhere to all the forms suitable to the European ones and noted that "*unity* does not require complete uniformity."[2] The North Carolina deputies essentially endorsed the statement of their Pennsylvania Brethren. It is not insignificant that, by 1818, the American leadership was willing to back the membership in their demand for recognition that the situation in America called for an alteration in practice.

In addition to the issue of the marriage lot, the American Brethren voiced some concerns that were the result of events in the post-Revolutionary period. They demanded that the *Gemeine* Council be reorganized to include all adult communicants, as it had before 1769, with the notable exception of the women, who were to be excluded from the new council, and that the UEC always have one American member. As we have seen, this latter demand expressed frustrations that had arisen much earlier regarding the governance of the American *Gemeinen* by officials who were an ocean's distance away. More significant in light of the restlessness evident in the 1780s and 1790s, the American Brethren asked that competition be permitted among the various businesses in the *Gemeine*. These requests on the part of the Brethren manifested changes in the attitudes of many members that had already led them to rebel against and, occasionally, simply ignore the statutes. By officially voicing their desire for independence from the regulations, the American Brethren shattered the ideal on which the *Ortsgemeine* had been built.

The argument made by the Pennsylvania deputies effectively put the European leadership over a barrel. The deputies made it clear that the existence of the Unity across the ocean was at stake. Ironically, to prevent worse consequences, such as complete separation between the American and the European Brethren, the synod confirmed the distance that had developed between the American Brethren and their heritage. The members agreed, without consulting the lot, to eliminate its use in marriages in the American *Gemeinen* for all members except officials charged with spiritual duties. They also agreed to the reorganization of the *Gemeine* Council according to local preferences and to allow limited economic competition.

On learning of the concession regarding the lot that had been granted to the American Brethren, the European Brethren expressed considerable consternation over what they claimed was an undesirable "distinction" between the Americans and the Europeans. Their reaction reveals the continued power of the indirect method of resistance. When initially asked about attitudes toward the marriage lot, the deputies of the German *Gemeinen* declared without exception that they did not want any changes made in its use.[3] The synod sensed potential difficulties, however, and, after much discussion, asked the Savior whether the European *Gemeinen* could implement a voluntary use of the marriage lot. They drew a negative answer, which effectively closed the issue, but decided that the UEC could grant individual exceptions on the request of the Elders Conferences.

The synod members soon learned what a storm lay beneath the apparently placid surface of the German *Gemeinen*. The Brethren in Herrnhut were particularly vocal and criticized the synod for allowing the Americans release from a regulation that others also opposed. They asked the synod to take up the matter again and to "give them the freedom and opportunity to express themselves frankly over the marriage lot etc." Two members of the local leadership expressed continued support for the lot but condemned the "essential differentiation" that now existed between Europe and America.[4] The synod sent someone to discuss matters with the Herrnhut Brethren. In the aftermath of this discussion, only four of the original one hundred signatories of the petition remained intransigently in opposition. The others agreed to submit to the authority of the synod but indicated that they preferred a voluntary marriage lot.

By this time, however, the news had spread, and, fanned by the initial Herrnhut petition, the other German *Gemeinen* also expressed their dismay over this "distinction." The synod summed up their sentiments as follows: "If the American *Gemeinen* are permitted by the synod to use the marriage lot or not, it is also just to grant the same freedom to the German *Gemeinen;* only because it was viewed as a pillar of our constitution . . . was it not outspokenly requested to eliminate the current regulations, as it was by the American *Gemeinen*."[5] In all of these protests, two important points emerge. In contrast to the American *Gemeinen,* the German *Gemeinen* did not feel free to express their opposition to the marriage lot. In addition, the lifting of the restriction for the American Brethren opened the door to the German Brethren to demand a restoration of unity that would result in freedom for them as well. In the end, the synod threw the responsibility onto the shoulders of the UEC, which, not surprisingly, granted all the European *Gemeinen* the desired freedom from the marriage lot.

It seems significant that the American Brethren acted as the voice for a desire for greater individual independence that was shared by the second generation on both sides of the Atlantic. The American Revolution gave the American Brethren the vocabulary to express a feeling shared by their counterparts in Europe. The experience of the Brethren thus adheres to the pattern laid out by

R.R. Palmer in his *Age of Democratic Revolution,* in which he argued that the American experience inspired political change in Europe. In the context of the history of the Unity, developments in the *Gemeinen* of America and of Germany indicate that the distance across the Atlantic evident in the eighteenth century was at least partially bridged by the early nineteenth century with planks made of new wood hewn from the "wilderness" of America.

Notes

Preface

1. LaVopa, *Grace, Talent, and Merit*, 137.
2. Outram, *Enlightenment*, 1–13, especially 3 and 12.
3. See Darnton, *Literary Underground*, in which he discussed the fine line between "high" and "low" versions of eighteenth-century philosophy.
4. Professor Pocock made this remark in an address he gave at the 1994 meeting of the American Historical Association.

Introduction

1. Holmes, *Protestant Church*, 1.
2. Langton, *Moravian Church*), 27; *A Brief History of the Moravian Church* (Raleigh, N.C.: Edwards and Broughton Printing, 1909), 21; Edmund Alexander de Schweinitz referred to "a little band of awakened Calixtines" in *The Moravian Manual: Containing an Account of the Protestant Church of the Moravian United Brethren or Unitas Fratrum* (Philadelphia: Lindsey and Blakiston), 17.
3. Langton, *Moravian Church*, 28. The most detailed modern study of the Ancient Unity in English is Peter Brock's *The Political and Social Doctrines of the Unity of the Czech Brethren in the Fifteenth and Early Sixteenth Centuries*. He emphasized the radical character of the Unity before the Brethren split into two branches in the 1490s. This study provides a balance to the more apologetic accounts that dominate the histories written by the Brethren themselves.
4. Brock, *Unity of the Czech Brethren*, 30.
5. Ibid., 87.
6. Zinzendorf, *Augsburg Confession*, 273–75.
7. Langton, *Moravian Church*, 34; de Schweinitz, *Unitas Fratrum*, 130.
8. Hutton, *Moravian Church*, 58 n.
9. de Schweinitz, *Unitas Fratrum*, 638, 641.
10. Hutton, *Moravian Church*, 196.
11. Holmes, *Protestant Church*, 256.
12. J.T. Hamilton, *History*, 14.
13. Erbe, "Zinzendorf," 9.
14. Weinlick, *Count Zinzendorf*, 33.
15. Ibid., 14.
16. Ibid., 16.

17. Ibid., 34.

18. Spangenberg, *Count Zinzendorf*, 2; Weinlick, *Count Zinzendorf*, 21.

19. Weinlick, *Count Zinzendorf*, 30.

20. Ibid., 31.

21. Addison, *Renewed Church*, 18.

22. This is mentioned by Spangenberg, *Count Zinzendorf*, and by Lewis, *Zinzendorf, the Ecumenical Pioneer*.

23. Brecht and Deppermann, *Geschichte des Pietismus*, vol. 2, 10.

24. Those of us who cannot read Hebrew are profoundly grateful for this. Zinzendorf's writings and many of the Unity records are peppered with French, Germano-French, and the occasional Greek. The information on Zinzendorf's education is taken from Weinlick, *Count Zinzendorf*, 27.

25. Ibid., 34.

26. Sawyer, "Religious Experience," 25–27.

27. Weinlick, *Count Zinzendorf*, 37.

28. Brecht and Deppermann, vol. 1, 16–17.

29. Pinson, *Pietism*, 118.

30. Kurt Aland argued that Pietism was the most socially leveling of all church movements. While the history of the Brethren suggests that it may have had this effect spiritually, the noble Brethren seem to have been of divided mind regarding how far Christian equality should affect social relations. Aland, "Der Pietismus," 123, 126–27.

31. Erbe, *Zinzendorf*, 121.

32. Lewis, *Zinzendorf, the Ecumenical Pioneer*, 55.

33. Gollin, *Moravians in Two Worlds*, 255 n.

34. This is noted in Sawyer, "Religious Experience," 55.

35. K.G. Hamilton, *Moravian Church*, 108.

36. Spangenberg, *Count Zinzendorf*, 50; Lewis, *Zinzendorf, the Ecumenical Pioneer*, 48.

37. Weinlick, *Count Zinzendorf*, 79.

38. Taken from the Herrnhut Diary (hereafter referred to as HD), excerpted in Hahn and Reichel, *Zinzendorf und die Herrnhuter Brüder*, 95. The reference to separatists may refer to a group of Schwenckfelders to whom Zinzendorf had also offered asylum.

39. Holmes, *Protestant Church*, 172.

40. Erb, *Pietists*, 325.

41. HD, Hahn and Reichel, *Zinzendorf und die Herrnhuter Brüder*, 106.

42. Sawyer, "Religious Experience," 38.

1. Forming the Ideal

1. Uttendörfer, *Wirtschaftsgeist*, 50–51. In 1766, the Herrnhut *Aufseher Collegium* issued a warning to the inhabitants to desist from extensive farming and leave it to the other tenants because large-scale agriculture was "not suitable" for a town economy [*bürgerliche Hantierung*].

2. Zinzendorf was exiled as a result of Baron Huldenberg's complaint that he

was seducing the Baron's tenants by the religious attraction of the group at Herrnhut.

3. Marienborn, 1736; Herrnhaag, 1738; Neudietendorf, 1742; Niesky, 1742; Gnadenberg, 1743; Gnadenfrei, 1743; Neusalz, 1744; Ebersdorf, 1746; Zeist (Netherlands), 1746; Barby, 1747; Neuwied, 1750; Kleinwelke, 1751; Christiansfeld (Denmark), 1764; Sarepta (Russia), 1765; Gnadau, 1767; Gnadenfeld, 1782; Königsfeld, 1807. This list includes only settlements on the continent.

4. See, for example, Stoeffler, *German Pietism*; Peter Erb, *Pietists: Selected Writings*; Lehmann, *Pietismus*.

5. Müller, *Zinzendorf als Erneuerer*, 9.

6. Ibid., 9.

7. Ibid., 10–12. Writing in 1747, Zinzendorf said of Ebersdorf, "Ich habe in Ebersdorf angetreffen einen Haufen Seelen, die ohne Unterschied der Religion, der Privatideen die jegliches hatte, *ohne Distinction der außeren Verfaßungen* sich geschloßen hatten" (emphasis mine).

8. Uttendörfer, *Alt Herrnhut*, 14.

9. Ibid., 16.

10. Müller, *Zinzendorf als Erneuerer*, 15. In fact, in 1731, Christian David claimed that Rothe's delegation of duties made the Brethren "all the more certain to continue further and to become a closed Gemeine." Quoted in Hahn and Reichel, *Zinzendorf und die Herrnhuter Brüder*, 86.

11. Ludwig von Zinzendorf, *Historische Begriff von der Beschaffenheit der Brüder aus Mähren und Böhmen*. Included in Müller, "Die altesten Berichte Zinzendorf's über sein Leben," 113.

12. Müller, *Zinzendorf als Erneuerer*, 23.

13. "Von Dienstbarkeit, Leibeigenschaft u.s.w., mit allen seinen statutmäßigen Einwohnern frei gesprochen sein." This and all other references to the *Obligations and Prohibitions* are taken from the supplement to Müller, *Zinzendorf als Erneuerer*, 107–18. The form used in the translation is taken from the 1728 revised version of the statutes.

14. Blum, "European Village Community," 561.

15. Sabean, *Power in the Blood*, 28.

16. Burke, *Popular Culture*, chap. 8.

17. Uttendörfer, *Alt Herrnhut*, 61.

18. Müller, *Zinzendorf als Erneuerer*, 49.

19. Quoted in ibid., 49.

20. Ibid., 56.

21. Reference mislaid. Gollin noted that by 1747 the population was more than eight hundred. *Moravians in Two Worlds*, 150.

22. Müller, *Zinzendorf als Erneuerer*, 58. He ultimately established Herrnhaag, from which the Brethren were expelled in 1749 after a quarrel over feudal authority. Many of those from Herrnhaag ended up in Salem.

23. Uttendörfer, *Alt Herrnhut*, 53, 56.

24. Uttendörfer, *Wirtschaftsgeist*, 51.

25. Uttendörfer, *Alt Herrnhut*, 98.

26. Uttendörfer, *Wirtschaftsgeist*, 52.

27. Extract of the Synod Report of 1749, n.pag. Moravian Archives of the

Southern Province (hereafter referred to as MA-SP), B20:2. The text reads, "Sie denckt, wenn sie uns darum bringen könnte, so hätte sie uns um alles gebracht . . . Aber der mächtige Schirm-Herrn dieser Constitution, des große Protector und Advocatus dieser Ecclesiae Anatolicae et Unitas Sclavonicae ist der Heiland selbst."

28. Cranz, *History of the Brethren,* 37.

29. Müller, *Zinzendorf als Erneuerer,* 97.

30. Uttendörfer, *Wirtschaftsgeist,* 112. The text reads, "Damit wir zwar alles machen, was in der Welt gethan wird, aber nicht so wie sie, sondern wie es Gliedern am Leibe Jesu ziemet."

31. Uttendörfer, *Alt Herrnhut,* 49.

32. Uttendörfer, *Wirtschaftsgeist,* 112.

33. According to Zinzendorf, the term "city on the hill" was used in reference to Niesky by Christian David, Georg Neißer, and other early leaders of the Renewed Unity. This information is taken from an entry in Zinzendorf's diary for Nov. 11, 1752, quoted in *Niesky 1742,* 5.

34. Synod Report of 1764, sect. 2, 4 (no chapter number), MA-SP, B20:4. The report goes on to make it clear that this government by Christ does not replace their obedience to worldly governments.

35. Ibid., sect. 2, 5.

36. Ibid., sect. 43, 49.

37. Synod Report of 1769, chap. 6, pt. B, no. 5, n.pag., MA-SP (bound manuscript; no catalog number).

38. Ibid., chap. 6, pt. A, no. 1.

39. Synod Report of 1764, sect. 7, 19. The Directorate was established in 1764 as the central ruling body (referred to as the Unity Elders Conference after 1769). It should be noted that it was broken down into three branches, or committees, which allowed for some differentiation of duties.

40. Uttendörfer, *Alt Herrnhut,* 16; idem., *Wirtschaftsgeist,* 51.

41. This status was not confined to Zinzendorf's estates. The Synod Report of 1775 noted that the settlement of Gnadau could continue to receive the annual profit from the *Wirtschaft* of the hereditary lease of the *Doben* because they could not survive otherwise.

42. *Aufseher, Ermahner, Lehrer, Diener,* and *Krankenwärter.* Müller, *Zinzendorf als Erneuerer,* 15.

43. Blum, "European Village Community," 560.

44. Uttendörfer, *Alt Herrnhut,* 27. In theory, Zinzendorf was subordinate to the elders who also served in the capacity of assistant justices. Ibid., 25.

45. They were Christian David, Georg Nitschmann, Christian Hoffmann, and Melchior Nitschmann.

46. Although the common translation of the term *Vorsteher* is "superintendent," the Brethren used the term "warden" in their English writings.

47. Sabean, *Power in the Blood,* 18. When the term *Vorsteher* was eliminated by the Synod of 1769, it was specified that this term would continue to be used in all outside correspondence and documents.

48. Uttendörfer, *Alt Herrnhut,* 26. Taken from the Herrnhut Diary. The text reads, "Die Aeltesten nur die voluntariam iurisdictionem der Statuten auf

herrschaftlichen Commission eine Zeitlang exerzieren, die sämtliche Streitigkeiten aber und Begünstigungen (Konzessionen, Privilegien, u.s.w.) in die Berthelsdorfischen Gericht gehören sollten."

49. Ibid., 26–27.

50. Ibid., 29–30.

51. Ibid., 30.

52. Nicholas Ludwig von Zinzendorf, *Apologetische Schluß-Schrift*, 419.

53. Uttendörfer, *Alt Herrnhut*, 31. The text reads, "Weil bei etlichen Ungezogenen in der Gemeine nicht bloß Liebe helfe, sondern auch Ernst anzuwenden sei und man hier das geistliche Priestertum und obrigkeitliche Amt verbinden könne, weil die Obrigkeit zugleich Christen wären, so wolle man sich nach I Kor. 6 hier richten und zum Besten der Seelen gebrauchen, die der geistlichen Arbeiternund ihrer Arbeit nicht achteten. Darum sollten alle Sachen die nicht ins Reich Gottes gehoren und zu einem Anstoß gereichen könnten, bald von gewissen aus der Gemein gewählten Männern abgetan und nach Gelegenheit hart von ihnen verfahren werden."

54. Blum, *European Village Community*, 54. The basis for comparison of the *Ortsgemeine* with the European village and town structure is taken from Blum's article; from Sabean, *Power in the Blood;* and from Walker, *German Home Towns*.

55. Despite this change, the Unity referred to the *Aufseher Collegium* as the "Gemeine Justice" when speaking to outsiders.

56. The restriction of village assembly membership is discussed in Blum, *European Village Community*, 561.

57. Synodal Compendium., vol. 1, chap. 6, pt. C, sect. 221, 258.

58. Taken from Zinzendorf's *Theologica Bedenken* of 1742. Excerpted in Hahn and Reichel, *Zinzendorf und die Herrnhuter Brüder*, 136.

59. Cranz, *Nachricht von der Brüder Kirche*, 27.

60. Müller, *Zinzendorf als Erneuerer*, 89. Although the term "civil elder" was unique to the Unity, David Cranz used the term "magistrates" in his *Account of the Church of the Brethren* written for the English authorities in 1757 during the period in which the church government was based in London: "They are the overseer of those matters that do not directly enter into the sphere of souls, and therein have to see that everything proceeds orderly and honorably. They direct all *Gemeine* justice at home and appoint agents in foreign lands." Cranz, *Nachricht von der Brüder Kirche*, 24.

61. Müller, *Zinzendorf als Erneuerer*, 89.

62. Taken from Christian David's *Schweitzer Bericht* of 1731, excerpted in Hahn and Reichel, *Zinzendorf und die Herrnhuter Brüder*, 89.

63. G. Beyreuther, "Sexualltheorien im Pietismus," 45.

64. Hamilton, K.G., *History*, 73. Those present at the conference were Zinzendorf; Countess Erdmuthe Dorothea von Zinzendorf; Benigna von Zinzendorf; Leonard Dober; Anna Maria Lavatsch, interim head eldress; Friedrich von Watteville; Rosina Nitschmann, wife of Bishop David Nitschmann; David Nitschmann Syndic; August Gottlieb Spangenberg; and his wife, Eva Maria Spangenberg.

65. J.T. Hamilton, *History*, 115. The largest numbers were in Upper Lusatia

(2,450), Silesia (2,000), Yorkshire (1,200), the Wetterau (850), and Denmark (500).

66. K.G. Hamilton, *Moravian Church*, 97.

67. J.T. Hamilton, *History*, 153. The board consisted of Count von Damnitz, Baron Heinrich von Zeschwitz, Julius von Seidliz, Anthony von Ludecke, Charles von Schachmann, Leonard Köber, Weinel (no first name given), and Johann Gotthold Wollin (the latter two as secretaries).

68. These three units were the *Directorium*, for general administration; the *Syndicus Collegium*, for civil matters; and the *Vorsteher Collegium*, for finances.

69. K.G. Hamilton, *Moravian Church*, 167–68. See also J.T. Hamilton, *History*, 217–18. The latter edition of *History* lists the members of the original Unity Elders Conference as: (the *Aufseher Collegium*) Abraham von Gersdorf, Leonard Köber, Count Heinrich XXVIII Reuß; (the *Helfer Collegium*) Bishop August Gottlieb Spangenberg, Johannes von Watteville, Christian Gregor, Johann Friedrich Reichel; (the *Vorsteher Collegium*) Johannes Loretz, Paul Eugene Layriz, Friedrich Nießer, Johann Christian Quandt, Peter Boehler, and Renatus van Laer.

70. Synodal Compendium, vol. 1, chap. 6, sect. 410, 409.

71. Schmidt, "Die Banden oder Gesellschaften," 150.

72. Uttendörfer, *Alt Herrnhut*, 83.

73. Ibid., 86. This concept of the consecrated nature of the Single Brothers House also surfaced in the Synod Report of 1764, which said the Choir houses should be "die Sacristeyen und Tempel."

74. Ibid., 87.

75. Walker, *German Home Towns*, 83.

76. Uttendörfer, *Alt Herrnhut*, 92.

77. This practice persists in the modern Moravian Church in Europe and in America.

78. Erbe, *Zinzendorf*, 320.

79. Synod Report of 1769. Appendix reserved for the Elders Conference. The text reads, "In so ferne die ledige Brüder Chorhäuser als eine Familie in der Gemeine anzusehen, in so ferne repraesentirten die Vorsteher und andere Vorgesetzen den Haus-Väter dieser Familie."

80. The *Gemeine* at Herrnhaag was the center of the excesses of the Sifting Period. It was dispersed after the new count of Büdingen, from whom the Brethren held their lease, required them expressly to abjure their ties to Count Zinzendorf as a condition of lease renewal.

2. Order in the Wilderness

1. Thorp, *Moravian Community*, 83–86.

2. Merrens, *Colonial North Carolina*, 35. The report was published in several editions from 1709 to 1722.

3. Thorp, "Moravian Colonization," 71–73.

4. Walker, *German Home Towns*, 112–19.

5. Thorp, "Moravian Colonization," 43.

6. This information is based on a list provided by Thorp in "Moravian Colonization," 34. He said that, in addition to Zinzendorf and Spangenberg, those

involved in planning Salem were probably Cornelius van Laer, Johannes von Watteville, Jonas Paulus Weiß, James Hutton, Henry Cossart, Abraham and Siegmund von Gersdorf, David Nitschmann Syndic, and Friedrich von Marschall. Ibid., 70.

7. Ibid., 70.

8. The following discussion of this plan is taken from Thorp, "City," 36–54.

9. Thorp noted the protective element in the circular plan in light of historical geographer Manfred Büttner's claim that the grid pattern normally used by the Brethren is "outer-directed." Büttner also pointed out, however, that even in the grid pattern the whole settlement focused on the square with the Saal and Choir houses. See Büttner, "Religion and Geography," 163–93. The Salem *Gemeine* never grew large enough to warrant separate Choir houses for the Widows and Widowers Choirs, nor were separate buildings for the Boys and Girls Choirs ever built, although boarding schools for each sex were in place by the early nineteenth century.

10. Reflection über den Riss der Salem der von Europa geschickt werden, July 7, 1759. Quoted in Thorp, "City," 53.

11. Merrens, *Colonial North Carolina*, 142.

12. Thorp, *Moravian Community*, 129–30.

13. Memorandum concerning the Wachau, Feb. 1, 1764, n.pag., MA-SP, B65:2, box 5A:7:1.

14. Ekirch, *Poor Carolina*, 29.

15. Spangenberg to the Wachovia Congregation, Feb. 27, 1756. Quoted in Sensbach, "A Separate Canaan," 150.

16. Thorp, "Moravian Colonization," 270.

17. Smaby, *Transformation of Moravian Bethlehem*, 33.

18. Fogelman, *Hopeful Journeys*, 139–49.

19. The figures for the expulsion rate pre-1772 are taken from Thorp, *Moravian Community*, 101. Although the adolescent and adult population of Salem was larger than that of early Bethabara, by 1801 it was not even double that of Bethabara in 1771, while the rate of expulsion had tripled.

20. Fries, *Records of the Moravians* (hereafter referred to as *RM*), vol. 2, 818.

21. Thorp, "Moravian Colonization," 109. Thorp suggested that Spangenberg favored the foundation of Bethania as a means of preventing Bethabara from growing too large and rivaling the central *Ortsgemeine*.

22. Synod Report of 1764, 70, MA-SP. The *Arbeiter* for one of the Wachau *Landgemeinen* requested that they be put under the *Gemeine* statutes, but Marschall held fast to the Unity principle that they not be obligated to accept such. Minutes of the Salem Elders Conference (hereafter referred to as Min. EC.), May 28, 1771, no. 3, MA-SP, J299C:1.

23. By 1775, these two *Landgemeinen* were joined by a third, Hope, made up of English immigrants from Maryland.

24. *RM*, vol. 2, 725. A small book held in the Unity Archives in Herrnhut containing the statutes for Herrnhut, Niesky, Neudietendorf, Gnadenberg, Gnadenfrei, Ebersdorf (all issued in 1770), and Gnadau (issued in 1773) reveals that in most cases the articles are reproduced verbatim for each of these *Gemeinen*. There are, however, some significant differences in certain articles between the

Salem statutes and their German model. These primarily pertain to the relationship with the outside government and are discussed in chap. 5.

25. This information is taken from an indenture between Georg Hauser Jr. and Friedrich von Marschall, Sept. 29, 1796, MA-SP, D155:7b.

26. Brotherly Agreement and Contract (hereafter referred to as Brotherly Agreement), 1773 version, introduction, n.pag., MA-SP, R699:4. The archive holds a translation of this document by Frances Cumnock. All quotations cited here are taken from the German original.

27. Ibid. The text reads, "Und dabey der menschlichen Schwachheit diese heilsame Absicht ohne vestzustellende und durchgängig zu beobachtende, der Lehre Jesu und Seiner Apostel, auch den Umständen des Orts allenthalben gemäße Ordnungen, sich zu erreichen stehet; so ist beschloßen worden, die gegenwärtigen der Brüder Kirche Disciplin gemäße Gemeinordnungen zusammen zu tragen, als zu welche die ganze Gemeine in Salem . . . sich zu bekennt, und zu derselben treulichen Beobachtung sich vor unserm lieben Herrn und Heiland freiwillig einverstehen und brüderlich verbindet."

28. Ibid., sect. 2, article 2.

29. Reiter, "Moralische Subjektkonstitutionen," 85.

30. Brotherly Agreement, sect. 2, article 7, and sect. 4, article 2.

31. Robisheaux, *Rural Society*, 119; Medick, "Village Spinning Bees," 321–22.

32. Brotherly Agreement, sect. 5, article 4. The text reads, "Wir erkennen für eine der wichtigsten und ersprieslichsten Gemeinordnungen, daß zu Verhutung aller Seelen-Schadens und alles Bekränkung des Ruhms an Christo unter uns, über die Auseinanderhaltung beyderley Geschlechte in gebührende Ordnung und Anständigkeit unwandelbar gehalten werde."

33. Ibid., sect. 5, article 5f.

34. Ibid., sect. 5, article 5a.

35. Ibid., sect. 5, article 5e.

36. Berdahl, *Prussian Nobility*, 56.

37. Brotherly Agreement, sect. 5, article 8.

38. Ibid., sect. 7, articles 12, 2, 3, and 7.

39. The one exception to this is found in the section that deals with trades. The 1786 version of the statutes added a statement to article 9 on the relationship between masters and journeymen. This statement required that all masters report to the *Aufseher Collegium* or *Gemeine Diener* what had been agreed regarding wages so that these wages could be maintained in a "just and proper relationship" for all parties. This statement undoubtedly was added in an effort to prevent another incident such as that of 1778, when several Single Brothers walked out on the job to protest unjust wages. Brotherly Agreement, 1786 version, sect. 7, article 9.

40. Herrnhuter Diarium, Aug. 15, 1727, quoted in Reiter, "Moralische Subjektkonstitutionen," 80–81.

41. This view of a "lenten" Christian culture has been echoed in other studies of religion and culture. See, for example, Muchembled, *Popular Culture;* Joseph Klaits, *Servants of Satan: The Age of the Witch Hunts* (Bloomington: Indiana Univ. Press, 1985); John Bossy trained his sights specifically on Protestantism in *Christianity in the West, 1400–1700.*

42. I am grateful to Craig Atwood for letting me see a draft of his then-in-progress dissertation for the divinity school of Princeton University, "The Impact of Zinzendorf's Theology on Colonial Bethlehem, 1742–1762." This information is taken from chap. 7, which provides much fascinating detail on the aesthetics of worship in Bethlehem.

43. I am indebted to W.R. Ward for this particular description, but I have often been struck by the same observation. Significantly, Ward said this combined culture is "most *movingly expressed*" in the worship building at Herrnhut. I most heartily concur. The culture of the Brethren was, and is, one of feeling. Ward, "Zinzendorf and Money."

44. Ted Campbell recently explored the common emphasis on the heart in early modern European religious movements. See *Religion of the Heart*.

45. Hahn, "Theologie," 289, 293.

46. For a discussion of the role of Communion within community, see Bossy, *Christianity*. Sabean discussed the implications of refusal of communion in *Power in the Blood*.

47. Reiter, "Moralische Subjektkonstitutionen," 82.

48. Synod Report of 1775, sect. 912, MA-SP. Bound manuscript; no catalog number. Quotation taken from Nelson, "Herrnhut," vol. 1, 182. The information contained in the following discussion of the devotional cycle is taken largely from Nelson.

49. Atwood, *Zinzendorf's Theology*, chap. 7. Atwood summarized one of the verses of a hymn used at the kiss of peace as follows: "The kisses each member gives and receives come from the Triune God, especially from the 'Savior with the bleeding face,' but in the act of kissing all of the *Gemeine* is joined."

50. These anniversary festivals commemorated the following: the martyrdom of Jan Hus; the founding of the Ancient Unity; the Protestant Reformation; the Augsburg Confession; the felling of the first tree in Herrnhut; the building of the first *Saal* in Herrnhut; the first Brotherly Union; the Communion of Aug. 13, 1727; the founding of the *Stundengebet*, or Hourly Intercessions; the first mission to St. Thomas; the first mission to Greenland; the naming of the Savior as chief elder; and the announcement of His Eldership to the *Gemeine*.

51. The *Nachrichten* were manuscript newsletters containing information from and about all of the *Gemeinen* of the Unity. The officials of each *Gemeine* gathered together what they considered to be the most significant news items from their settlement and sent them to the Unity Elders Conference. The Elders Conference then selected some of these items and put them together in one manuscript. A second manuscript contained selected *Lebensläufe*, the autobiographies or biographies of members from various *Gemeinen*; these were read at funerals. A third section consisted of information from the Unity Elders Conference and was usually directed solely at the local Elders Conferences.

52. After 1750, the Single Sisters wore deep-pink ribbons (designated in at least one source as red), the Married Sisters wore blue, and the widows wore white. Thus, a ceremonial change of ribbon accompanied the change of Choir. The ritual of this ceremony emphasized the change of Choir in a way very similar to the giving of the bride at a wedding ceremony. The head of the former Choir removed

the current ribbon, and the head of the receiving Choir attached the new ribbon. The practice of passing the kiss of peace was based on the Scriptural injunction "greet one another with an holy kiss." The documentary evidence suggests that the various Choir colors were changed occasionally over time. Clearly, work remains to be done in this area.

53. *Lebenslauf* of Rachel Bagge, 1734–99, English version, MA-SP. All of the *Lebensläufe* are in manuscript form. Most are in German, although a few are also in an English manuscript version. They are filed alphabetically in the memoir file. Selected *Leben* in the Salem archives have been translated.

54. Nelson, "Herrnhut," 288–89.

55. *Lebenslauf* of Friedrich Wilhelm von Marschall, 1721–1802, MA-SP. The quotation is taken from the English translation of the German original (translator undesignated).

56. *Lebenslauf* of Maria Elisabeth Praezel, 1750–1821, MA-SP (quotation taken from the translation by Bishop Taylor Hamilton); *Lebenslauf* of Carl L. Meinung, 1748–1817, MA-SP (quotation taken from the translation by Frances Cumnock).

57. *Lebenslauf* of Gottlieb Strehle, 1756–1815, MA-SP.

58. *Lebenslauf* of Christina Dixon Biwighaus, 1756–1835, MA-SP. Translated by Elisabeth Marx. The quotation cited is taken from the German original.

59. Synodal Compendium., vol. 1, chap. 6, sect. 405, 405.

60. In the early years of the Unity, discipline could be quite painful. In November 1732, Zinzendorf, acting as judge, declared, "As Johann Jacob Liebich has given offense among the children . . . [he] is not only in like manner put out of the orphanage [i.e., the current *Anstalt*] but has to avoid Herrnhut and moreover, should be treated as a convict with hard work and severe blows for four weeks." In 1734, two youths who went out into the countryside during devotional time received twelve blows and a "sharp reprimand," In 1735, an apprentice was imprisoned after frequent disobedience to his master. In 1736, three apprentices were whipped and confined for insubordination. In the same year, two young men who spoke "light-mindedly" to one of the Sisters had to cart grain for six days. And, in 1737, a member of the College of Judges wrote, "My son has been imprisoned and whipped . . . because he has taken some *Groschen* and frittered them away." Nor was harsh punishment always confined to males. In 1744, four Sisters were discovered to have been meeting (in what was referred to as an *unerlaubte Zusammenkunfte*) with a "stranger" who worked in the tavern. One received 300 blows; the others received 170 and 160, respectively, and were sent to the manorial farm as servants. The fourth initially refused to admit guilt but later submitted and was expelled from Herrnhut. Uttendörfer, *Alt Herrnhut*, 99, 101–2; Uttendörfer, *Wirtschaftsgeist*, 189.

61. Minutes of the Salem Elders Conference (hereafter referred to as Min. EC.), July 18, 1778, no. 1.

62. All information regarding the members of the Elders Conference is taken from their *Lebensläufe*.

63. The German records do often refer to him as von Marschall.

64. *Lebenslauf* of Gertraut Graff, 1721–84, MA-SP. The quotation cited is taken from the translation by Bishop Hamilton.

65. The information used to create this profile is taken from the *Lebensläufe* of the various members.

3. Battling Chaos

1. Minutes of the Salem Gemeine Council (hereafter referred to as Min. GC.), Sept. 5, 1786, MA-SP, J297A:1. The text reads, "Es sey den Geschwister schon öfters, . . . dringend zu Gemuthe geführt worden, nicht zu vergessen, daß uns der Heiland zu Seinem Zeugenvolk berufen, und wir uns daher allen Werke des Fleisches and der Vernunft und was irgend Seine Absicht mit uns hindern könnte, zu reinigen verbunden wären. Wir müssten aber mit Schaam und Schmerz gestehen, daß ohngeachtet solcher wiederhalten Aufmunterungen und Warnungen noch manches in dem Wandel mehrerer hiesigen Einwohner übrig bliebe, was zur Ueppigkeit und Wollust dieser Lebens, und zum Welt und Fleisches Sinn gehöre."

2. Jack Greene gave a good overview of the declension issue in *Pursuits of Happiness*, 58–61.

3. These figures have been adjusted to exclude children under twelve who were neither subject to expulsion nor eligible for Communion. The adult population of Salem in 1801 was 180 (this figure only accounts for those who were official inhabitants and does not include day laborers or "strangers"). A comparison with the number of those excluded by the consistory of Geneva from 1559 to 1569 serves to point up how seriously the Brethren took discipline. Over a ten-week period at the height of its activity, the consistory excluded an average of five per week and twenty per month. If we look at the figures for Salem during the 1780s, we find that the number of those excluded from Communion averaged twenty per month. Given the vastly larger population of Geneva during the sixteenth century, the activity of the Salem Elders Conference actually exceeds that of the Geneva consistory during Calvin's tenure. The figures for Geneva are taken from Monter, "Consistory of Geneva," 467–87.

4. These figures have been gathered by combining information available in the extracts of the minutes of the Herrnhut *Aufseher Collegium,* which include a monthly list of all people expelled from the *Gemeine,* and information in the extracts of the Herrnhut Elders Conference.

5. Minutes of the Salem Aufseher Collegium (hereafter referred to as Min. Auf. Colleg.), Oct. 22, 1778, MA-SP, J298A:1. The passages cited from the Min. Auf. Colleg. are from the translation by Erika Hubner, unless otherwise noted. Passages from the records of all other ruling bodies are taken from the German original and are my translation.

6. Minutes of the Single Brothers House Conferences (hereafter referred to as Min. SBC.), Feb. 5, 1783, no.1, MA-SP, J302B:1. A similar admonition appears in the minutes for April 22, 1787, and for Feb. 24, 1788.

7. Ibid., Sept. 23, 1787, no. 2.

8. Min. Auf. Colleg., Aug. 15, 1797, no. 3.

9. Min. EC., Feb. 8, 1797, no. 3.

10. Extracts of the Minutes of the Herrnhut Elders Conference (hereafter referred to as Extracts Min. EC. Herrnhut), Jan. 14, 1792, UA-Herrnhut,

R6.A.b.41.b; Minutes of the Unity Elders Conference (hereafter referred to as Min. UEC.), Sept. 11, 1793, 315, UA-Herrnhut, R3.B.4.f (all of the minutes of this body have the same catalog number).

11. Extracts of the Minutes of the Herrnhut Aufseher Collegium (hereafter referred to as Extracts Min. Auf .Colleg. Herrnhut), Oct.-Dec. 1791, pt. 7, no. 1; ibid., Jan.-March 1792, pt. 6, no. 1, UA-Herrnhut, R6.A.b.49.a.

12. Min. EC., Dec. 11, 1782, no. 7.

13. Caldwell, *Puritan Conversion Narrative*, chap. 6.

14. Min. Auf. Colleg., Oct. 31, 1780; Min. EC., Feb. 24, 1781, no. 3; The *Collegium* specified that the boys should not ask about the life of a soldier or about details of military maneuvers.

15. Min. EC., Nov. 4, 1780, no. 1.

16. Single Brothers Diary (hereafter referred to as SB Diary), Dec. 15, 1787, MA-SP, J302A:19.

17. Min. Auf. Colleg., Nov. 3, 1795, no. 4; ibid., July 4, 1797, no. 3. The problem did not diminish with time. In 1801, one young Brother was "severely" admonished for continuing his connection with stranger day laborers and "often being in their company in the tavern, especially in the evening." Min. EC., Dec. 9, 1801, no. 3.

18. Extracts Min. Auf. Colleg. Herrnhut, Jan.-March 1795, pt. 4, no. 2. The text reads, "Da das vor einige Zeit ins Land ergangene Pulicandum zur Erläuterung des Mandats wider Tumult und Aufruhe eigentlich nur die Dorfgemeinden betrifft."

19. Czok, *Geschichte Sachsens*, 306-10.

20. It is worth noting that one of the rare direct references is a positive one. In 1791, the UEC remarked that as a result of the current "freedom of conscience" in France, the Brethren had a freer hand to evangelize. This was, of course, before the Revolution took a more radical direction. Min. UEC., Jan. 20, 1791, 145-46.

21. Synod Report of 1764, sect. 43, 49.

22. Min. EC., Feb. 20, 1788, no. 8; ibid., Nov. 11, 1795, no. 4.

23. Erbe, "Erziehung und Schulen," 320. Even after the responsibility for raising children was turned back to the parents, many still placed their children in the nursery when the parents were called to another *Gemeine* or were in deep financial difficulty.

24. Uttendörfer, *Wirschaftsgeist*, 51.

25. Friedrich Wilhelm von Marschall to Peter Boehler, Feb. 1775, UA-Herrnhut, R14.B.b.11.a.

26. Because the Unity forbade guilds in its settlements, the artisans raised in the *Gemeine* were not eligible for guild membership. Although, by 1775, the UEC was willing to make exceptions and allow some to become guild members, evidence suggests that this remained relatively rare. The lack of guild training made getting a position or establishing a trade difficult in most German towns.

27. Min. UEC., Nov. 3, 1784, no. 1, 291-92.

28. Ibid., Nov. 1, 1792, no. 6, 183.

29. Ibid., April 6, 1793, no. 6, 25-26.

30. Min. EC., Feb. 1, 1792, no. 4; ibid., Feb. 15, 1792, no. 3.

31. Ibid., March 22, 1797, no. 1.

32. The other expelled family man was the town doctor. The course of his discipline serves as further confirmation of the tendency to excuse heads of households from the most severe discipline. He was first warned of impending expulsion in February 1787 (after being excluded from Communion for nine months in a year and a half), then given notice in April but allowed to stay. He was finally expelled in December of that year, although he did not leave until the spring of 1788. The Elders Conference initially contented themselves with a warning because they did not want to deprive his wife of the benefits of the *Gemeine*. Ibid., Feb. 21, 1787, no. 2.

33. Ibid., March 26, 1783, no. 1.

34. Ibid., May 3, 1796, no. 5.

35. Ibid., May 3, 1796, no. 6.

36. Min. UEC., Sept. 17, 1793, no. 4, 336.

37. Ibid., Nov. 12, 1791, no. 5, 251.

38. Min. UEC., Dec. 1, 1800, 223; Ibid., Dec. 20, 1800, 300–1.

39. Andreas Schober to Marschall, March 21, 1773, MA-SP, Letter File A-13:3.

40. Extracts Min. EC. Herrnhut, Nov. 11, 1793, no. 2.

41. Extracts of the Minutes of the Neuwied Elders Conference (hereafter referred to as Min. EC. Neuwied), Nov. 20, 1779; ibid., Nov. 27, 1779, UA-Herrnhut, R7.G.b.4.b.

42. See, for example, the visitation reports for Gnadau in 1797 and for Neusalz in 1799.

43. Min. EC., March 22, 1780, no. 3.

44. The figures cited for the increase in courtships and so forth err on the side of caution, as two of the cases in the 1780s involved more than one couple (in one case, five were involved), and one incident in the 1790s involved four couples. The Brethren tended to elope en masse.

45. Min. UEC., Dec. 21, 1785, 600.

46. Ibid., Oct. 22, 1787, 130.

47. Ibid., July 20, 1790, 113. The visitation report indicates that things had been allowed to come to this pass because the former Single Brothers *Diener* had maintained that stopping this commerce would injure other businesses. Part of the difficulty involved the need to set aside a special room to accommodate such traffic. Neusalz Visitation Report, 1787, UA-Herrnhut, R7.E.a.9.

48. Jonathan Briant to Johann Christian Geisler, March 5, 1795, UA-Herrnhut, R7.C.I.a.12.a (no. 11).

49. Extracts Min. Auf. Colleg. Herrnhut, Oct.-Dec. 1791, pt. 7, no. 1; ibid., July-Sept. 1793, pt. 6, no. 1. As an added precaution, the Elders Conference admonished the older girls who served as nursemaids to stick carefully to the times and places prescribed for their walks. Extracts Min. EC. Herrnhut, June 22, 1793, no. 2. It is also worth noting that by 1795 the UEC expressed unhappiness with the "mixing" that occurred in choral groups. They feared that this occasioned an "inadmissible connection" between musicians. Min. UEC., May 10, 1795, 168.

50. Min. Auf. Colleg., May 26, 1779.

51. Reuß expressed his views in a conversation with his *Gemeine* authorities,

who then relayed them to the UEC. Carl August Baumeister and M. Winckler to Johannes Loretz, Dec. 31, 1787, UA-Herrnhut, R6.D.I.b.12 (no. 161).

52. Visitation Report for Barby, Feb. 10, 1784, 68, and Feb. 16, 1784, 101, UA-Herrnhut, R6.D.I.a.30.

53. Min. EC., Aug. 2, 1780, no. 2.

54. Min. UEC., Sept. 22, 1795, 384–85.

55. Ibid., March 27, 1788, 425.

56. Extracts Min. EC. Herrnhut, March 3, 1792, no. 1.

57. Min. EC., Sept. 23, 1801, no. 6.

58. Ibid., Dec. 2, 1801, no. 3. A similar situation had arisen in Herrnhut in 1797 when a journeyman potter was expelled for becoming engaged to his master's daughter after the lot had negated the match. The UEC commented that the Elders Conference should not have asked the lot because the couple's "inclination toward each other had gone so far." They also took the master potter to task for keeping the journeyman in his house "when he knew the marriage between him and his daughter had fallen away." Although the UEC labeled this behavior "incautious," it is possible that Brother Rosler favored the match and deliberately turned a blind eye to the "danger." Min. UEC., Aug. 8, 1797, 126–27.

59. Extracts of the Minutes of the Gnadenberg Elders Conference (hereafter referred to as Extracts Min. EC. Gnadenberg), March 17, 1785, UA-Herrnhut, R7.C.I.b.5.b.a2. All following references to this incident are taken from this entry.

60. Sabean, *Property*, 330–34.

61. Extracts Min. EC. Gnadenberg, June 6, 1794, no. 1.

62. Ibid., Nov. 15, 1794, no. 15.

63. Extracts of the Minutes of the Niesky Elders Conference (hereafter referred to as Extracts Min. EC. Niesky), Nov. 3, 1784; Min. UEC., Nov. 6, 1784, 334, UA-Herrnhut, R6.B.I.b.15.b-c. The same entry also reports the troublesome discovery of a "sinful connection" between two Single Brothers. The sin in question was sexual, but it is not clear whether one encouraged the other to frequent "loose women" or to engage in homosexual acts.

64. Min. UEC., Jan. 21, 1797, 101–2.

65. Ibid., Dec. 19, 1793, 318–19.

66. Min. Auf. Colleg., Oct. 18, 1785; Min. EC., March 3, 1794, no. 2.

67. Extracts Min. EC. Herrnhut, Nov. 3, 1791, no. 2.

68. Christian Gregor to Jeremias Risler, May 14, 1792, UA-Herrnhut, R7.C.I.a.12.a (no. 15).

69. Extracts Min. EC. Neuwied, July 4, 1792, no. 4.

70. In his work on the cult of sensibility in eighteenth-century Britain, G.J. Barker-Benfield cited the importance of the novel in establishing "sentimental fashion" because of its stress on the "language of feeling." Barker-Benfield identified the resemblance between the "language of feeling" and Methodist devotion, but this language was also very much a part of the Moravian devotional world. The similarity underscores the rivalry between the culture of holiness and the culture of sensibility. More important for the issue at hand, Barker-Benfield pointed to the frequent association of novel reading with becoming "sexually inflammable." This was thought to be especially true when the readers were young women. The leader-

ship of the Brethren seem to have shared this assumption. See Barker-Benfield, *Culture of Sensibility, xix,* 325–26. Jeffrey Watt also connected contemporary literature with changing ideas on marriage in his study *The Making of Modern Marriage.* See especially 265–70.

71. Extracts Min. EC. Herrnhut, April 21, 1792, no. 1.

72. Extracts of the Minutes of the Kleinwelke Elders Conference (hereafter referred to as Extracts Min. EC. Kleinwelke), Sept. 4, 1797, no. 3, UA-Herrnhut, R6.C.b.4.b.

73. Guido Ruggiero included a discussion of the relationship between "correct" passion directed at family, state, and God and "unbound" passions of the flesh in *Binding Passions: Tales of Magic, Marriage, and Power at the End of the Renaissance* (New York: Oxford Univ. Press, 1993), chap. 1, especially 11–12.

74. A couple of examples from the records do underscore the fact that practical considerations could still override romantic attraction. In one case, a Single Sister became engaged without approval, but when her intended proved unable to find work in a nearby town, she thought better of her decision and withdrew from the match. In another case, a young Single Sister had been courted by a watchmaker at a hunt in Großwelke and had given him her written promise of marriage. When the Elders Conference pointed out that both parties were only nineteen and had no possessions, she wrote a letter taking back her promise. Min. EC. Herrnhut, Feb. 3, 1800; ibid., Feb. 15, 1800, no. 2.

75. Single Sisters Diary, June 29, 1794, MA-SP, J303A:1a.

76. Min. EC., July 9, 1794.

77. Extracts Min. EC. Herrnhut, March 30, 1797, no. 3.

78. Ibid., March 30, 1797, no. 8.

79. Min. UEC., March 16, 1789, 349.

80. Extracts Min. EC. Herrnhut, Nov. 15, 1790; April 10, 1794, no. 3; March 30, 1797, no. 8

81. In the North Carolina *Gemeinen,* this insistence on personal choice also surfaced in the slave community. In 1803, the governing committee in Bethania noted, "Negroes and Negresses here in town would not marry each other, because for their part they wish to make their own choices. One Brother remarked that if he had an adult Negro and an adult Negress they would not want to marry each other because one would not be right for the other." Minutes of the Bethania Committee, May 30, 1803. Quoted in Sensbach, *A Separate Canaan,* 485.

82. Jonathan Briant to Johann Christian Geisler, Feb. 28, 1795, UA-Herrnhut, R7.C.I.a.12.a (no. 10). The text reads, "Dann sind auch freilich Leute da, und nicht geringer Anzahl, die nicht wissen was sie in der Gemeine wollen, noch einen Eindruck davon haben, was der Heiland für einen Zweck darunter hat, daß Er sie zur Gemeine gebracht hat; sondern so unbekümmert drauf los leben, wie andere Leute auch."

83. Ritual as a means of marking a distinction from the world is discussed by Hall in *Worlds of Wonder,* 117.

84. Reichel, "Samuel Christlieb Reichel," 12.

85. Isaac, *Transformation of Virginia.* See also Ekirch, *Poor Carolina.*

86. Min. EC., Feb. 7, 1775.

87. Ibid., March 13, 1783, no. 11; Min. Auf. Colleg., June 2, 1795, no. 3.

88. Min. EC., Dec. 30, 1777, no. 2. See also Jan. 11, 1786, no. 8. The Salem Elders held authority over the outlying settlements such as Bethania.

89. See, for example, Min. EC., Sept. 14 and Oct. 19, 1779; also Oct. 13, 1796. In September 1779, one of the Bethanians "rudely opposed" the prohibition on attendance at the cornhuskings. The practice of cornhuskings seems to mirror the European spinning bee gatherings as a potential meeting ground for young people.

90. For an overview of spinning bees and their role in courtship, see Hans Medick, "Village Spinning Bees."

91. Min. EC., June 14, 1783, and March 22, 1786, no. 16.

92. There is even today a notable difference in the cultural life and social structure of Herrnhut and its neighboring villages.

93. Min. UEC., Oct. 23, 1793, 90; ibid., June 14, 1794, 294. In referring to the June incident, the minutes specify that "*more* Single Sisters" went to the Bernstadt soothsayer and lament that this happens all too often. It is also well worth noting that the minutes strongly suggest that the Sisters went to the wise woman to inquire about their future marital status. The text in question reads, "Mehrere ledige Schwestern daselbst sich von einen Frau in Bernstadt wegen ihrer künftigen Schicksale habe wahrsagen lassen, welches bereits vorm Jahr geschehen, aber erst kürzlich entdeckt worden ist. Einige dieser Schwestern sind jetzt schon verheirathetes ist zu bedauern daß jetzt so oft dergleich vorkommt." Earlier the problem had been thought serious enough to warrant a new admonition against "superstitious ideas and customs" in the synod report of 1789. Extract of the Report of the Synod of 1789, chap. 1, article 11, MA-SP.

94. See, for example, Extracts Min. EC. Herrnhut, July 11, 1795, no. 4; ibid., July 13, 1795, no. 5; Min. UEC., July 9, 1795, 37–38; ibid., July 30, 1796, 90; Extracts Min. EC. Herrnhut, March 10, 1798, no. 3; ibid., Oct. 25, 1798, no. 2. Although the leadership of the Brethren consistently opposed theatrics, a discussion of an incident in 1795 indicates an intriguing shift in thinking. Several Single Brothers in Herrnhut justified their attendance at a play in Strahwalde by pointing out that "some reputable people in the *Gemeine* had watched the shadow play in Zittau, and even a magician's show here in their houses." The Herrnhut Elders Conference failed to note the incursion of "superstitious" entertainment and instead noted that there was a "big difference" between "mechanical art" and dramas designed to heat and arouse the emotions. Perhaps, they sensed a rival to their own sacred drama. Clearly, they viewed the pull of the passions as a greater threat than "superstition," however deplorable the latter. They also said they would "gladly" allow the Brethren to go to see circus riders, "outlandish animals," and giants. It should be noted, however, that this entry has a question mark and double lines in the margin beside it. Because the UEC members read the extracts and often discussed them, it seems reasonable to assume that these are their marks. They appear to have disagreed with the Elders Conference on this matter. Extracts Min. EC. Herrnhut, July 13, 1795.

95. Min. UEC., May 23, 1796, 215; Extracts Min. EC. Herrnhut, June 30, 1798. The use of expulsion can probably be attributed to the fact that he also

admitted that he had tried to establish "an epistolary [*schriftliche*] connection" with young Dorothea Geillichin.

96. Min. UEC., Jan. 23, 1790, 132–33.

97. Ibid., Aug. 10, 1793, 156; Extracts Min. EC. Herrnhut, March 7, 1795, no. 5. The complete text of the 1795 entry reads, "Weil zu vermuthen war, daß zu der in Ottenheyn bevorstehenden Execution einer Mörderin verschiedene junge Brüder gehen wollen; so hielt man für nöthig es zu widerathen, wegen der dabey zu bevorgehenden Unordnung und der unangenehmen Eindrücken, die eine solche Execution auf ihrer Gemuthe, durchs ansehen derselben, haben könnte."

98. Johann Christian Geisler to Jacques Duvernoy, May 15, 1799, UA-Herrnhut, R7.E.a.9. The text reads, "So wie nun die Geschwister sahen, daß der Gemeinhelfer da war, so strömtz jung und alt auch dahin, und sahen die geilsten Posituren, die insonderheit eine Frauensperson machte sich auf ein Seit hinlegte, und Mannspersonen auf ihren Leib sich legten und drauf herum traten, worauf sie schrie mehr Manns Leute her [zu ihr] und dergleich."

99. Extracts Min. EC. Herrnhut, Nov. 11, 1797, no. 3. Another Single Brother who had gone to a fair in Neukirch after being told not to left the *Gemeine*. Ibid., Oct. 21, 1799.

100. See, for example, Extracts Min. EC. Herrnhut, March 2, 1786, Jan. 14, 1792, and Dec. 12, 1796, as well as Extracts Min. Auf. Colleg. Herrnhut, Feb. 11, 1780. The Elders Conference reported the following of the 1796 incident: "We must very much disapprove of the incautious conduct of the two Single Brothers Königheer and Burckhardt, who drank brandy and smoked tobacco here in the inn before an appointed sleigh journey. As a result they became so drunk [*benebelnt*] that they went straight to sleep in the sleigh and on their return had to be carried out of it, which gave much offense."

101. Extracts Min, Auf, Colleg. Herrnhut, Nov. 23, 1793; Dec. 21, 1797; Jan. 14, 1792. The Herrnhut Elders Conference minutes also refer to the exclusion from Communion of the cook in the Single Brothers House for dancing at a tavern in a neighboring village. Jan. 16, 1797. The prohibition on "partying" in taverns extended to the villages over which the Unity had manorial authority, but the Unity came to recognize the futility of the restriction. In a discussion of a request for permission to have music and dancing at the tavern in Großhennersdorf, the UEC considered lifting the restriction for that village and for Berthelsdorf. The elders observed that prohibiting music and dance simply led people to turn to "outside taverns," which led to "fist fighting and all sorts of disorderly conduct" so that one could not say the "morality of these people" was helped by the restriction. They did not, however, discuss allowing dancing in the *Ortsgemeinen*. Min. UEC., Nov. 20, 1797, 182–84.

102. Min. UEC., April 27, 1790, 143–44.

103. Briant to Geisler, March 23, 1795, UA-Herrnhut, R7.C.I.a.12.a (no. 15).

104. Uttendörfer, *Wirtschaftsgeist*, 30.

105. Min. UEC., Oct. 20, 1785, 150–52. The text defines the following as "obscene" male clothing: "when the fastening of the jacket . . . is too narrow at the bottom, the vests made without fastenings or too short, and so broadly cut out in front that the lower part of the body is not decently and properly covered on either

side; further, when Brothers wear an open shirt furnished with a shirt frill [*Busenstreifen*] under an unbuttoned vest so that the bare breast is visible." For women, "when these do not cover their throat sufficiently; so too *otherwise* much vanity often radiates from *their* clothing." The remainder of the note concerning female dress detailed the various "vanities" to which they were prone.

106. Extracts Min. EC. Neuwied, Dec. 29, 1792, no. 2.

107. Extracts Min. Auf. Colleg. Herrnhut, April-June 1793, pt. 6, no. 1; Extracts Min. EC. Herrnhut, Aug. 24, 1793, no. 5.

108. Briant to Geisler, Feb. 28, 1795. The following references are also taken from this letter.

109. Min. UEC., May 11, 1793, 184. Both Gnadenfrei and Gnadenberg had a relatively large number of noble members.

110. Geisler to Samuel Liebish, Aug. 4, 1799, UA-Herrnhut, R7.F.a.3.a-b. The minutes of the UEC for 1797 contain a similar note about the wearing of gowns by poor women. In this case, the head of the Single Sisters, Marianne von Watteville, spoke of the incursion of "vanity" and expressed specific concern that daughters of families on poor relief went about in gowns. Min. UEC., May 23, 1797, 207–8.

111. Barker-Benfield identified a similar trend in England, which he tied to the role of resort towns in exposing servants to upper-class recreation and, thus, upper-class tastes. A quotation he gave from Bernard de Mandeville echoes Geisler's sentiments: "The poorest Laborer's wife . . . will half starve herself and her Husband to purchase a secondhand Gown and Petticoat . . . because . . . it is more genteel." 178.

112. Min. UEC., May 6, 1782, 156–57.

113. Hall, *Worlds of Wonder*, 55–57.

114. Enclosures of the Synod of 1789, vol. 1, n.pag., UA-Herrnhut, R2.B.48.e. Aside from novels and "free-thinking pamphlets," the seminary library itself, at least after 1788, contained several works by thinkers associated with the Enlightenment including Voltaire, Montesquieu, Wolff, Moses Mendelsohn, Leibnitz, and Rousseau. This information is taken from Catalogus der von den Erben der selig Bruder Köber künftig ubernammenen Bibliothec [*sic*] and Catalogus von aus der von Schrautenbachischen Bibliothec, UA-Herrnhut.

115. Min. UEC., June 11, 1785, 459. The text reads, "Seine Seele ist mit lauter nur einern Bildern erfüllt; er verfertigt Gedichte solchen Inhalts, und sein Gemuthe ist ganz darauf gestellt, sich allen Lusten zu ergeben."

116. Ibid., May 16, 1787, 259; July 19, 1787, 127–28. In 1790, Spangenberg expressed distress "that so many journals are kept in the seminary" and feared that the young Brothers "could suffer harm through this." Min. UEC., Nov. 6, 1790, 251.

117. Ibid., May 10, 1794, 167; Oct. 1, 1794, 4.

118. Ibid., May 7, 1791, 216; Feb. 27, 1794, 301. The seminary director also referred specifically to the influence of Kant's philosophy. Ibid., Aug. 21, 1794, 200–1.

4. Gambling with God

Much of the material in this chapter has appeared previously in Elisabeth Sommer, "Gambling with God: The Use of the Lot among the Moravian Brethren in the Eighteenth Century," *Journal of the History of Ideas* 59 (1998): 267–86. I thank the journal for permission to use material from this article.

1. Fix, *Prophecy and Reason*, 3, 5.

2. Becker, "Pietism's Confrontation," 140, 143–45. Count Nicholas Ludwig von Zinzendorf, the dominant influence in the development of the new Unity, attended the pädegogium at Halle from 1710 to 1716. Ironically, Enlightenment ideas penetrated the University of Halle, and, consequently, it became a source of trouble to the Unity in the late eighteenth century. This trouble resulted in part from the proximity of the university and its students to the Unity seminary at Barby. In an attempt to remove the prospective leaders from its influence, the Synod of 1789 decided to move the seminary to Niesky in the Oberlausitz. While this location lessened the "danger," as far as the seminary students were concerned, many other Brethren, particularly those from noble families, continued to have contact with Halle and other universities.

3. Ibid., 146, 149. See also LaVopa, *Grace, Talent, and Merit*, chaps. 5 and 6.

4. On free prophecy, Becker, "Pietism's Confrontation," 162.

5. This situation throws some doubt on the generalized association of Enlightenment views with elite culture and of continued adherence to the supernatural with popular culture because the members of the Unity as a whole were quite literate and the leadership often came from noble families.

6. E. Beyreuther, "Lostheorie," 112.

7. Ibid., 113; on pilgrimage image, ibid., 126.

8. G. Brenner and R. Brenner, *Gambling and Speculation*, 1–3. The Moslem Arabs and American Indians also used the lot in a similar sense, with the Moslems limiting its use to judges and priests. Ibid., 4.

9. Ibid., 6.

10. Schlatter, *Richard Baxter*, 107. I am grateful to Erik Midelfort for steering me to Baxter's comments on the lot.

11. Ibid., 108. The following quotation is also from this page.

12. It should be noted, however, that Baxter's attitude toward science has been classed as generally critical. Becker, "Pietism's Confrontation," 143, 148.

13. This may well have been Baxter's attempt to offset any objection that election was less divinely ordained than was hereditary monarchy.

14. Luther, *Werke*, vol. 19, 212–13.

15. Ibid., 213.

16. Ibid., 212–13. I am indebted to a note in the English-language edition of Luther's works for the observation regarding games of chance. Martin Luther, *Works* (St. Louis, Mo.: Concordia Publishing House, 1964), 19:62. The German original reads, "Die ist nichts arges, sondern eyn fridliche vereynigunge und verwilligung, des dings zu emperen oder zu haben, nach dem das messer mal odder unmal tregt, nach dem es gerade oder ungerade ist und so fort an."

17. Luther, *Werke*, 214.

18. Fix, *Prophecy and Reason*, 12.

19. E. Beyreuther, "Lostheorie," 119.

20. Hahn, "Theologie," 248.

21. Shapiro, *Probability and Certainty*, 77; Fix, *Prophecy and Reason*, 86–119.

22. According to Erich Beyreuther, it is for this reason that Zinzendorf was so fond of Pierre Bayle, who mercilessly attacked the "reasonableness" of religion. E. Beyreuther, "Paradoxie," 201–11.

23. Hahn, "Theologie," 247.

24. E. Beyreuther, "Lostheorie," 130.

25. Spangenberg, *Count Zinzendorf*, 4.

26. E. Beyreuther, "Lostheorie," 117–18.

27. Ibid., 118–19. Proverbs 8:31 reads, "And my [wisdom's] delights were with the sons of men."

28. E. Beyreuther, "Ehe-Religion," 36.

29. Hahn and Reichel, *Zinzendorf und die Herrnhuter Brüder*, 246.

30. Zinzendorf, *Büdingsche Sammlungen*, vol. 1, 521.

31. E. Beyreuther, "Lostheorie," 130–31.

32. Ibid., 127.

33. The blank lot was also used in the process for admission to membership in the *Gemeine* (1769) and candidature for Communion (1764). In these cases, if the blank were drawn, the leadership could either ask what the Savior meant or use only the blank and a "yes" when the individual next came up for admission or candidature. Synod Report of 1769. Special appendix reserved for the Elders Conference. MA-SP.

34. Minutes of the Synod of 1769, vol. 1, session 12:204, UA-Herrnhut, R2.B.45.1.a. During the Synod of 1764, one Brother remarked that the blank lot allowed for more "certainty." Minutes of the Synod of 1764, vol. 1, session 10:579, UA-Herrnhut, R2.B.44.1.c.

35. Minutes of the Synod of 1764, vol. 1, session 10:553, UA-Herrnhut, R2.B.44.1.c.

36. Extract of the Minutes of the Synod of 1764, n.pag.

37. Minutes of the Synod of 1764., vol. 1, session 10:575.

38. Ibid., vol. 1, session 10:574.

39. Ibid., vol. 1, session 10:559.

40. Ibid., vol. 1, session 10:554.

41. Ibid., vol. 1, session 11:582–84. It is worth noting that although the word *anbeten* translates as "worship," the Unity had a special service designated as the *Anbeten* in which they literally prostrated themselves before the Lord.

42. This was actually done, and several of these lot books survive. A study of them would give much insight into such things as marriage patterns and the process of decision making.

43. Becker, "Pietism's Confrontation," 148; LaVopa, *Grace, Talent and Merit*, 147. This dual strain within Pietism is also discussed in a recent bibliographical survey by Ward, "German Pietism," 479–505, especially 478–79.

44. Minutes of the Synod of 1769, session 15:246–47.

45. Ibid., vol. 1, session 26:465–66.

46. Ibid., vol. 1, session 26:466.

47. Ibid., vol. 1, session 12:200.

48. Ibid., vol. 1, session 14:224. It is possible that the biblical image of paternal care had been reinforced by years of its use in the service of state-building. Although, clearly, the Brethren did not have an absolutist system, they still faced the similar problem of subordinating individual wills to the good of the whole. For them, the problem was complicated by their conviction that this subordination had to be free-willing and come from the heartfelt love of Christ.

49. Ibid., vol. 1, session 12:207–8.

50. Ibid., vol. 1, session 12:201.

51. Ibid., vol. 1, session 14:233–34, and 242. The synod also declared that no decision regarding the outward circumstances of a member should ever be put to the lot without hearing from the member first.

52. Petitions to the Synod of 1769, n. pag., UA-Herrnhut, R2.B.47.b.a.2.b.2.

53. Minutes of the Synod of 1769, vol. 1, session 12:204. Interestingly, in my own research, I have only been able to identify one clear case of manipulation of the lot.

54. Ibid., vol. 1, session 26:468.

55. Hall, *Worlds of Wonder*, 139.

56. Min. UEC, Dec. 2, 1773, 353.

57. Ibid.

58. Ibid., 354.

59. Ibid., July 4, 1778, 32–33, no. 7.

60. These figures come from the extracts of the Minutes of the Herrnhut Aufseher Collegium.

61. Minutes of the Synod of 1782, vol. 1, session 10:222–23, UA-Herrnhut, R.2.B.47.b.a.2.b.2.

62. Ibid., vol. 1, session 10:233.

63. Ibid., 233.

64. Ibid., session 12:250.

65. Ibid., session 12:251.

66. Sommer, "Serving Two Masters," 208.

67. Min. UEC, Oct. 20, 1784, 188; Extracts of the Minutes of the Gnadenfrei Elders Conference (hereafter referred to as Extract Min. EC. Gnadenfrei), Oct. 25, 1788, no. 5, UA-Herrnhut, R7.D.I.d.5.

68. Count Heinrich 39th Reuß to Carl August Baumeister and M. Winckler, Dec. 29, 1787, UA-Herrnhut, R6.D.I.b.12 (no. 160).

69. Baumeister and Winckler to Johannes Loretz, Dec. 31, 1787.

70. G. Beyreuther, "Sexualltheorien im Pietismus," 49.

71. Baumeister and Winckler to Loretz. The following observations are also from this letter.

72. Enclosures of the Synod of 1789, vol. 2, n.pag..

73. Extract of the Minutes of the Gnadau Elders Conference (hereafter referred to as Extracts Min. EC. Gnadau), June 10, 1786, no. 2, UA-Herrnhut, R6.D.II.b.4.a. The term used by the Elders Conference was actually *schlechten Gang*, which indicates a specific concern with the spiritual development of the boys. *Gang* most commonly referred to a member's spiritual "walk."

74. La Vopa, *Grace, Talent, and Merit,* 166–67.

75. Enclosures of the Synod of 1789 (Remarks on the *Harmony of the Four Synods*). In Beilagen der Synod 1789. R2.B.48.e. The following remark is also from this source.

76. Minutes of the Synod of 1789, vol. 2, session 25:596.

77. Schlatter, *Richard Baxter,* 108.

78. Minutes of the Synod of 1789, vol. 2, session 25:599–600.

79. Ibid., session 25:607–8.

80. Ibid., session 25:613–17.

81. Ibid., vol. 4, session 27:1239. The debate was sparked by the fact that the Synod of 1782 had allowed the city and country *Gemeinen,* which were congregations rather than congregation *settlements,* to dispense with the use of the lot in marriages.

82. Ibid., vol. 4, session 27:1243–44, 1247. One Brother's remark about the dependence on the Savior indicates a continued sense of the immediacy of Christ's presence: "When a circumstance arises which makes a human decision difficult, who could we better ask for counsel than our dearest Savior who is always ready to do more for us than we ask?" Ibid., session 27:1244.

83. Ibid., vol. 4, session 27:1245.

84. Ibid., vol. 2, session.. 25:597.

85. Min. UEC., Sept. 11, 1793, 3:313, no. 4e. Four years later, things were no better. Jacques Duvernoy spoke of the inability to continue coping with "the determined free spirits," who only laughed at admonitions to adhere to the *Gemeine* regulations. Ibid., 1797, 2:206.

86. Briant to Geisler, March 5, 1795. These complaints echo those voiced by the Puritan clergy as they watched their youth increasingly attracted to "worldly" culture. See Hall, *Worlds of Wonder.*

87. Min. UEC., March 21, 1796, 407.

88. Min. UEC., 1797, 4:205, no. 3, and 209, no. 1.

89. Ibid., 1796, 4:229, no. 7.

90. Ibid., 1797, 3:126–27, no. 2.

91. Surratt, *Gottlieb Schober,* 91.

92. Gottlieb Schober to Johann Daniel Köhler, Sept. 16, 1800, UA-Herrnhut, R2.B.49.d.

93. Minutes of the Synod of 1801, vol. 1, session 22:28, UA-Herrnhut, R2.B.49.a-b2.

94. Ibid., vol. 1, session 22:29–30.

95. Ibid., vol. 1, session 25:80.

96. Ibid., vol. 1, session 10:30 and session 23:41.

97. Ibid., vol. 1, session 10:158–60.

98. Ibid., vol. 1, session 4:113.

99. Ibid., vol. 1, session 5:123–26. The Elders Conferences supporting the lot included Litiz (in Pennsylvania), Ebersdorf, Barby, Gnadau, Gnadenberg (all in Germany), and, surprisingly, Herrnhut. The original of the dissenting memorandum is missing, so it is difficult to determine which Brethren opposed the decision of the Herrnhut Elders Conference.

100. Ibid., vol. 1, session 5:119–20.

5. Testing Authority and Defining Freedom

1. Minutes of the Synod of 1818, Session 6:84–5, UA-Herrnhut, R2.B.50.a-b.
2. Krieger, introduction to *Freedom*.
3. The American mind-set is nicely summarized by Jack Greene in *Imperatives*, 174–75.
4. Roeber, *Palatines*, 1, 19. In the same vein, the term *Willkür* underwent a transformation in meaning from "free choice" to "lawlessly individualistic" over the course of the eighteenth century. Walker, *German Home Towns*, 38. The tradition of local autonomy has been explored by Peter Blickle, Thomas Brady, and others. Perhaps the most thorough analysis is that of Brady in *Turning Swiss: Cities and Empire, 1450–1550* (Cambridge and New York: Cambridge Univ. Press, 1985).
5. Uttendörfer, *Alt Herrnhut*, 134.
6. Ibid., 134.
7. Ibid., 135.
8. Extract of the Report of the Synod of 1749, n. pag.
9. Zinzendorf, *Apologetische Schluß-Schrift*, 494.
10. Minutes of the Synod of 1789, special section on Unity statutes, pt. 2, 1389, no. 7.
11. Extracts of the Minutes of the Synod of 1764, n. pag.
12. Min. UEC., Dec. 21, 1771, 898. The text reads, "Alle Brüder waren darin vollkommen einig, daß die Aeltesten Conference der Unitaet zwar nicht um ihrer selbst willen auf der Ausübung mehrere Macht und Authorität zu bestehen habe; daß es aber gleichwol um der Sache des Heilands Willen, damit eine Ihm wohlgefällige Gang in Seinem Hause befördert, und Schaden verhütet werden könne, unumgänglich nöthig sey, daß sie einen reallern Einfluß und gehörige Authorität habe. Man kan und will nicht indeßen die Schranken des von Heiland approbirten Regulativs nicht überschreiten."
13. Brotherly Agreement, sect. 4, article 2.
14. Extracts Min. EC. Neuwied, Oct. 16, 1779, UA-Herrnhut.
15. See, for example, Bailyn, *Voyagers to the West*, 4; also see Zuckerman, "Identity in British America," 115–17.
16. Hall, *Worlds of Wonder*, 4.
17. The Prussian *Ortsgemeinen* were Neusalz, Gnadenberg, Gnadenfrei, Gnadenfeld, and Neuwied (on the Rhine). The Saxon *Ortsgemeinen* were Herrnhut, Kleinwelke, Niesky, Gnadau, and the seminary at Barby. Ebersdorf stood under the authority of the Reuß family, and Neudientendorf, under the dukes of Gotha.
18. Min. UEC., March 25, 1789, 162–63.
19. See, for example, Min. UEC., May 20, 1775, 264; ibid., Oct. 12 and 18, 1791, 86–87, 116–17; Extracts of the Minutes of the Neudietendorf Elders Conference (hereafter referred to as Extracts Min. EC. Neudietendorf), Oct. 1, 1791, UA-Herrnhut, R9.B.b.4.a; Johann Traugott Bluher to Johann Friedrich Reichel, Oct. 5, 1791, UA-Herrnhut, R9.B.b.8.c (no. 172). At the bottom of Bluher's letter is the following sentence: "May the act of homage [in Neudietendorf] be as short as possible! There are still many doubtful feelings among the Brethren." It should be noted that the manorial lords held the estates in trust for the Unity, which

received the income, and that not all of the inhabitants of the estates were *Gemeine* members.

20. Extracts Min. EC. Herrnhut, Dec. 6, 1792, no. 1.

21. Min. UEC., July 31, 1798, 139.

22. Extracts Min. EC. Herrnhut, March-June 1789, no. 1.

23. Brotherly Agreement (Salem), sect. 3, article 1, UA-Herrnhut, NB.V.R.1.23. Quotation is from the translation by Frances Cumnock.

24. Brotherly Agreement (Herrnhut), sect. 3, article 1, UA-Herrnhut, NB.V.R.1.23.

25. Extracts Min. Auf. Colleg. Herrnhut, Nov. 22, 1776.

26. Min. UEC., July 31, 1772, 281. A very similar comment appears in the minutes of July 24, 1787.

27. Ibid., March 2, 1780, 216–17.

28. Neusalz Visitation Report of Christian Gregor, 1787.

29. Extracts Min. EC. Gnadenfrei, Aug. 16, 1788, no. 6, UA-Herrnhut. The UEC simply noted that the Savior had approved the noble members. The difficulties involved in serving a dual role as *Gemeine* member and lord of the manor emerges in a remark from a month later, when the Gnadenfrei nobles asked that they be given prior notice when one of their subjects was received into the *Gemeine* or became a communicant. Ibid., Sept. 6, 1788, no. 1.

30. Min. UEC., May 31, 1794, 250.

31. Ibid., Feb. 20, 1796, 264.

32. Ibid., Feb. 11, 1777, 205.

33. Ibid., Feb. 15, 1782, 263.

34. Greene, *Imperatives*, 174–75.

35. Thorp, *Moravian Community*, 171.

36. Roeber, "'He read it to me,'" 213.

37. Min. EC., Jan. 4, 1783.

38. Connor, *North Carolina*, vol. 1, 393; Ekirch, *Poor Carolina*, 6.

39. Thorp, "Assimilation," 32–33. Thorp attributed the shift in landholding patterns to the Unity's recognition of the strong lure that individual farm ownership held for potential settlers.

40. SB Diary, April 2, 1778; Min. SBC., Sept. 23, 1787, no. 2.

41. Min. UEC., Feb. 28, 1771, 391. Research by A.G. Roeber and Aaron Fogelman has emphasized the importance of landholding to other groups of German immigrants.

42. Min. EC., March 28, 1781, no. 5b.

43. Min. GC., May 30, 1782, no. 2.

44. Min. Auf. Colleg., Aug. 16, 1780 (my translation).

45. Min. EC., Sept. 5, 1790, no. 2.

46. Greene, *Pursuits of Happiness*, 196.

47. Uttendörfer, *Wirtschaftsgeist*, 54.

48. Thorp, "Assimilation," 38; Gollin, *Moravians in Two Worlds*, 167.

49. Min. Auf. Colleg., Feb. 4, 1794, no. 2 (my translation).

50. Min. EC., Jan. 5, 1785, no. 1.

51. Min. Auf. Colleg., Dec. 10, 1793, no. 4, and April 7, 1795, no. 1.

52. The statistics on landholding come from charts that are part of Scott Rohrer's dissertation "Planting Pietism: Religion and Community in the Moravian Settlements of North Carolina, 1750–1830," in progress at the University of Virginia. I am grateful to Scott for allowing me to have a copy of these charts. He also argued that the larger amounts of land bought by Salem residents were purchased almost exclusively for speculation. Scott Rohrer, "Pietism and Profits: Landholding in Wachovia, North Carolina, 1753–1830" (paper presented at the 1998 meeting of the Organization of American Historians, Indianapolis, Indiana), 4–5.

53. Surratt, *Gottlieb Schober*, 74–80.

54. The royal edict issued in 1792 makes the contrast with land purchase in America plain: "It cannot be a matter of indifference to us if the official leases become the occasion for rampant speculation and the officials barter a right for which they have *only us to thank*"(emphasis mine). H.H. Müller, "Domänen und Domänenpächter," 171, 187.

55. Jerome Blum showed that in many places in eastern Europe serfdom was barely distinguishable from slavery. Blum, *End of the Old Order*.

56. Jack Green made this point far more eloquently than I. See *Imperatives*, chap. 11, especially 276–80.

57. The first Salem slave was purchased in 1769 with the approval of the lot.

58. Sensbach, *A Separate Canaan*, 136, 166–67. All the information on Moravian slaves is taken from this work. Any historian interested in the Brethren or in African American history cannot but be grateful to Professor Sensbach for giving us this truly groundbreaking study of the African Moravian world.

59. These forms of indirect resistance have been identified as not uncommon among the early modern German peasantry. Winfried Schulze cited a "graded spectrum of peasant resistance to feudal or state demands." This spectrum included careless performance of labor and litigation. He pointed out that actual open revolt was the exception rather than the rule. Schulze, "Peasant Resistance," 64. Robert Berdahl pointed out that in the relations between masters and servants in the Prussian manorial system, deference and conflict existed side by side. These were expressed by means such as "exaggeratedly slow" obedience to commands and blank looks when given instructions. Berdahl defined this as a "secret war" against authority. Berdahl, *Prussian Nobililty*, 51–52.

60. Johann Christian von Damnitz to the UEC., Nov. 25, 1782, UA-Herrnhut, R9.B.a.25.4.

61. Wilhelm Schmidt, Connau Roemming, Heinrich Heinz, Johann Sauermann, and Heinrich Gottlieb Petsch to the UEC., Nov. 20, 1782, UA-Herrnhut, R9.B.b.8.c (no. 123).

62. David W. Sabean identified the demand for an oath as a form of "indirect violence" on the part of manorial lords because it required the oath taker to lay one's soul on the line. Because the leaders of the Brethren were viewed as bound to protect and preserve their spiritual privileges, the accusation that von Damnitz required an oath of them undoubtedly carried special weight. Sabean, *Power in the Blood*, 22. The Brethren's stress on their own basic obedience, in contrast to von Damnitz's behavior, reflects an incident in the 1790s cited by Winfried Schulze in which peasants in the electorate of Köln appealed to the law against their lords and

stressed their own obedience and restraint under the circumstances. Schulze, "Peasant Resistance," 126.

63. Johann Christian Gebauer to the UEC., Nov. 23, 1782, UA-Herrnhut, R9.B.b.8.c (no. 122). Gebauer's letter generally backs up the version given by the Single Brothers and focuses on von Damnitz's demand for an oath. It also indicates that von Damnitz argued that ignorance of the law was no excuse for disobeying a direct order.

64. The reference to the "fire" occurs in a letter from Spangenberg to von Damnitz, Nov. 27, 1782, UA-Herrnhut, R9.B.b.9.c (no. 125). The UEC faulted von Damnitz for acting "more in the letter than in the sense of the law" but later scolded the Neudietendorf Elders Conference for supporting "ignorant *Gemeine* members who quickly took the opportunity to oppose each ordinance." Min. UEC., Jan. 2, 1783., 17, and June 12, 1783, 479.

65. Extracts Min. EC. Gnadenfrei, Feb. 4, 1789, no. 1.

66. Extracts Min. EC. Herrnhut, Sept. 18, 1794, no. 2.

67. Briant to Geisler, Feb. 18, 1795, UA-Herrnhut, R7.C.I.a.12.a (no. 9). The following quotation is also from this source.

68. Briant to Geisler, March 23, 1795. The letter also indicates that one of these lampoons took the form of sexual innuendo.

69. Extracts Min. Auf. Colleg. Herrnhut, Jan.-March 1793, pt. 9; Extracts Min. EC. Herrnhut, Sept. 5, 1791; ibid., July 11, 1796. This latter entry specifies that a Brother needs to be appointed to keep a daily watch on the tower to ensure that it remains free of offensive writing.

70. Min. UEC., Jan. 5, 1780, 29. This remark reflects the alternative view of authority cited by Roeber, who pointed specifically to a concern with protecting household sustenance as a hallmark of the southwest German tradition. See Roeber, *Palatines*, chaps. 2 and 9. This topic is also discussed by Winfried Schulze in "Peasant Resistance," 84.

71. Min. UEC., Jan. 25, 1780, 167.

72. Ibid., Jan. 11, 1780, 74; Nov. 25, 1780, 580. Teutsch had failed to answer a summons, claiming he was ill.

73. David Sabean noted the need to reevaluate resistance in light of this fact. Sabean, *Power in the Blood*, 26. The tradition of symbolic protest has also been explored as an integral part of popular culture. See, for example, Burke, *Popular Culture,* and Robert Darnton, *The Great Cat Massacre and Other Episodes in French Cultural History* (New York: Basic Books, 1984), chap. 2.

74. Min. UEC., April 11, 1774, 42.

75. Ibid., June 2, 1789, 8. It is well worth noting with regard to the association of freedom with passion that Friedrich Schleiermacher and Novalis attended the Brethren's educational institutions. A description of life at university by a friend of Novalis illuminates the attractions of this life for the young Brethren and the danger it posed to the Unity. He wrote to Friedrich Schlegel's brother, "That lovely time in Jena . . . was one of the most radiant and delightful periods of my life. You and your brother . . . all of us young and stirring . . . these spirits and their multiple plans . . . constituted almost uninterruptedly a festival of wit, esprit, and philosophy." Jena, in particular, seems to have had a reputation as a "party school," so it is

no wonder that the Brethren preferred to send their boys to Halle if university attendance could not be avoided. Ziolkowski, *German Romanticism*, 219, 229–30.

76. LaVopa, *Grace, Talent, and Merit*, 148.

77. Min. UEC., April 26, 1792, 119; Briant to Geisler, Feb. 28, 1795.

78. Extracts Min. EC. Herrnhut, Nov. 18, 1793, no. 1.

79. Briant to Geisler, March 5, 1795.

80. In his study of German liberal and romantic political thought, Frederick Beiser pointed out that, although they varied on political and economic theories, many Enlightenment, liberal, and early-romantic thinkers agreed in supporting freedom of conscience and freedom of speech and of the press. Most important for this context, they believed "that individuals were the best judge of their own welfare, religion, and morality." Beiser, *Enlightenment*, 18, 24. Diethelm Klippel pointed out the particular importance of the 1790s to the development and spread of political concepts of freedom and natural rights in German thought. Klippel, "True Concept of Liberty."

81. Schlumbohn, *Freiheit*, 112.

82. This information is taken from the appendix to van Dülmen, *Society of the Enlightenment*.

83. Min. UEC., April 8, 1800, 26. The Brethren did not necessarily depend solely on reading societies to provide them with controversial material. The general number of publications rose dramatically in Germany in the later eighteenth century. In the 1740s, 176 new journals appeared, but, by the 1790s, the number had reached 1,225. The number of newspapers also rose in this period. Schlumbohn, *Freiheit*, 39–40.

84. Min. Auf. Colleg., Jan. 17, 1776, no. 3. It should be noted, however, that Aust defended his stance by claiming that when he had acceded to the *Collegium*'s suggestions in the past, the result had been harmful to "the entire *Gemeine*." This echoes the modes of indirect defiance seen in the German *Gemeinen* and may reflect the fact that Aust was born and raised in Germany. He was called to service in America at age thirty-two.

85. Min. EC., Nov. 3, 1778, no. 1. The Elders Conference made a similar complaint with regard to domestic service on July 4, 1781, no. 5.

86. Min. Auf. Colleg., Feb. 29, 1780.

87. Min. EC., July 4, 1781, no. 5, and Feb. 7, 1787, no. 6.

88. Ibid., May 2, 1791, no. 6 (my translation). The Elders Conference also complained about the general "perverted spirit" by which many in the *Gemeine* took various actions without informing the officials. Min. EC., June 18, 1787.

89. Min. EC., April 10, 1793, no. 5.

90. Min. GC., April 24, 1788. A similar frustration over inattention to the admonitions of the Single Brothers leaders appeared earlier. See Min. SBC., Sept. 15, 1784, no. 2.

91. Min. EC., Aug. 30, 1780, no. 3a.

92. Ibid., Dec. 28, 1782, no. 1.

93. Hunter James pointed out the uniqueness of the Brethren's apprenticeship practices in *Quiet People*, 30.

94. Min. Auf. Colleg., June 23, 1789 (my translation).

95. Ibid., May 2, 1790, no. 1.

96. Ibid., June 21, 1774 (my translation).

97. Min. EC., Dec. 12, 1783; Min. Auf. Colleg., Oct. 15, 1799, no. 4.

98. Min. EC., March 28, 1778, no. 3, and March 31, 1778, no. 2; Min. Auf. Colleg., April 1, 1778 (no number).

99. Min. EC., April 3, 1778 (special conference). All information on the actual walkout and reaction to it is taken from this source. It is worth noting that the recalcitrant Brothers included Gottlieb Schober and Johannes Flex.

100. Ludwig Moeller to the Salem Elders Conference, n.d., 1778, MA-SP, B65:2 box 5, no. 33.

101. Min. Auf. Colleg., Jan. 3, 1776 (my translation). The text reads, "In Ansehung des Topfer Gesellens Rudolph Christ, welcher seinen eigenen Gang geht, sich über alles wegsezt, und nach niemand was fragt, sondern schon eine geräume Zeit, wenn es nicht nach seinen aufgeblasenen Kopf geht, den Stuhl vor die Thure sezt, weil er glaubt, dass die Topferey ohne ihn nicht gehen kan; so wurde dieser Vorschlag proponirt: Wenn Ludwig Moeller sich wirklich und ganz bekehrt, dass man sich auf ihn Fussen kan, vielleicht eine Probe mit Christ machen konne, ihm seinen Gang im Shop, seine Nachlässigkeit in der Arbeit, balde mit der Flinte auf der Jagd zu gehen, ein ander mal Vogel stellen, und dergleichen vorzuhalten, und nacher sehen, wo es mit ihm hinaus will, und zu was er sich verstehen wird" (spelling left as in original).

102. Ibid., July 5, 1780; Min. SBC., Jan. 21, 1784, no. 4.

103. These books were apparently being passed around. The Elders Conference discussed the need to speak with William Eldridge about his reading of "bad books . . . which, from time to time Charles Bagge procures for him." Min. EC., April 23, 1794, no. 6. See also Min. Auf. Colleg., Jan. 7, 1794, no. 8. Bagge was his father's assistant in the Salem store; he must have used his commercial contacts to procure the books. I have attempted to track down a more specific reference to these books but without success.

104. Brotherly Agreement, sect. 6, no. 5.

105. I am indebted to A.G. Roeber for emphasizing this point. Roeber, *Palatines*, 1. Although the late eighteenth century did see the appearance of specific calls for economic freedom in Germany, such voices remained "relatively isolated." Schlumbohn, *Freiheit*, 123. Jack Greene argued that the connection between property and freedom became an integral part of the American mind-set: "In this emerging secular and commercial culture, the central orientation of people in the littoral became the achievement of personal independence, a state in which a man and his family and broader dependents could live 'at ease' rather than in anxiety, in contentment rather than in want, in respectability rather than in meanness, and, perhaps most importantly, in freedom from the will and control of other men." *Pursuits of Happiness*, 195.

106. Min. EC., March 14, 1781, no 4.

107. Ibid., Aug. 15, 1775, no. 3. The Elders Conference also declared that, in the future, letters from Pennsylvania to individuals in Salem were to be read by the Elders Conference before being sent to their destination if, indeed, it was deemed advisable to send them on. The Pennsylvania connection may well have been a

conduit for revolutionary ideals. In 1775, the UEC observed that several of the Brethren there "were not only inclined to the spirit of opposition that reigned in the colonies, but sought to bring others to the same inclination." Min. UEC., March 18, 1775, 527–28.

108. Min. EC., July 6, 1785, no. 3. The text reads, "Man kam hierbey darauf daß in der Gemeine bey einigen ein *Geist* wahrgenommen wird, *der die Amerikanische Freyheit etabliren will* und hielt für gut, darüber in einem Geemeinrath eine cordate Aeusserung und Nachfrage zu thun, um auf den Grund zu kommen und ein so schädliche Sache unter uns abzustellen." The Elders Conference had remarked earlier that the Brethren in Bethabara had probably put this idea into Krause's head and should be admonished not to discuss such things in the future. Min. EC., June 15, 1785, no. 1.

109. Min. GC, Aug. 4, 1785, no. 4. The text reads, "Wurde angebracht, daß es seit einige Zeit bey einigen gewöhnlich zu werde anfangen, sich in Contradiction gegen menschliche Ordnung auf die Amerikanische Freyheit zu berufen. Siene Ausdruck beweist wenigstens einen grossen Unverstand; denn es wird ja in den sogenannten freyen Ländern eben so gut als in andern, über der gehörigen Subordination, ohne welche keine menschliche Gesellschaft bestehen kan, gehalten. So muß z.b. ein Gesell sich allerdings darnach richten, was der Meister in der Handthierung verordnet. Wolte aber jemand, wie man auch bereits Spuren hat, erwehnte Freyheit gegen die Orts-Ordnungen verwenden, der beweise dadurch, daß er seinen Aufenthalt besser anderswo hätte."

110. In his study of deviant behavior among the Puritans, Kai Erikson suggested that communities often redefine and identify deviant behavior in response to historical changes that alter or threaten their social structure. Erikson, *Wayward Puritans*, 23, 68–70. With regard to this theory, it is worth noting that the Lutheran pastor Melchior Mühlenberg identified "American liberty" with the struggle over the right to choose and dismiss pastors. Under conditions in America (i.e., no state support system), this particular liberty came to be associated with the monetary contributions to the upkeep of the congregation. Roeber, *Palatines,* 291, 295.

111. Walker, *German Home Towns,* 134.

112. Min. GC., Oct. 30, 1794, no. 2.

113. Min. Auf. Colleg., June 30, 1774.

114. Andreas Schober to Marschall, March 21, 1773. The text (original spelling and punctuation intact) reads, "Mein liebe Marschall ich kann nicht umhin, durch ein mal zu fragen, wie es doch komt, das du meinen Sohn verbunden hast, ohne mich zu fragen oder mir zu melden, ich glaube das dir doch bekannt ist das wir nicht in Deutschland seyn und also niemand Macht hat, meinen Kinder zu verbunden, so lang ich lebe kommt es mir allein zu, ich kan nicht laugnen, ich habe mich sehr gewundert dazu sich jemand unterstehe kan in Englischen Landen so was zu thun und dar zu eine Provision die vielleicht seinen Temprament entgegen ist. Was denkst du?"

115. Min. EC., May 18, 1773, no. 1.

116. Marschall to Böhler, Feb. 1775. The text reads, "Für Bruder Wallis sind wir herzliche dankbar, und ich in specie weil ich hoffen kan, daß nun in meiner Abwesenheit die äußerliche regulariaet von Salem nicht verwildern werden, wie es

dem Indianischen Landes genio änlich ist, und auch auf der innerlichen Gang einer Gemeine einen großen Effect hat."

117. On German immigrant views of America as unregulated, see Roeber, *Palatines,* 17.

118. Min. UEC., 1782, vol. 1, 400ff. The text reads, "Leztere waren es eigentlich die sich zu laut für Amerikaner erklärten."

119. Marschall to von Lüdecke, June 24, 1782, UA-Herrnhut, R14.B.b.11.a.

120. Ibid.

121. Gregor to Marschall, Nov. 12, 1783, MA-SP, Letter File A-12:3.

122. Marschall to Gregor, June 26, 1788, UA-Herrnhut, R14.B.b.11.a. The text reads, "Wenn sie nicht falschen suppositiones mitbringen, als ob hier eine Indepedenz von Gemeine Ordnung wäre."

123. "Colonisten nach der Wachau betreffend," Marschall to the Unity Vorsteher Conference, July 1786, MA-SP, B28:9. Marschall contrasted this "harmful" focus on individual prosperity with the proper focus on what the Savior wanted.

124. Ibid. The complete text reads, "Es ist also nöthig, Leute die zu so etwas Lust haben, von vorne her zu verständen, ob des Ihr Sinn sey, denn des Veränderung vom Land, der Landes Constitution und Gebrauchen, eine Idee als ob hier eine Freyheit existire, die durch keine Gesetze eingeschränkt sey, oder daß man sich hier weniger an Gemein-Ordnung binden dürfe, verändern auf die Denkart, oftmals ehe noch Personen an Ort und Stelle angelangt sind."

125. Min. UEC., March 21, 1796, 407.

126. As Mack Walker has shown, guilds continued to thrive in many parts of Germany into the eighteenth century and often held considerable power over local economic life.

127. Various remarks about the problems with guild membership or the lack thereof are found in the following sources: Min. Herrnhut Auf. Colleg. Jan.-March 1790, pt. 7, no. 1; ibid., April-June 1790, pt. 7, no. 7; Min. Herrnhut EC., Aug. 15, 1791; Min. Herrnhut Auf. Colleg., Jan.-March 1793, pt. 7, no. 8; Min. Herrnhut EC., May 28, 1796.

128. Min. EC., Aug. 13, 1789, no. 4 and Aug. 19, 1789, nos. 2 and 7.

129. Min. GC., Sept. 10, 1789, no. 1. The text reads, "Manchen Gemeingliedern an Willigkeit fehlt, sich dem Regiment des Heilands zu überlaßen, und dagegen eine Neigung ihren Gang und Umstände selbst zu dirigiren; und daß es ferner an Willigkeit fehlt, sich zu den Gemein-ordnungen und Einrichtungen zu bequemen, . . . Dabey zeige sich bey manchen die Idee, als ob man hier, als in einem freyen Lande, nicht so nöthig hätte, sich nach den Gemeinordnungen zu richten als etwa in den Europäische Gemeinen, wenn man nur die Landes Gesetz befolgte." The leadership most likely had Christoph Loesch in mind in particular. In a letter written in response to his denial of any wrongdoing, the Elders Conference observed, "Since you thus go your own way in all matters, and will be restricted merely by *the law of the land,* but not by a brotherly mind and way of thinking, which underlies even the Bethania statutes, who can recommend you to a *Gemeinort?*" (emphasis mine). Min. EC., Oct. 21, 1789, no. 7.

6. Hands across the Water

1. Marianne Wokeck discussed the German immigrants' ties to their homeland in "Charting Courses," 3, 7.

2. Roeber, *Palatines*, 209, 323–25.

3. Greene, *Imperatives*, 174–77. Gordon Wood made a similar point about the divided American mind-set in *The Radicalism of the American Revolution* (New York: Random House, 1991). See especially pt. 1.

4. *RM*, vol. 2, 605.

5. Synod Report of 1764, sect. 7, 21.

6. Synod Report of 1769, chap. 5, paragraph 5 (ignoring numeration).

7. Ibid., paragraph 11, no. 6 of the second set of numbers.

8. Ibid., no. 4 of second set.

9. Synod Report of 1775, sect. 264A, MA-SP.

10. Synod Report of 1789, chap. 14, sect. 154, 129.

11. von Boetticher, *Geschichte*, vols. 2 and 3.

12. One letter, for instance, includes the observation, written in English within a German-language letter, possibly to keep it from prying eyes, that M. Childs "went to France, some think, in order to drink claret cheap of which he is very fond." Heinrich Wollin to Marschall, June 12, 1771, MA-SP, B81:11.

13. Johannes von Watteville (hereafter referred to as Johannes because this is how he was normally addressed) to Johann Michael Graff, Jan. 19, 1778, MA-SP. Roeber noted that images of water are not prominent in the devotional literature of German Americans in the colonial period. While my study does not encompass the devotional literature of the American Brethren, their correspondence is replete with references to the ocean. Marianne Wokeck pointed out that most German immigrants came to America in search of opportunity, and, thus, "homesick exiles" were rare among them. The Brethren as a whole and the leadership in particular do not fit comfortably into either the willing immigrant or the exile category. While they did leave Germany voluntarily, many of them and all of those in leadership positions viewed the departure as submission to the Savior's will rather than as a personal choice. Therefore, it is not surprising that their letters express a strong sense of attachment to their home *Gemeinen*. The Unity ideal, however, stressed the need to have a "pilgrim mindset" [*Pilgerdenkweise*].

14. Marschall to Gregor, Sept. 15, 1788, UA-Herrnhut, R14.B.b.11.a. The text reads, "Ich wünsche du könnst nach dem Synodo her, und fährst dir die Wachau noch einmal an, ob du mich aber noch anträfest, weiß nicht zu beurthielen."

15. Gregor to Marschall, June 4, 1790, MA-SP, Letter File A-12:3; Gregor to Stotz, Feb. 3, 1794, MA-SP, Letter File A-15:1. The text of the latter reads, "Was du liebster Brüder, von dir selbst und deinen Ergehen schreibst, das kan ich dir von mir auch erwiedern: Schämen und Danken, Loben und Abbitten, wechßelt alle Tage zwischen mir und dem Heiland."

16. Wollin to Marschall, Feb. 4, 1772, MA-SP, B81:11.

17. Johann Heinrich Andersen to Graff, Jan. 23, 1777, MA-SP, B82:5.

18. Spangenberg to the American Brethren, Jan. 15, 1778, MA-SP, B65:2, box 2 no. 44.

19. Min. EC., Oct. 29, 1783, no. 8.

20. Gregor to Marschall, Jan. 19, 1797, MA-SP, Letter File A-12:3.

21. Johann Friedrich Reichel to Marschall, July 28, 1781, MA-SP (unable to locate catalog number).

22. Reichel to Marschall, Aug. 14, 1783, MA-SP, Letter File A-12:5.

23. Marschall to Anton von Lüdecke, June 24, 1782, UA-Herrnhut, R14.B.b.11.a.

24. UEC to the Elders Conference, Sept. 17, 1778, MA-SP (unable to locate catalog number).

25. Marschall to Andersen, Sept. 29, 1780, UA-Herrnhut, R14.B.b.11.a (no.23). All further references are taken from this letter.

26. Benzien to Gregor (unsigned), April 20, 1786, MA-SP, Letter File A-15:1. This letter is actually his annual Choir report for 1785–86. The Choir year began with the celebration of their central festival in early April.

27. Min. EC., Nov. 26, 1785, no. 1. All of these declarations of gratitude and joy regarding the visitations from the UEC might well be taken as the wishful thinking of the leadership. The records of the Elders Conference, however, yield a pattern of Communion attendance around the time of these visitations that indicates that they did have some real impact on the laity. In two of the three months of the Reichels' visitation in 1780, no one abstained from Communion, and two members were readmitted. Although the number of abstentions and exclusions had been relatively low before the arrival of the Reichels in July, it is worth noting that in the two months following their departure, the pattern of no abstentions continued.

28. The Wachau settlement had been begun as a communal economy. Only with the foundation of the central town of Salem were the various businesses and individual holdings separated.

29. Thorp, "Paying for Paradise," 1.

30. Ibid., 2–9.

31. All financial figures are taken from the Min. UEC., 1790, 2:509; 1797, 3:319; 1799, 3:211–12.

32. UEC to the Provincial Helpers Conference (hereafter referred to as PHC), Jan. 4, 1773, B81:12; Reichel to Marschall, July 14, 1783, Letter File A-12:5; Reichel to Marschall, Aug. 14, 1783; Gregor to Marschall, Nov. 24, 1788, Letter File A-12:3. All MA-SP.

33. Marschall to Böhler, Feb. 1775.

34. Marschall to von Lüdecke, July 12, 1783.

35. Andersen to Graff, Jan. 23, 1777. See also, Johannes to Graff, Jan. 19, 1778, and UEC to EC, Sept. 17, 1778.

36. Gregor to Marschall, June 4, 1790. The difficulties in correspondence also created uncertainty and anxiety on a personal level. In a letter to her uncle, Catherina Margaretha Trübel wrote the following: "Since an opportunity of a Brother from here going to America presents itself, I will gladly make use of it, and in these couple of lines greet my dear uncle right tenderly, as does my sister Martha. Of course we cannot know whether these lines will find my uncle still alive or not." Catherina Margaretha Trübel to Christian Trübel, Feb. 28, 1786, MA-SP, C141:6.

37. Marschall to Andersen, Sept. 29, 1780. He expressed a similar frustration in a letter to Johann Friedrich Reichel written Oct. 1, 1781. *RM,* vol. 4, 1912. The reference to a "regulated post" was especially apt for Saxony, which had a notably efficient communications network. Czok, *Geschicht Sachsens,* 266.

38. Marschall to von Lüdecke, June 24, 1782.

39. UEC to EC, Sept. 17, 1778, MA-SP.

40. Gregor to Marschall, Sept. 25, 1783, MA-SP, Letter File A-12:3.

41. Gregor to Marschall, Aug. 4, 1796; Gregor to Marschall, April 17, 1790; Gregor to Johannes Stotz, Nov. 15, 1796; Gregor to Marschall, July 19, 1797, both MA-SP, Letter File A-12:3.

42. Gregor to Marschall, June 6, 1795, MA-SP, Letter File A-12:3.

43. Marschall to Böhler, Feb. 1775. The text reads, "Ich setze zum voraus, daß auf der einen Ecke nichts unter uns vorkommen müßen das nicht aus den völligen Sinne der Subordination herfließe, und sich von Herzen gar darin füge, weil wir aber nicht unter einem Jahr eine Antwort von Europa bekommen, so ists für bekannt angenommen worden, daß manche Sachen in loco decidirt werden müßten."

44. Andersen to Graff, Jan. 23, 1778.

45. Extract of the Minutes of the Synod Revision Committees, 1789, no. 25b, n.pag.; Gregor to Marschall, Oct. 30, 1790, Letter File A-12:3. Gregor had said much the same thing in his letter of April 17, 1790. All MA-SP.

46. Min. UEC., July 22–23, 1801, 78.

47. At each synod, special committees were chosen to deal with necessary changes in specific areas of Unity responsibility. These committees were termed "revisions committees." One such committee held responsibility for the American *Gemeinen.* A copy of the minutes of each committee was then sent to the *Gemeine* or *Gemeinen* to which they pertained.

48. Minutes of the Synod Revision Committees, 1789, 41, UA-Herrnhut, R2B48i; Extract of the Minutes of the Synod Revision Committees 1789, no. 3, n.pag., MA-SP.

49. For example, Wollin to Marschall, Oct. 21, 1772, MA-SP, B81:11; UEC to PHC, Dec. 17, 1772, MA-SP, B81:11; Marschall to Loretz, May 5, 1773; Gregor to Marschall, July 21, 1791, MA-SP, Letter File A-12:3; Min. UEC., May 22, 1790, 302.

50. Marschall to UEC, Jan. 12, 1791, UA-Herrnhut, UVCx, no. 171–78.

51. Minutes of the Synod Revision Committees, 1775, session 8, n.pag., UA-Herrnhut, R2.B.46.6.

52. Min. UEC., March 15, 1779, 434.

53. It is revealing that although this visitation was approved in January 1783, the Salem Elders Conference decided in April to admit Brother Praezel's new wife to the Elders Conference despite the fact that, lacking a bishop in America, she had not been officially consecrated to her new office as *Helfer* for the Married Choir. The protocol official noted, "Since it might be a good while before we receive a visit from the UEC we believed that in our present situation we might be sufficiently excused if we admitted her for now." Min. EC., May 21, 1783, no. 1b. It is difficult to determine the influence that female members of the Elders Conference possessed, so it is also difficult to determine what effect Sister Praezel's lack of consecration had on her authority.

54. Min. UEC., Dec. 13, 1791, 427; ibid., April 18, 1792, 691; ibid., May 28, 1793, 250; ibid., Jan. 14, 1795, 40; ibid., March 2, 1795, 250; ibid., Jan. 16, 1797, 76. The decision to call a synod, reached in 1798, suspended any further consideration of a visitation until the Synod of 1801, at which point it was approved. The UEC members wanted to ask the Savior about a visitation in 1794, but Brother Ettwein in Pennsylvania told them that it was unnecessary that year. The UEC rejected a suggestion that a member of the UEC stay in America until the next synod because a synod would not even come up for consideration for another five years. They did not want one of their members stuck in America for such a length of time. Ibid., Sept. 27, 1794, 374; Dec. 11, 1794, 354.

55. Marschall to Gregor, June 26, 1788.

56. Marschall to Reichel, Sept. 18, 1796, UA-Herrnhut, R14.B.b.11.a. It should be noted, however, that Marschall followed this by stating his assurance that "the Savior will bring forth counsel within it" (i.e., the UEC) regarding the Wachau because they *were* a part of the Unity.

57. Min. UEC., Feb. 16, 1801, 198.

58. Minutes of the Synod Revision Committees, 1769, vol. 2, session 57, no. 2, n.pag., UA-Herrnhut, R2.B.45.1.c.

59. Min. UEC., June 20, 1783, 559.

60. EC to UEC, Aug. 1, 1787, UA-Herrnhut, R14.B.b.11.a. All further references are taken from this letter.

61. The text reads, "Wo eine religio dominans ist in welcher Leute ihr Kinder taufen laßen, zum heiligen Abendmahls gehen, und daneben sich zu unsern Societaets Versammlungen halten können, kan der Gemein-Zirkel enger gefaßt werden ohne daß Leute, denen die enge Regel nicht paßt, darum von brüderlicher Gemeinschaft ausgeschloßen wären, oder das heilige Abendmahl ihre Lebenzeit entbehren müßten. Hier zu Lande aber, wo jede Secte gleiche Befügniß und Gerechtsame hat, ja auch in denselben noch keine Christliche Ordnungen und Einrichtungen existiren, würde unsers Bedünckens kein Nützen für die Sache des Heilands heraus kommen, wenn man die Leute nöthigen wolte, sich zu der Denomination zu halten, aus welcher sie oder ihre Eltern hergekommen, und die hier keine kirchliche Verfassung haben noch weniger aber, wenn sie darum gar nicht zum heilige Abendmahl gelangen könten: Diesem Mangel ab zu helfen, dünkt uns daß unsre Landgemeinen von Heilands destinirt sind."

62. Min. UEC., Jan. 24, 1788, 131.

63. Min. EC., April 14, 1790, no. 5.

64. Min. UEC., June 22, 1773, 565. The text reads, "Es hat sich Bruder Friedrich von Marschall in einem Brief an Bruder Johannes darüber beschwert, daß unsren nach America deputirt gewesenen Brüder ihn durch das getrofene Arrangement außer Stand gesezt haben, das beste der Wachau, so wie bisher, zu befördern, weil ihm die freye disposition über die dasigen Fonds und Effecten, und also auch die Mittel zur Bestreitung gewißer allgemein Expensen zu sehr dadurch beschrenkt und einiger maßen benommen wären."

65. Ibid., June 22, 1773, 566.

66. Ibid., March 8, 1774, 476–77.

67. Although, in most instances, the UEC urged the claims of piety over prac-

ticality with regard to the Brethren in America, evidence exists of one case in which the opposite was true. Toward the end of the eighteenth century, the Brethren in America began equipping substitute soldiers rather than paying the stiff fine for nonparticipation. Historian Jerry Surratt ("From Theocracy to Voluntary Church and Secularized Community") has cited this as an example of the American Brethren's increasing secularization; they had originally paid the fine in order to avoid the personal equipping of a substitute, which they considered a mode of indirect service. The records of the UEC reveal a very different story, however. The UEC learned of the American *Gemeinen's* practice of paying the fine from reading the extracts of the minutes of their Elders Conference and were not pleased with the local *Arbeiter* who had given those instructions. They admonished the American Elders Conferences not to be "so scrupulous" because the fine laid a far heavier financial burden on the members than did the cost of equipping a soldier.

68. Min. UEC., Feb. 16, 1775, 303. The text reads, "Es nicht ohne Nachtheil und Versäumniß der unsern Gemeinen und Orte geschehen könte, wenn dieser Bruder allein an Salem gebunden wurde."

69. Andersen to Graff, Jan. 23, 1778. The text reads, "Und wenn wir fallens davon denken daß unser lieber alter treuer Bruder Graff fast wie ganz allein gelaßen . . . so wird es uns recht weich zumuthe."

70. Min. UEC., March 30, 1780, 560–1. The text reads, "Und man zweifelt nicht daß ein solcher Bruder, auch als denn wenn Bruder Köhler hinkommt . . . auf eine andre Weise sehr wohl werde zu gebrauchen seyn."

71. Marschall to von Lüdecke, July 12, 1783. The complete text reads, "Daß die Americanische Committee biß auf die lezte verschoben, und auf als denn erst in Barby zu stande gekommen, haben wir sehr gut faßen können da Euch damals noch die Nachrichten von dennen verschiedenen Heimgegangen gefehlt haben und also auch die Deliberationes über die Besezungen sehr unvollkommen gewesen seyn wurden. Hier in der Wachau ist unser Provincial Helfer Conferenz eingegangen unser Episcopus ist Heimgegangen, ein Prediger wozu Bruder Koehler destinirt war fehlt ohnedem, und verschiedenen Bruder wurden Wittwerer daß sie ihre Gemeine nur halb vorstehen konten [sic]."

72. Reichel to Marschall, Feb. 17, 1783, MA-SP, Letter File A-12:5.

73. Zuckerman, "Identity in British America," 118.

74. Marschall to the UEC, Memorandum concerning the Wachau, Feb. 1, 1764, MA-SP.

75. Min. UEC., June 15, 1773, 519. It is possible, of course, that such expressions were simply part of the "unworthy servant" topos, but, given the very real stress involved in positions of authority, especially in the Wachau, it seems likely to have been based in real fears.

76. Ibid., Feb. 27, 1776, 459.

77. Reichel to Marschall, Feb. 17, 1783. Unfortunately, Reichel gave no hint as to why he thought Single Sisters would be reluctant to go to America.

78. Min. UEC., March 16, 1789, 344.

79. Ibid., Feb. 4, 1799, 138.

80. Ibid., Aug. 6, 1795, 174. At least two candidates for a new master tailor

"forbad" a transfer to America. von Schweinitz to Marschall, Feb. 6, 1800, MA-SP, Letter File A-12:8.

81. Gregor to Marschall, June 6, 1795; Gregor to Schröter, Gambold, and Petersen, June 4, 1795, Letter File A-15:1. All MA-SP. The text reads, "Man solte freylich denken, daß bey den trübseligen Zeiten in Teutschland, genug Brüder seyn würden, die gern nach America, wo Ruhe und Friede ist, gehen würden. Allein wenn sie nicht Aussichten haben, sich dort zu verbeßern, so denken sie leicht: Wenn ich dort wieder wie hier als Geselle Schustern oder Schneidern oder Webern soll, so bleibe ich lieber wo ich bin. Der ehemalige Sinn, zu allem da zu seyn, wozu man begehrt wird, ist nicht so allgemein zu finden wie in vorigen Zeiten."

82. Gregor to Gambold, Aug. 20, 1798, MA-SP, Letter File A-15:1.

83. Min. UEC., Jan. 8, 1801, 40.

84. Thus, when Marschall wrote to request a potter and a tanner, the UEC remarked that it was unlikely they could provide them, for these professions were rare. The same was true of their request for a clock maker who could also serve as a silversmith. Min. UEC., March 14, 1776, 586–87; Gregor to Stotz, May 23, 1798, MA-SP, Letter File A-15:1.

85. Min. UEC., July 7, 1778, 48–49.

86. Gregor to Marschall, June 6, 1795; Gregor to Marschall, July 16, 1795. MA-SP, Letter file A-12:3.

87. von Schweinitz to Marschall, Feb. 6, 1800. Von Schweinitz wrote the following from Herrnhut: "An einem Schneider Meister für des Salemer Brüder Haus wird fleißig in der UAC gedacht und herumgeschrieben; die Noth ist aber in die hiesigen Gemeinen selbst sehr groß: seit ich hier bin, sind schon zwei Vice-Meister aus dem hiesigen Brüder Haus abgegangen."

88. Min. UEC., Oct. 25, 1785, 167–79. Out of the forty-eight rejections, fourteen were rejected by the UEC and thirty-four by the lot.

89. Ibid., Jan. 30, 1779, 190.

90. Ibid., March 24, 1787, 507. Also, May 29, 1795, 269.

91. Roeber, "Origins," 258–59.

92. The majority of the vocabulary exceptions listed in the text occur after 1780. An overview of the minutes of the Elders Conference from 1778 through 1801 turns up two hundred different English words.

93. Min. Auf. Colleg., Aug. 20, 1799, no. 2.

94. Christian Thomas Pfohl to Gregor, March 29, 1793, UA-Herrnhut, R14.B.b.11.a.

95. Min. UEC., April 29, 1795, 126.

96. Ibid., Aug. 2, 1796, 104. The text reads, "Man glaubte aber, daß sich in America manche Heilands Schule für ihn finden."

97. Ibid., Jan. 12, 1801, 47.

98. Ibid., Feb. 11, 1772, 370; Böhler to Marschall, Nov. 1, 1773, MA-SP.

99. Min. UEC., April 11, 1788, 96; ibid., April 20, 1791, 129.

100. Ibid., March 2, 1795, 245; Gregor to Schröter, Gambold, and Petersen, June 4, 1795.

101. Koehler to Daniel Strümpfler, Aug. 20, 1795, UA-Herrnhut, R14.B.b.11.a.

102. Böhler to Marschall, Nov. 1, 1773, MA-SP.

103. Min. EC., Aug. 25, 1778, no. 3. The Elders Conference left it as a matter of conscience whether the Brethren felt they could accept this affirmation, although, by 1782, the elders were urging them to do so.

104. Min. EC., March 7, 1781, no. 2; Marschall to the UEC, March 7, 1782, UA-Herrnhut, R14.B.b.11.a. The Brethren received this advice while hosting a meeting of the assembly.

105. Minutes of the Synod of 1782, vol. 1, session 9:205, UA-Herrnhut, R2B47.b.a. The motivating factor behind this move was the UEC's desire to protect the *Gemeine* by attaining the acknowledgement of the Brethren as "faithful subjects."

106. Gregor to Marschall, June 4, 1790.

107. Min. UEC., May 5, 1778, 138.

108. Marschall to the UEC, Nov. 3, 1787, UA-Herrnhut, R14B11a.

109. Marschall to Gregor, Jan. 16, 1792. From a draft copy held in MA-SP, Letter File A-13:4.

110. Min. UEC., March 19, 1792, 524.

111. Min. Auf. Colleg., June 3, 1800, no. 4.

112. Min. UEC., March 16, 1779, 453.

113. Ibid., April 16, 1791, 95. The following reference is from the same page.

114. Gregor to Marschall, Jan. 28, 1791. In his letter of July 21, 1791, Gregor repeated that the American Brethren would celebrate the jubilee with "the collected European *Gemeinen*."

Epilogue

1. The information on the requests made by the American Brethren is taken from Smaby, *Transformation of Moravian Bethlehem*, 42–44.

2. Minutes of the Synod of 1818, session 6, 84–85, 88.

3. Minutes of the Synod of 1818, session 4, 46–54. In the case of Neudietendorf and Neuwied, the deputies ignored memoranda sent to the synod suggesting alterations in its use. Ibid., 37–39.

4. Ibid., session 16, 232–33.

5. Ibid., session 51, n.pag. The memoranda from the various *Gemeinen* are in *Beilagen*, nos. 88–97.

Bibliography

PRIMARY SOURCES

Manuscripts

Moravian Archives, Southern Province, Winston-Salem, N.C.
Brüderliche Einverständniß und Vortrag 1773. R699:3.
Brüderliche Einverständniß und Vortrag 1786. R699:4.
Business Correspondence. Letter File C.
Compendium of the Four Synods: 1764, 1769, 1775, 1782. Two bound vols. No catalog number assigned.
Correspondence to Official Boards. VN3, Box 5–6.
Diarium der ledige Brüder (Single Brothers Diary), 1771–1801. J302A:19.
Diarium der ledige Schwestern (Single Sisters Diary), 1786–1801. J303A:1a.
Extracts of the Minutes of the Synod of 1764. General Correspondence. Letter File A.
General Early Correspondence. VN3, Box 3–4.
Indenture between Georg Hauser Jr. and Friedrich Wilhelm Marschall, Sept. 29, 1796. D155:7b.
Lebensläufe of various members of the Salem *Gemeine* (classified as *Memoires*).
Memorandum wegen der Wachau (Friedrich W. Marschall), Feb. 1, 1764. B65:2 box 5A:7:1.
Protokolle der Aeltesten Conferenz Salem (Minutes of the Elders Conference), 1771–1801. J299C:1.
Protokolle der Aufseher Collegium Salem (Minutes of the Aufseher Collegium), 1771–1801. J298A:1.
Protokolle der Gemeinrath (Minutes of the Gemeine Council), 1783–96. J297A:1.
Protokolle der ledige Brüder Haus Conferenz (Minutes of the Single Brothers House Conference), 1774–88. (August 1777, August 1780 are not extant) J302B:1.
Spangenberg Correspondence. VN3, Box 1–2.
Synodal Verlaß 1749 (Synod Report of 1749—extract only). B20:2.
Synodal Verlaß, 1764, 1769, 1775, 1782, 1789, 1801. 1764 is unbound; the remaining years are all bound in separate volumes. An extract of 1775 has been translated by Bishop Kenneth Hamilton and is available in the archive.
Wachau Kirchen Buch, 1771–1801. No catalog number assigned.

Unity Archive, Herrnhut, Germany.

Allegemeine Correspondenz, 1773–95. R13.D.47.a-d.

Beilagen der Synod 1789. R2.B.48.e.

Bericht über einem ausgebrochenen Sträfling (1782 Neudietendorf). R9.B.a.25.4.

Briefe an C.G. Reichel. R12.A.138.b1–2.

Briefwechsel der Aeltesten Conferenz mit der Unitäts Aeltesten Conferenz, 1765–1809 (Barby). R6.D.I.b.12.

Briefwechsel der Unitäts Aeltesten Conferenz und anderer mit Herrnhut, 1777–1800. R6.A.b.52.a.

Briefwechsel mit der Unitäts Aeltesten Conferenz, 1765–1819 (Gnadenberg). R7.C.I.b.8.a.

Briefwechsel mit der Unitäts Aeltesten Conferenz und andern, 1745–1823 (Gnadenfrei). R7.D.I.b.9.a.

Briefwechsel mit der Unitäts Aeltesten Conferenz und andern, 1765–1811 (Neudietendorf). R9.B.b.8.c.

Briefwechsel zwischen der Unitäts Aeltesten Conferenz und die Aeltesten Conferenz in Neusalz. R7.E.a.5.

Diarien, Berichte, und Memorabilien, 1770–79 (Neudietendorf). R9.B.b.1.b.

Ebersdorf Briefwechsel mit der Unitäts Aeltesten Conferenz, 1785 and 1791. UA-Herrnhut. R9Ab9c.

Eingeben an die Synod 1769. R2.B.47.b.a.2.b.2.

Extracte aus dem Protokolle der Aeltesten Conferenz Gnadau, 1771–89. R6.D.II.b.4.a.

Extracte aus dem Protokolle der Aeltesten Conferenz Gnadenberg, 1780–93 and 1794–1804. R7.C.I.b.5.a-b.

Extracte aus dem Protokolle der Aeltesten Conferenz Gnadenfeld, 1783–94. R7.F.b.3.a.

Extracte aus dem Protokolle der Aeltesten Conferenz Gnadenfrei, 1788. R7.D.I.b.5.b.

Extracte aus dem Protokolle der Aeltesten Conferenz Herrnhut, 1787–92 and 1793–97. R6.A.b.41.b-c.

Extracte aus dem Protokolle der Aeltesten Conferenz Kleinwelke, 1767–93 (1770–78 not extant) and 1794–1803. R6.C.b.4.a-b.

Extracte aus dem Protokolle der Aeltesten Conferenz Niesky, 1784–91 and 1792–98. R6.B.I.b.15.b-c.

Extracte aus dem Protokolle der Aeltesten Conferenz Neudietendorf, 1773, 1775–88 and 1789–1801. R9.B.b.4.a-b.

Extracte aus dem Protokolle des Aufseher Collegium Gnadenfrei. R7.D.I.b.7.a.

Extracte aus dem Protokolle des Aufseher Collegium Herrnhut, 1773–99 and 1800–22. R6.A.b.49.a-b.

Lebenslauf of Anna Johanna Köhler. R22.78.30.

Lebenslauf of Carl Christian Siegmund von Seidlitz. R22.44.66.

Lebenslauf of Carl Friedrich Schröter. R22.117.4.

Lebenslauf of Franz Wenzelaus Neißer. R22.29.

Lebenslauf of Friedrich Rudolph von Watteville. R22.34.36.

Lebenslauf of Heinrich XXVIII Reuß. R22.49.48.
Lebenslauf of Jacob Heinrich Andersen. R22.1.a.
Lebenslauf of Jacques Christoph Duvernoy. R22.31.15.
Lebenslauf of Johann Daniel Köhler. R22.32.10.
Lebenslauf of Johannes Loretz. R22.54.
Lebenslauf of Johannes Renatus Verbeek. R22.152.60.
Nachrichten von der Brüderkirche, 1802. No catalogue number.
Protokolle des Revisionskommitees, 1789. R2.48.i. (an incomplete extract of these
    minutes is available in the Southern Province Archive)
Protokolle des Synod 1764. R2.B.44.1.c.
Protokolle des Synod 1769. R2.B.45.a2–b2.
Protokolle des Synod 1782. R2.B.47.b.a2–b2.
Protokolle des Synod 1789. R2.B.48.b.
Protokolle des Synod 1818. R2.B.50.a.b.
Protokolle des Synodalkommittees, 1769 and 1775. R2B45.1.c. and R2B46.6.
Protokolle der Unitäts Aeltesten Conferenz, 1771–1801. 120 vols. R3B4f.
Reichel, Levin Thomas. Amerikanische Brüdergeschichte. R3.23.C.
Visitationen und darauf bezügliche Correspondenz (Gnadenberg). R7.C.I.a.12.a-c.
Visitations Berichte (Gnadenfeld). R7.F.a.3.a-b.
Visitations Berichte von Gregor 1787 und Geisler 1789 (Neusalz). R7.E.a.9.
Visitations Berichte von Johann Friedrich Reichel über Gnadenfrei, 1788–89.
    R7.D.I.d.5.

Published Works

Cranz, David. *The Ancient and Modern History of the Brethren.* Trans. Benjamin
    LaTrobe. London, 1780.
———. *Nachricht von der Brüder Kirche.* N.P., 1757. Bd. 2, Nikolaus Ludwig von
    Zinzendorf Ergänzungsbände zu den Hauptschriften. Herausg. Erich
    Beyreuther und Gerhard Meyer. Hildesheim: Georg Olms Verlag, 1965.
Erb, Peter C., ed. *Pietists: Selected Writings.* New York: Paulist Press, 1983.
Fries, Adelaide L., ed. *Records of the Moravians in North Carolina.* Vols. 2–7. Ra-
    leigh: North Carolina Historical Commission, 1925–43.
Hahn, Hans-Christoph, and Helmut Reichel, herausg. *Zinzendorf und die
    Herrnhuter Brüder.* Hamburg: Friedrich Witting Verlag, 1977.
Luther, Martin. *Werke: Kritische Gesammtausgabe.* Weimar ed., 1964.
Müller, Josef Theodore, herausg. "Die Aeltesten Berichte Zinzendorf's über sein
    Leben, seine Unternehmungen und Herrnhuts Entstehen." In *Zeitschrift für
    Brüdergeschichte.* Vol. 6, 1912, pp. 45–118. Reihe 3. Bd. 2. Nikolaus Ludwig
    von Zinzendorf Materialien und Dokumente. Herausg. Erich Beyreuther,
    Gerhard Meyer, und Amedeo Molnár. Hildesheim: Georg Olms Verlag, 1973.
Nachrichten von der Brüdergemeine. Gnadau: 1823, 1834, 1838, 1845–48, 1851–
    52, 1872, 1874, 1877, 1880, 1880–82 (various Lebensläufe printed in these
    vols.).
Niesky 1742: Die Dokumente der Brüdergemeine zur Grundun von Niesky.
    Brüdergemeine Niesky, 1992.

Rimius, Henry. *A Candid Narrative of the Rise and Progress of the Herrnhuters Commonly Called Moravians or Unitas Fratrum.* London: 1753.

Schlatter, Richard, ed., *Richard Baxter and Puritan Politics.* New Brunswick, N.J.: Rutgers Univ. Press, 1957.

Spangenberg, August Gottlieb. *The Life of Nicholas Lewis Count Zinzendorf.* Trans. Samuel Jackson. London:1838.

Zinzendorf, Nicholas Ludwig von. *Apologetische Schluß-Schrift, Worinn über tausend Beschuldigungen gegen die Brüder Gemeinen und Ihren zeitrigen Ordinarium nach der Wahrheit beantwortet werden,* Erster Theil. Leipzig und Görlitz, 1752. Bd. 3, N.L. von Zinzendorf Ergänzungsbände zu den Hauptschriften. Herausg. Erich Beyreuther und Gerhard Meyer. Hildesheim: Georg Olms Verlag, 1966.

———. *Büdingsche Sammlungen.* Vol. 1-3. Büdingen, 1744. Bd. 9, N.L. von Zinzendorf Ergänzungsbände zu den Hauptschriften.

———. *Nine Public Lectures on Important Subjects in Religion . . . 1746.* Ed. and Trans. George W. Forrell. Iowa City: Univ. of Iowa Press, 1973.

———. *Twenty-One Discourses on the Augsburg Confession.* Trans. Francis Okeley. London: 1753.

SECONDARY SOURCES

Addison, William George. *The Renewed Church of the United Brethren, 1722–1930.* London: Macmillan, 1932.

Aland, Kurt. "Der Pietismus und die soziale Frage." In *Pietismus und moderne Welt.* Wittenberg: Luther Verlag, 1974.

Atwood, Craig. "The Impact of Zinzendorf's Theology on Colonial Bethlehem, 1742–1762." Ph.D. diss., Princeton University, 1995.

Bailyn, Bernard. *Voyagers to the West: A Passage in the Peopling of America on the Eve of the Revolution.* New York: Alfred A. Knopf, 1986.

Barker-Benfield, G. J. *The Culture of Sensibility: Sex and Society in Eighteenth-Century Britain.* Chicago: Chicago Univ. Press, 1992.

Becker, George. "Pietism's Confrontation with Enlightenment Rationalism: An Examination of the Relationship between Ascetic Protestantism and Science." *Journal for the Scientific Study of Religion* 30 (June 1991): 139–55.

Beiser, Frederick C. *Enlightenment, Revolution, and Romanticism: The Genesis of Modern German Political Thought.* Boston: Harvard Univ. Press, 1992.

Berdahl, Robert. *The Politics of the Prussian Nobility: The Development of a Conservative Ideology, 1770–1848.* Princeton, N.J.: Princeton Univ. Press, 1988.

Beyreuther, Erich. "Ehe-Religion und Eschaton." In *Studien zur Theologie Zinzendorfs.* Verlage der Buchhandlung des Erziehungsvereins Neukirchen-Uluym, 1962.

———. "Lostheorie und Lospraxis." In *Studien zur Theologie Zinzendorfs.* Verlage der Buchhandlung des Erziehungsvereins Neukirchen-Uluym, 1962.

———. "Die Paradoxie des Glaubens: Zinzendorfs Verhältnis zu Pierre Bayle und zur Aufklärung." In *Studien zur Theologie Zinzendorfs.* Verlage der Buchhandlung des Erziehungsvereins Neukirchen-Uluym, 1962.

Beyreuther, Gottfried. "Sexualltheorien im Pietismus." Ph.D. diss., Ludwig-

Maximilians Universität zur München, 1963. Reihe 2, Bd. 13, N.L. von Zinzendorf Materialien und Dokumente. Hildesheim: Georg Olms Verlag, 1975.

Blum, Jerome. *The End of the Old Order in Rural Europe.* Princeton, N.J.: Princeton Univ. Press, 1978.

————. "The Internal Structure and Polity of the European Village Community from the Fifteenth to the Nineteenth Century." *Journal of Modern History* 43, no. 4 (1971): 542–62.

Boetticher, Walter von. *Geschichte des OberLausitzer Adels und seiner Güter, 1635–1815.* 3 vols. Görlitz: Oberlausitzer Gesellschaft der Wissenschaften, 1912.

Bossy, John. *Christianity in the West, 1400–1700.* Oxford and New York: Oxford Univ. Press, 1985.

Brecht, Martin, and Klaus Deppermann, eds. *Geschichte des Pietismus.* Vols. 1 and 2. Göttingen: Vandenhoeck and Ruprecht, 1995.

Brenner, Gabrielle, and Reuven Brenner. *Gambling and Speculation: A Theory, a History, and a Future of Some Human Decisions.* Cambridge and New York: Cambridge Univ. Press, 1990.

Brock, Peter. *The Political and Social Doctrines of the Unity of the Czech Brethren in the Fifteenth and Early Sixteenth Centuries.* 'S-Gravenhage: Mouton, 1957.

Burke, Peter. *Popular Culture in Early Modern Europe.* New York: Harper and Row, 1978.

Büttner, Manfred. "Religion and Geography." Fasc. 3. *Numen* 21 (1974): 163–93.

Caldwell, Patricia. *The Puritan Conversion Narrative: The Beginning of American Expression.* Cambridge and New York: Cambridge Univ. Press, 1983.

Campbell, Theodore. *Religion of the Heart: A Study of European Religious Life in the Seventeenth and Eighteenth Centuries.* Columbia: Univ. of South Carolina Press, 1991.

Connor, R.D.W. *North Carolina: Rebuilding an Ancient Commonwealth, 1584–1925.* 2 vols. Chicago and New York: American Historical Society, 1929. Spartanburg, S.C.: Reprint, 1973.

Czok, Karl, ed. *Geschichte Sachsens.* Weimar: H. Beohlaus Nachf., 1989.

Darnton, Robert. *The Literary Underground of the Old Regime.* Cambridge and New York: Cambridge Univ. Press, 1982.

van Dülmen, Richard. *The Society of the Enlightenment: The Rise of the Middle Class and Enlightenment Culture in Germany.* Trans. Anthony Williams. New York: St. Martin's Press, 1992.

Ekirch, Roger. *Poor Carolina: Politics and Society in North Carolina, 1729–1776.* Chapel Hill: Univ. of North Carolina Press, 1981.

Erbe, Hans Walther. "Erziehung und Schulen der Brüdergemeine." In *Unitas Fratrum: Herrnhuter Studien.* Herausg. Mari P. van Buijetenen, Cornelis Dekker, Huib Leeuwenberg. Utrecht: Rijksarchief, 1975.

————. "Zinzendorf und der fromme hohe Adel seiner Zeit." Ph.D. diss. Universität Leipzig, 1928. Reihe 2, Bd. 12, N.L. von Zinzendorf Materialien und Dokumente.

Erikson, Kai. *Wayward Puritans: A Study in the Sociology of Deviance.* New York: John Wiley and Sons, 1966.

Fix, Andrew. *Prophecy and Reason: The Dutch Collegiants in the Early Enlightenment.* Princeton, N.J.: Princeton Univ. Press, 1991.

Fogelman, Aaron. *Hopeful Journeys: German Immigrants, Settlement, and Political Culture in Colonial America, 1717–1775.* Philadelphia: Univ. of Pennsylvania Press, 1996.

Gollin, Gillian Lindt. *Moravians in Two Worlds: A Study of Changing Communities.* New York: Columbia Univ. Press, 1967.

Greene, Jack. *Imperatives, Behaviors, and Identities: Essays in Early American Cultural History.* Charlottesville: Univ. Press of Virginia, 1992.

———. *Pursuits of Happiness: The Social Development of Early Modern British Colonies and the Formation of American Culture.* Chapel Hill: Univ. of North Carolina Press, 1988.

Hahn, Hans-Christoph. "Theologie, Apostolat und Spiritualität der Evangelischen Brüdergemeine." In *Unitas Fratrum: Herrnhuter Studien.* Herausg. Mari P. van Buijetenen, Cornelis Dekker, Huib Leeuwenberg. Utrecht: Rijksarchief, 1975.

Hall, David D. *Worlds of Wonder, Days of Judgment: Popular Religious Beliefs in Early New England.* New York: Alfred A. Knopf, 1989.

Hamilton, John Taylor. *A History of the Church Known as the Moravian Church or the Renewed Unitas Fratrum.* Bethlehem, Pa.: Times Publishing, 1900.

Hamilton, Kenneth Gardiner. *History of the Moravian Church: The Renewed Unitas Fratrum, 1722–1957.* Bethlehem, Pa.: Interprovincial Board of Christian Education, Moravian Church in America, 1967.

———. *John Ettwein and the Moravian Church.* Bethlehem, Pa.: Times Publishing, 1940.

Holmes, John B. *History of the Protestant Church of the United Brethren.* Vol. 1. London: 1825.

Hutton, Joseph E. *History of the Moravian Church.* 2d ed. London: Moravian Publications Office, 1909.

Isaac, Rhys. *The Transformation of Virginia, 1740–1788.* Chapel Hill: Univ. of North Carolina Press, 1982 (published for the Institute of Early American History and Culture, Williamsburg, Va.).

James, Hunter. *The Quiet People of the Land: A Study of the North Carolina Moravians in Revolutionary Times.* Chapel Hill: Univ. of North Carolina Press, 1976 (published for Old Salem Inc.).

Klippel, Diethelm. "The True Concept of Liberty: Political Theory in Germany in the Second Half of the Eighteenth Century." In *The Transformation of Political Culture: England and Germany in the Late Eighteenth Century.* Ed. Eckhart Helmut. New York and Oxford: Oxford Univ. Press, 1990.

Krieger, Leonard. *The German Idea of Freedom.* Boston: Beacon Press, 1957.

Langton, Edward. *History of the Moravian Church.* London: Allen and Unwin, 1956.

La Vopa, Anthony. *Grace, Talent, and Merit: Poor Students, Clerical Careers, and Professional Ideology in Eighteenth-Century Germany.* Cambridge and New York: Cambridge Univ. Press, 1988.

Lehmann, Hartmut. *Pietismus und weltliche Ordnung in Württemberg von 17. bis zum 19. Jahrhundert.* Stuttgart: W. Kohlhammer Verlag, 1969.

Lewis, A.J. *Zinzendorf, the Ecumenical Pioneer: A Study in the Moravian Contribu-tion to Christian Mission and Unity.* Philadelphia: Westminster Press, 1962.

MacMaster, Richard K. *Land, Piety, and Peoplehood: The Establishment of the Men-nonite Communities in America.* Scottdale, Pa.: Herald Press, 1985.

Medick, Hans. "Village Spinning Bees: Sexual Culture and Free Time among Ru-ral Youth in Early Modern Germany." In *Interest and Emotion: Essays on the Study of Family and Kinship.* Ed. Hans Medick and David W. Sabean. Cam-bridge and New York: Cambridge Univ. Press, 1984.

Merrens, Harry R. *Colonial North Carolina in the Eighteenth Century: A Study in Historical Geography.* Chapel Hill: Univ. of North Carolina Press, 1964.

Monter, William. "The Consistory of Geneva, 1559–1569." *Bibliotheque d'Humanisme et Renaissance* 38 (1976): 469–87.

Muchembled, Robert. *Popular Culture and Elite Culture in France, 1400–1750.* Trans. Lydia Cochrane. Baton Rouge: Louisiana Univ. Press, 1985.

Müller, H.H. "Domänen und Domanenpächter." *Jahrbuch für Wirtschaftsgeschichte* 4 (1965): 152–92.

Müller, Josef Theodore. *Zinzendorf als Erneurerer der alten Brüderkirche.* Leipzig: Verlag von Friedrich Jansa, 1900. Reihe 2, Bd. 12, N.L. von Zinzendorf Materialien und Dokumente. Herausg. Erich Beyreuther, Gerhard Meyer, Amadeo Molnár. Hildesheim: Georg Olms Verlag, 1975.

Nelson, James David. "Herrnhut: Friedrich Schleiermacher's Spiritual Homeland." Vol. 1. Ph.D. diss., University of Chicago, 1963.

Outram, Dorinda. *The Enlightenment.* Cambridge and New York: Cambridge Univ. Press, 1995.

Peschke, Erhard. *Kirche und Welt in der Theologie der Böhmischen Brüder: Vom Mittelalter zur Reformation.* Berlin: Evangelische Verlaganstalt, 1981.

Philipp, Guntram. "Wirtschaftsethik und Wirtschaftspraxis in der Geschichte der Herrnhuter Brüdergemeine." In *Unitas Fratrum: Herrnhuter Studien.* Herausg. Mari P. van Buijetenen, Cornelis Dekker, Huib Leeuwenberg, 401–63. Utrecht: Rijksarchief, 1975.

Pinson, Koppel Shub. *Pietism as a Factor in the Rise of German Nationalism.* New York: Columbia Univ. Press, 1934.

Reichel, Werner. "Samuel Christlieb Reichel in seine Entwicklung zur Vertreter des Ideal Herrnhutismus." In *Zeitschrift für Brüdergeschichte.* Vol. 6, 1912. 1–44. Reihe 3, Bd. 2, N.L. von Zinzendorf Materialien und Dokumente.

Reiter, Michael. "Moralische Subjektkonstitutionen in deutschen Pietismus." In *Der Innere Staat des Bürgertums: Studien zur Entstehung bürgerlicher Hegemonie-Apparate in 17. und 18. Jahrhundert.* Herausg. Herbert Bosch et al. West Ber-lin: Argument Verlag, 1987.

Robisheaux, Thomas. *Rural Society and the Search for Order in Early Modern Ger-many.* New York: Cambridge Univ. Press, 1989.

Roeber, A.G. *Palatines, Liberty, and Property: German Lutherans in Colonial British America.* Baltimore: Johns Hopkins Univ. Press, 1993.

———. "'He read it to me from a book of English law': Germans, Bench, and Bar in the Colonial South, 1715–1770." In *Ambivalent Legacy: A Legal History of the South.* Ed. David Bodenhamer and James Ely. Jackson: Mississippi Univ. Press, 1984.

———. "The Origins of Whatever Is Not English among Us." In *Strangers within the Realm: Cultural Margins of the British Empire.* Ed. Bernard Bailyn and Philip D. Morgan. Chapel Hill: Univ. of North Carolina Press, 1991.

Sabean, David Warren. *Power in the Blood: Popular Culture and Village Discourse in Early Modern Germany.* New York: Cambridge Univ. Press, 1984.

———. *Property, Production, and Family in Neckarhausen, 1700–1870.* Cambridge and New York: Cambridge Univ. Press, 1991.

Sante, Georg Wilhelm, herausg. *Hessen.* Bd. 4. Handbuch der Historischen Stätten Deutschlands. Stuttgart: Alfred Kröner Verlag, 1967.

Sawyer, Edwin Albert. "The Religious Experience of the Colonial Moravians." *Transactions of the Moravian Historical Society* 18, pt. 1 (1961):47–61.

Schmidt, Gottfried. "Die Banden oder Gesellschaften in alten Herrnhut." In *Zeitschrift für Brüdergeschichte.* Vol. 3, 1909. 145–207. Reihe 3, Bd. 1, N.L. von Zinzendorf Materialien und Dokumente.

Schlumbohn, Jürgen. *Freiheit: Die Anfänge des bürgerlichen Emanzipationsbewegung in Deutschland im Spiegel ihres Leitwortes.* Düsseldorf: Pädagogishche Verlag Schwann, 1975.

Schulze, Winfried. "Peasant Resistance and Politicization in Germany in the Eighteenth Century." In *The Transformation of Political Culture: England and Germany in the Late Eighteenth Century.* Ed. Eckhart Helmut. New York and Oxford: Oxford Univ. Press, 1990.

———. "Peasant Resistance in the Sixteenth and Seventeenth Centuries in a European Context." In *Religion, Politics, and Social Protest.* Ed. Kaspar von Greyertz. London: Allen and Unwin Press, 1984.

de Schweinitz, Edmund Alexander. *The History of the Church Known as the Unitas Fratrum or Unity of the Brethren, Founded by the Followers of John Hus, the Bohemian Reformer and Martyr.* Bethlehem, Pa.: Moravian Publications Office, 1885.

Sensbach, Jon F. "A Separate Canaan: The Making of an Afro-Moravian World in Salem, North Carolina, 1763–1856." Ph.D. diss., Duke University, 1991. Ann Arbor, Mich.: University Microfilms, 1991, 92–20321.

Sessler, Jacob John. *Communal Piety among Early American Moravians.* New York: Holt, 1933; New York: AMS Reprints, 1971.

Shapiro, Barbara. *Probability and Certainty in Seventeenth-Century England: A Study of the Relationship between Natural Science, Religion, History, Law, and Literature.* Princeton, N.J.: Princeton Univ. Press, 1983.

Smaby, Beverly Prior. *The Transformation of Moravian Bethlehem: From Communal Mission to Family Economy.* Philadelphia: Univ. of Pennsylvania Press, 1988.

Sommer, Elisabeth. "Serving Two Masters: Authority, Faith, and Community among the Moravian Brethren in Germany and Salem, North Carolina, in the Eighteenth Century." Ph.D. diss., University of Virginia, 1991.

Stoeffler, F. Ernest. *German Pietism during the Eighteenth Century.* Leiden: Brill, 1973.

Surratt, Jerry L. *Gottlieb Schober of Salem.* Macon, Georgia: Mercer Univ. Press, 1983.

────. "From Theocracy to Voluntary Church and Secularized Community: A Study of the Moravians in Salem, North Carolina, 1722–1860." Ph.D. diss., Emory University, 1968. Ann Arbor, Mich.: University Microfilms, 1968, 68–15763.

Thorp, Daniel B. "Assimilation in North Carolina's Moravian Community." *Journal of Southern History* 52 (1986): 19–42.

────. "The City that Never Was: Count Zinzendorf's Original Plan for Salem." *North Carolina Historical Review* 61, no. 1 (1984): 36–58.

────. "The Moravian Colonization of Wachovia, 1753–1722: The Maintenance of Community in Late Colonial North Carolina." Ph.D. diss., Johns Hopkins University, 1982. Ann Arbor, Mich.: University Microfilms, 1982, DDJ82–13236.

────. *The Moravian Community in Colonial North Carolina: Pluralism on the Southern Frontier.* Knoxville: Univ. of Tennessee Press, 1989.

────. "Paying for Paradise: How the Moravians Financed the Establishment of Wachovia." Paper presented at a conference of the Society for Communal Studies, Winston-Salem, North Carolina, 1989.

Uttendörfer, Otto. *Alt Herrnhut.* Verlager Missionsbuchhandlung Herrnhut, 1925. Reihe 2, Bd. 22. N.L. von Zinzendorf Materialien und Dokumente. Hamburg: Georg Olms Verlag, 1984.

────. *Wirtschaftsgeist und Wirtschaftsorganisation Herrnhuts und der Brüdergemeine von 1743 bis zum Ende des Jahrhunderts.* Verlager Missionsbuchhandlung Herrnhut, 1926. Reihe 2, Bd. 22, N.L. von Zinzendorf Materialien und Dokumente.

Vierhaus, Rudolph. *Germany in the Age of Absolutism.* Trans. Jonathan B. Knudsen. New York: Cambridge Univ. Press, 1988.

Walker, Mack. *German Home Towns, Community, State, and General Estate, 1648–1871.* Ithaca, N.Y.: Cornell Univ. Press, 1971.

Ward, W.R. "German Pietism, 1670–1750." *Journal of Ecclesiastical History* 44 (July 1993): 476–505.

────. "Zinzendorf and Money." In *The Church and Wealth.* Ed. W.J. Sheils and Diana Wood. London: Basil Blackwell, 1987.

Watt, Jeffrey. *The Making of Modern Marriage: Matrimonial Control and the Rise of Sentiment in Neuchâtel, 1550–1800.* Ithaca, N.Y.: Cornell Univ. Press, 1992.

Weczerka, Hugo, herausg. *Schlesien.* Bd. 12, Handbuch der historischen Stätten Deutschlands. Stuttgart: Alfred Kröner Verlag, 1977.

Weinlick, John R. *Count Zinzendorf.* New York: Abingdon Press, 1956.

Whaley, Joachim. "The Protestant Enlightenment in Germany." In *The Enlightenment in National Context.* Ed. Roy Porter and Mikulás Teich. Cambridge and New York: Cambridge Univ. Press, 1981.

Wokeck, Marianne. "Charting Courses between Assimilation and Persistence: German Settlements in the American Colonies." Paper presented at a conference sponsored by the German Historical Institute, Pennsylvania State University, 1992.

Zialkowski, Theodore. *German Romanticism and Its Institutions.* Princeton, N.J.: Princeton Univ. Press, 1990.

Zuckerman, Michael. "Identity in British America: Unease in Eden." In *Colonial Identity in the Atlantic World, 1500–1800*. Ed. Nicholas Canny and Anthony Pagden. Princeton, N.J.: Princeton Univ. Press, 1987.

Index

Acolyte (*Acoluthe*), 27
aesthetics, nobles' effect on, 48
Agapen, 49, 50
agriculture, 10–11, 35, 120–23
alienation, of American *Gemeinen*
    from Europe: over appointments
    of local officials, 142, 143, 153–
    54, 160; and balancing of needs,
    141, 142, 156–59, 160, 161–62,
    163; by distance, geographical,
    from UEC, 118, 151, 163 (*see
    also* visitations, to Wachau); over
    finances, freedom of, 159; by
    identity as Americans, 150, 151,
    165–70; by mail delays, 151–54,
    155; over the marriage lot, 109,
    140, 157–59, 171–73; in second
    generation, 140–41; by shortage
    of artisans, 143, 162–65; by
    shortage of leaders, 142, 143,
    160–62
Allgemeine Literatur Zeitung, 85
American *Gemeinen*, perceived as
    distinct: in the defiance of
    authority, 128–33; in their
    concept of freedom, 129, 133–
    39; through new identity as
    Americans, 150, 151, 165–70; in
    use of the marriage lot, 109, 140,
    157–59, 171–73. *See also*
    alienation, of American *Gemeinen*
    from Europe
Anbeten, 51
Ancient Unity, 1–4, 8, 27
anniversary celebrations, 49–50, 169
Anstalten, 31, 66, 67, 166
apprentices, 31, 46, 130–31

Arbeiter, 25, 151. *See also*
    Hauptarbeiter; Landarbeiter
aristocracy, in Renewed Unity. *See*
    nobles, in Renewed Unity
artisans: and guild system, 138;
    shortage of, 143, 162–65; society,
    ideal of, 10–11, 121; walkout of
    1778, 120, 131–32. *See also*
    Single Brothers Choir, Salem
Aufseher, 22
Aufseher Collegium: and artisans'
    walkout of 1778, 131–32; and
    "bad books," 133; and children,
    control over, 65, 70; and Christ,
    Rudolph, 132; and discipline,
    role in, 53, 54; in early
    Ortsgemeinen, 18, 25; and
    economic affairs, Salem, 46–47;
    on freedom, desire for, in Salem,
    129, 130; on land, desire for, 122;
    and property restrictions, Salem,
    46; Unity, established, 29; view
    of, in Salem ordinances, 44
Aust, Georg, 129
authority, judicial, in *Ortsgemeinen*,
    17, 20, 23–25, 112
authority *vs.* freedom, 110–39:
    defiance, forms of, in Germany,
    124–28; defiance, forms of, in
    North Carolina, 124, 128–33,
    171–74; and environment of
    German *Gemeinen*, 114–18, 123;
    and environment of North
    Carolina *Gemeinen*, 118–23;
    freedom, American concept of,
    129, 133–39; freedom, British
    constitutional tradition of, 111,

www.ingramcontent.com/pod-product-compliance
Lightning Source LLC
Chambersburg PA
CBHW030530100426
42813CB00001B/205